# RAISING TRANS KIDS

# RAISING TRANS KIDS

*What to Expect When You Weren't Expecting This*

REBECCA MINOR, LICSW

100 BLOCK
BY ROW HOUSE

Library of Congress Cataloging-in-Publication Data Available Upon Request
ISBN 978-1-955905-98-5 (TP)
ISBN 978-1-955905-99-2 (eBook)

Design by Neuwirth & Associates, Inc.

Printed in the United States

Distributed by Simon & Schuster
First edition

10 9 8 7 6 5 4 3 2 1

*To the clients and families who have entrusted me to guide them on their gender journeys—this book wouldn't exist without you. Thank you for your courage, vulnerability, and belief in our work together.*

# CONTENTS

## PART FOUR
## Family, Social, and Cultural Impacts



## PART FIVE
## From Understanding to Action

## PROLOGUE

# This Book Is for You

Thank you for being curious.

If even opening this book was hard, I'm so glad you are here. You may be grappling with a range of emotions about a young person in your life. Perhaps you're a parent, anxious about what your child's gender identity means for their future or mourning the path you once envisioned for them. Maybe you're an educator striving to create a more inclusive classroom, a healthcare provider aiming to offer better care, or a family member wanting to show more meaningful support for a transgender or gender-expansive young person. While this book centers on the unique concerns and experiences of parents, it's designed to be a valuable resource for anyone in a supportive role. Throughout this book, I will primarily use the word "parent" because they are often the ones most responsible for providing support. However, you don't need to be a parent to find value in these pages. Whether you're a caregiver, family member, or trusted adult in a young person's life, your role is just as essential, and your contribution matters. Whether you feel isolated, ashamed, confused, angry, hopeful, curious, or determined—or more likely, a combination of these emotions—you're here because you care deeply about the well-being of the young people in your life and want to learn how to support them better. This book is your companion.

There's no wrong way to read this book. Each chapter names, explores, and reframes a common concern that parents and caregivers of gender-expansive youth may experience. As a therapist who has spent thousands of hours working with gender-expansive youth and their families, I have learned that being a concerned caregiver and a supportive ally are not mutually exclusive. One of the primary reasons I wrote this book was to bridge a gap I noticed in available resources for parents and caregivers. Too often, it seemed like the advice out there fell into two extremes: either demanding unwavering support without acknowledging the complex emotions involved or dismissing concerns as bigotry in a way that left many feeling unheard and unsupported. I believe there's a vast, nuanced space between these poles and that's where this book resides. Your doubts, fears, and questions are welcome here. You may wish this wasn't happening, worry about the challenges ahead, or feel unprepared for this development. All of these feelings are to be expected at various points along your journey, and this book is here to guide you in showing up for your child despite (and alongside) these concerns.

It's important to recognize that loving your child and being apprehensive about their journey are not necessarily at odds. You can harbor fears while still showing up as an active ally for your child. As I often remind my clients, both of these realities can coexist. Your own journey of understanding and support is pivotal to your child's growth and happiness. While the circumstances are different, it's important to acknowledge that worrying about your child is normal. Many parents have fears and worries for their children, whether it's about solo adventure travel, engaging in extreme sports, or choosing a different spiritual path from their family of origin. Parents may worry about their children's choices in dating partners or friends, career choices, whether they are studying enough or practicing safe sex—the list goes on. Part of parenting is accepting that our children know their own minds, desires, joys, and needs. However, accepting this is not always easy.

The goal of this book isn't to convince you of anything, nor will it provide you insurance against ever having another pang of anxiety. Instead, it aims to provide you with accurate information, practical tools, resources, and real-life examples to help you support someone you care about. This book is crafted for those moments when worry or doubt creeps into your thoughts in the quiet of the night or amid the day's hustle. It's structured to be an easy-to-navigate resource for busy parents and individuals seeking immediate clarity and support on specific concerns regarding their child's gender identity that challenge their peace of mind.

Here's your open invitation to navigate this resource in a way that aligns with your journey. Skip, leap over, or dive deeper into sections that call out to you. There's no prescribed way to engage with the information shared within these pages. Your path through this material is yours to define. Just like your child's gender journey hasn't been linear, neither need be your use of this book.

In the pages ahead, you'll find a blend of evidence-based insights, heartfelt stories, summaries of key points for each chapter, and thoughtful reflection questions. These elements come together to enhance understanding, empathy, and actionable knowledge. Throughout this book, you'll encounter case studies that illustrate real-world experiences and challenges. It's important to note that these case studies are composites, carefully crafted from a wealth of sources. They draw from my own career as a clinician, as well as from the experiences shared by many other gender specialists, therapists, and members of the trans community. This includes parents of trans kids who have courageously shared their stories to empower others. While the specific details may be altered to protect privacy, each case study represents authentic experiences and common scenarios faced by families navigating gender identity journeys. I aim to strike a balance in these stories—I don't want to paint everything as perfect and easy because that's not always the reality, but I also don't want to leave you feeling disheartened. As you read, please bear in mind that these are just snapshots of a much longer journey, with moments of progress, setbacks, and hope along the way.

Additionally, there's a Trans Supportive Parent Self-Assessment designed to help you see where you are in your journey. It's not about getting a good grade or being the most supportive parent, but rather about guiding you to identify your strengths and areas where more education or support may be needed. By directly addressing common concerns about gender identity and providing actionable insights, this book empowers you to confidently support the young people in your life, whenever and however they need it.

As we embark on this journey together, let's move forward with compassion and an openness to learn, ready to embrace the lessons and transformations that await us. This path we're on is as much about unlearning old narratives as it is about embracing new truths. With every page turned, let us be guided by hope, by the potential for a more understanding and inclusive future.

Remember, we're in this together, so you don't have to worry or wonder alone.

## UNDERSTANDING THE 2SLGBTQIA+ ACRONYM

Recognizing the beautifully fluid and ever-evolving nature of language surrounding gender and identity within the 2SLGBTQIA+ community, I've created an online glossary to complement the printed one at the back of this book. This living digital resource will be regularly updated, ensuring you have access to the most current terminology. You can find a QR code at the back of the book.

**2S - Two-Spirit:** refers to a person who identifies as having both a masculine and a feminine spirit, and originated as a term Indigenous people used to describe their sexual, gender, and/or spiritual identity. As an umbrella term, it may encompass same-sex attraction and a wide variety of gender variance, including people who might be described in Western culture as gay, lesbian, bisexual, transsexual, transgender, genderqueer, cross-dressers, or who have multiple gender identities.

**L - Lesbian:** often defined as a woman who is attracted to other women. Current perspectives define it as a person, often a woman or femme (feminine gender identity or presentation), who is emotionally, romantically, or sexually attracted to other women, femmes, or non-men.

**G - Gay:** experiencing attraction solely (or primarily) to some members of the same gender. Can be used to refer to men who are attracted to other men and women who are attracted to other women. Also *adj.*: an umbrella term used to refer to the queer community as a whole, or as an individual identity label for anyone who is not straight *(see LGBTQ and queer)*.

**B - Bisexual:** often defined as a person who experiences attraction to some men and women. Current perspectives define it as a person who experiences attraction to some people of their gender and another gender (can include nonbinary genders). Bisexual attraction does not have to be equally split or indicate a level of interest that is the same across the genders an individual may be attracted to. Can be shortened to "bi" (pronounced "bye"). Often used interchangeably with "pansexual."

**T - Transgender:** an umbrella term covering a range of identities that transgress socially defined gender norms. Trans with an asterisk is often used in written forms (not spoken) to indicate that you are referring to the larger group nature of the term (Trans*) and specifically including nonbinary identities, as well as transgender men (trans men) and transgender women (trans women).

**Q - Queer:** an umbrella term to describe individuals who don't identify as straight and/or cisgender. Due to its historical use as a derogatory term, and how it is still used as a slur in many communities, it is not embraced or used by all LGBTQ+ people; however, over the past decades there has been a vast reclaiming of the word "queer," not only by those who identify as queer themselves but in political and academic circles, for example universities offering classes on "Queer Studies." For those who have reclaimed and embraced this term, "queer" can often be used interchangeably with LGBTQ+ (e.g., "queer people" instead of "LGBTQ+ people").

**I - Intersex:** term for a combination of chromosomes, gonads, hormones, internal sex organs, and/or genitals that differs from the two expected patterns of male or female. The terms formerly hermaphrodite or hermaphroditic have historically been used to describe intersex people, but these terms are now outdated and derogatory.

**A - Asexual:** experiencing little or no sexual attraction to others and/or a lack of interest in sexual relationships/behavior. Asexuality exists on a continuum from people who experience no sexual attraction or have any desire for sex, to those who experience low levels, or sexual attraction only under specific conditions. Many of these different places on the continuum have their own identity labels. Those who are asexual may also be lacking in romantic feelings and be aromantic, or they may experience romantic feelings and fall deeply in love, simply without the physical and emotional craving for sex. Asexual is sometimes abbreviated as "ace."

+ - **Plus:** signifies a spectrum of other identities not specifically covered by the eight initialisms above, recognizing the diversity of sexuality and gender identity.

A few more terms to ensure we are all on the same page:

**Cisgender:** a gender description for when someone's sex assigned at birth and gender identity correspond (e.g., someone who was assigned female at birth and identifies as a woman). A simple way to think about it is if a person is not transgender (which includes nonbinary and gender-fluid folks), they are cisgender. The word cisgender can also be shortened to "cis" and is not a slur.

**Nonbinary:** a gender identity label used by some people who do not identify with the binary of man/woman. Alternatively spelled "non-binary." Often abbreviated as "enby" or "enbie" (based on the pronunciation of N-B).

# TRANS SUPPORTIVE PARENT SELF-ASSESSMENT

**Instructions**

Answer the following questions honestly to better understand your current level of familiarity and comfort with topics relating to your child's gender identity. Each question is followed by four options: A, B, C, and D. Choose the one that best describes your current understanding or behavior.

*How familiar are you with the concept of gender identity?*

A. Very familiar, I understand the difference between gender identity and sexual orientation.
B. Somewhat familiar, I know the basics but could learn more.
C. Slightly familiar, I've heard about it but don't know much.
D. Not familiar, this is a new idea.

*How do you react when your child expresses their gender identity?*

A. I listen and support them unconditionally.
B. I try to be supportive but sometimes feel unsure about what to do.
C. I find it challenging to understand and often feel confused.
D. I struggle to accept it and often feel resistant.

*How often do you use your child's chosen name and pronouns?*

A. Always, I make a conscious effort to use them correctly.
B. Most of the time, I try but sometimes slip up.
C. Occasionally, I find it difficult to remember or adjust.
D. Rarely, I struggle to make this change.

*How informed are you about the medical and social transition options available for transgender youth?*

A. Very informed, I know the various options and their implications.
B. Somewhat informed, I know some options but not all the details.
C Slightly informed, I've heard of a few options but not in depth.
D. Not informed, I don't know much about this.

*How do you handle conversations about your child's gender identity with extended family and friends?*

A. I advocate for my child and educate others about their identity.
B. I support my child but sometimes find it hard to educate others.
C. I feel unsure and often avoid these conversations.
D. I struggle with these conversations and often don't address them.

*How do you educate yourself about transgender issues and experiences?*

A. I regularly read books, attend workshops, and engage with relevant resources.
B. I occasionally read articles or watch videos on the topic.
C. I rely on what I hear from others and don't seek out information actively.
D. Reading this book is the first step.

*How well do you understand the legal rights of transgender youth?*

A. Very well, I am knowledgeable about their legal protections and rights.
B. Somewhat well, I know some rights but not all the details.
C. Slightly well, I have a basic idea but lack depth.
D. Not well, I am not aware of their legal rights.

*How do you support your child in school-related matters concerning their gender identity?*

A. I actively work with the school to ensure a supportive environment.
B. I try to support but sometimes feel unsure how to address issues.
C. I occasionally support but often rely on the school to handle it.
D. I find it difficult to engage with the school on these matters.

*How comfortable are you discussing gender identity with your child's healthcare providers?*

A. Very comfortable, I advocate for my child's needs confidently.
B. Somewhat comfortable, I try but sometimes feel uncertain.
C. Slightly comfortable, I struggle with these conversations.
D. Not comfortable, I avoid discussing it.

*How often do you engage with other parents of transgender children or support groups?*

A. Regularly, I am an active participant in support groups.
B. Occasionally, I attend when I can.
C. Rarely, I have attended once or twice.
D. Never, I don't know any other parents of transgender children.

*How well do you understand the importance of affirming your child's gender identity?*

A. Very well, I recognize it's crucial for their well-being.
B. Somewhat well, I know it's important but struggle with consistency.
C. Slightly well, I need to understand more about its impact.
D. Not well, I am unsure why it's important.

*How do you address bullying or discrimination your child might face?*

A. I proactively address it and support my child through it.
B. I try to address it but feel unsure about the best approach.
C. I occasionally address it but often rely on others to handle it.
D. I struggle to address it and often feel overwhelmed.

*How do you incorporate your child's gender identity into family activities and traditions?*

A. Fully, I make sure all activities and traditions are inclusive.
B. Somewhat, I try but sometimes face challenges.
C. Slightly, I haven't made many changes yet.
D. Not at all, I struggle to incorporate changes.

*How informed are you about the mental health challenges transgender youth might face?*

A. Very informed, I know the potential challenges and ways to support.
B. Somewhat informed, I know some challenges but not all.
C. Slightly informed, I have a basic idea but need more knowledge.
D. Not informed, I don't know much about this.

*How do you support your child's social relationships and friendships?*

A. Actively, I help them build and maintain supportive friendships.
B. Somewhat actively, I support but could do more.
C. Slightly actively, I occasionally support their social life.
D. Not actively, I struggle to support their social relationships.

*How often do you reflect on and challenge your own biases about gender?*

A. Regularly, I actively work to understand and challenge my biases.
B. Occasionally, I try but sometimes avoid it.
C. Rarely, I don't often think about my biases.
D. Never, this book is the first time.

*Are you willing to learn and consider new ideas and perspectives to become a more supportive parent?*

A. Absolutely!
B. I am unsure, but open to it.
C. I need more information.
D. Not at this time.

## Scoring

Now, take a moment to tally your answers. This will help you gain insight into your current understanding and support for your child.

**Mostly A's: Embracing and Exploring**

You're doing a wonderful job understanding transgender issues and supporting your child.

*Next steps*: Keep learning and stay connected with the transgender community. Your experiences could be valuable in helping other families on similar journeys.

**Mostly B's: Growing and Developing**

You're on a positive path in supporting your child, with opportunities for further growth.

*Next steps*: Explore more learning opportunities like workshops or support groups. Practice using affirming language and learn more about various aspects of transition.

**Mostly C's: Learning and Progressing**

You've taken important first steps in understanding and supporting your child. There's room to build on this foundation.

*Next steps*: Explore resources like books and articles about transgender youth. Consider joining a support group for parents to share experiences and learn from others.

**Mostly D's: Beginning the Journey**

You're at the start of your learning journey, which is an important first step.

*Next steps*: Start with introductory resources about gender identity. Connecting with a support group or counselor could help you better understand your child's experience and how to offer support.

**Remember**

Every parent's journey is unique, and taking steps to learn and understand is what matters most. Your effort to support your child is commendable, regardless of where you are in this process.

PART ONE

# UNDERSTANDING GENDER AND IDENTITY

1

# AREN'T THERE ONLY TWO GENDERS?

**For some parents,** when your child confides in you that their gender identity doesn't match the one assigned at birth, it's like everything you thought you knew about your child and gender comes to a screeching halt. For other parents, their child's coming out as transgender or nonbinary may not be as earth-shattering, but they still feel unfamiliar with identities that aren't just "man" or "woman." This moment often prompts a pivotal question, challenging deep-seated beliefs: "Aren't there only two genders?"

Understanding gender's complexity can shake up what we've always believed, especially when it's about someone close to us. It's a bit like finding out that not everything we learned as kids holds up under scrutiny. If that isn't true, what else isn't true? This shift can be uncomfortable, but it's also the first step toward deeper empathy and understanding. Everyone adjusts to this change at their own pace, and it might be tougher for some, especially if it's about your kid stepping outside traditional gender lines. It's an ongoing journey, for both you and your child, and it's okay to navigate it one step at a time.

The gender binary is like the ultimate rulebook society handed us on day one, dictating everything from the team colors—blue or pink—to the toys we're supposed to play with. Even before a baby is conceived, it's common for people to hope for a child of a specific gender. This anticipation often leads to the most frequent question asked during pregnancy: "What are you having?" Traditionally, this question is expected to have one of two answers: a boy or a girl. Then, once the baby arrives, the first proclamation is usually "It's a boy!" or "It's a girl!" This initial binary classification—boy or girl—begins to shape our lives from the very beginning, influencing us in both overt and subtle ways throughout our lives.

What's more, this tends to be true globally, such that no matter what race, ethnicity, or nationality a family identifies with, the gender binary often serves as a constant. The gender binary is far-reaching—from marketing to language, shaping how we're seen and how we view others. But here's the thing: life and people aren't that straightforward—and they never have been.

The history of gender nonconforming and trans folks is long and rich across many cultures, but it has been hidden from mainstream history. It is important to stress this again: no matter what you may hear on television or read in the news, transgender people are not "new," and it is not a "fad" or a byproduct of so-called woke culture. Transgender individuals have always existed, and the increased visibility today is primarily due to a growing societal acceptance that has allowed many who once lived in secrecy to express their true identities openly. Now, while this is a welcome change, it also comes with certain new challenges and confusions that previous generations of parents did not experience in the same ways.

With our increased understanding of expansive gender identities, more individuals who previously had to conceal their gender identity are now able to openly share their true selves with their families, friends, and communities. These are people who have always been part of our lives, perhaps unbeknownst to us, but now they can live authentically and openly. This is reminiscent of how left-handedness was once punished. When society stopped penalizing children for being left-handed, there was a noticeable spike in the number of left-handed individuals. This wasn't because more left-handed children were suddenly being born, but because people were no longer being forced to conform to a right-handed standard. Similarly, the increasing visibility of trans identities isn't indicative of a new fad; it's a reflection of society becoming more accepting and allowing people to express who they truly are without fear of punishment. This book is a tool for those who are open to the possibility that the old rulebook might be too simple for the complex reality we live in, and that it is time we as a culture embrace rather than deny and persecute those who dare to be themselves.

Just as our understanding of the scientific world has evolved, so too has our grasp of gender. This evolution doesn't mean we need to throw out the rulebook or create a genderless world. Men and women still exist, and statistics tell us that about 95% of people identify as the sex they were assigned at birth (Williams Institute 2022). While society has become more open and affirming, transgender people remain a minority, which can make them vulnerable to discrimination and in need of support from cisgender allies. The goal is not to eliminate gender but to ensure the next generation isn't limited by rigid binary norms, allowing everyone to express their true selves.

You may have started this chapter with the belief that there are only two genders or thinking that a wider range of gender expression is a new and trendy idea. As you learn more and move forward, I encourage you to consider this empowering belief instead:

---

"I embrace the belief that gender is expansive and fluid; I celebrate and support the diverse expressions of identity."

---

## KEY POINTS

**Gender is More Than a Binary:** While many people were raised to see gender as strictly male or female, history and diverse cultures show that gender has always been more expansive.

**Trans and Nonbinary People Have Always Existed:** Increased visibility today reflects greater acceptance, not a sudden emergence of trans identities. Many have lived in secrecy due to societal constraints.

**Understanding Gender Can Be a Journey:** It's natural for parents and caregivers to feel unsettled when their child's identity challenges what they thought they knew. Shifting perspectives takes time and openness.

**Language Evolves to Reflect Experience:** Just as societal understandings of race, disability, and sexuality have expanded, so too has our ability to recognize and affirm diverse gender identities.

**Supporting a Child's Gender Identity Strengthens Connection:** A child's coming out isn't about rejecting their family—it's about seeking to be known and loved for who they truly are.

## REFLECTION QUESTIONS

1. What messages about gender did you receive growing up? How have they shaped your beliefs?
2. When your child (or someone close to you) shared their gender identity with you, what emotions or thoughts surfaced?

3. What do you need in order to feel more comfortable discussing gender outside of the binary?
4. How can you balance your own learning process while ensuring your child feels supported and affirmed?
5. In what ways does embracing gender diversity align with your values about love, family, and authenticity?

2

# HOW DOES THE BINARY LIMIT US?

**Binary thinking**—categorizing everything into two mutually exclusive groups—has profound implications for our perceptions and interactions. Either/or thinking oversimplifies the wide range of human emotions, behaviors, and identities. By forcing everything into two rigid categories such as good/bad, left/right, us/them, or male/female, we deny the nuances that make each person unique. A binary framework shapes not just our personal interactions but also societal structures, including marketing and language.

Take a moment to think about the language we use daily. Phrases like "we are on top of the world," "we've hit rock bottom," or "sink or swim," normalize and reinforce the idea that there are only two possible outcomes: the absolute best or the absolute worst. This kind of thinking limits our understanding and appreciation of the spectrum of human experience and behavior.

The language we use to describe cultural phenomena plays an important role in shaping our attitudes and policy decisions. Consider the phrases "War on Drugs" and the "Opioid Epidemic." The "War on Drugs" language implies a fight against a clear enemy, evoking images of criminality and conflict. It prescribes a value judgment, suggesting that those involved with drugs are on the wrong side of a battle and need to be eradicated. On the other hand, the term "Opioid Epidemic" frames the issue as a public health crisis, emphasizing compassion, treatment, and systemic failure. This shift in language changes how society perceives the problem and the solutions we consider acceptable. The phrase "War on Drugs," popularized in the 1980s and 1990s, was aimed primarily at Black Americans and resulted in mass incarceration. In contrast, the term "Opioid Epidemic" gained popularity when many white Americans became addicted to prescription opioid painkillers, with Big Pharma and doctors being seen as part of the problem. Consequently, those addicted were viewed more humanely and less criminally. Institutional racism, ingrained over time, guided political and media narratives, framing these problems differently depending on the perceived race of those involved.

Binary thinking extends beyond politics and the legal system and significantly impacts marketing. For instance, advertising frequently targets products to specific genders, reinforcing stereotypes. A car commercial might depict men as thrill-seekers and women as safety-conscious caregivers, ignoring that people of all genders can value both excitement and security. Gender stereotypes, like valuing beauty in women and ruggedness in men, contribute to phenomena such as the "pink tax," where products like women's razors cost more than men's razors due to their "feminine" design. Women face higher pressure to maintain smooth skin and may be more willing to pay a premium. These campaigns shape our understanding of what is normal or desirable, often perpetuating narrow definitions of gender roles.

However, some companies are beginning to recognize the limitations of binary thinking and are moving toward more inclusive marketing strategies. Brands that embrace diversity and complexity in their advertising are more likely to resonate with a broader audience. For example, campaigns that show diverse families, including those with same-sex parents or single parents, reflect a more accurate picture of society and appeal to consumers who see themselves represented.

The language used in marketing also shapes consumer perceptions. By framing issues in ways that either ascribe blame or evoke empathy, we can dramatically influence public opinion and policy. Consider how the framing of climate change as a "crisis" versus an "opportunity" affects public engagement and the types of solutions people support. Similarly, framing gender diversity as a problem to be solved versus a reality to be embraced can influence how society reacts to nonbinary and transgender individuals.

One of the most dramatic illustrations of binary thinking in regard to gender is the way in which children's toys are designed and marketed. Historically, many toys have been marketed strictly to boys or girls, and the toys in question often reinforce gender stereotypes. Dolls and play kitchens are for girls, while trucks and action figures are for boys. This binary approach limits children's experiences and can contribute to rigid gender roles. Studies show that girls' toys were associated with physical attractiveness, nurturing, and domestic skill, whereas boys' toys were rated as violent, competitive, exciting, and somewhat dangerous (NAEYC n.d.). The toys rated as most likely to be educational and to develop children's physical, cognitive, artistic, and other skills were typically categorized as neutral or moderately masculine. These associations tell us more about gender stereotypes and sexism than they do about which toys should be used by which children. In recent years, however, some companies have begun to market toys in a more gender-neutral way, allowing children to explore a wider range of interests and activities.

For starters, coming to grips with the fact that sex and gender are two different things is crucial. Sex is, as mentioned, assigned at birth based on physical characteristics, but gender is about who someone knows themselves to be on the inside and how they wish to express this externally through clothing or presentation, which might not fit the box they were initially put in based on their genitals or sex characteristics.

**What differentiates the sexes?** When a baby is born, their sex is typically assigned based on visible physical characteristics. The primary determinant is genitalia—presence of a penis usually leads to a male assignment, and a vulva to a female assignment. In some cases, particularly when there's ambiguity in genital features, other factors like chromosomes (XX for female, XY for male), gonads (ovaries or testes), and hormonal levels may be examined, though these are less common at birth. It's crucial to understand that these biological markers used for sex assignment at birth do not necessarily dictate a person's gender identity, which is how they perceive themselves and may evolve differently as they grow.

When we use the words "male" or "female," we are referring to sex, versus when we use the words "man" and "woman" or "boy" and "girl" to refer to gender. Society tends to mix up these two concepts, as exemplified by things like gender reveal parties. These parties, meant to be fun, ultimately end up boxing people into categories before they even have a chance to figure themselves out because they are not even born yet!

In fact, the mom who came up with gender reveal parties has said she regrets ever making them up, especially when she discovered her own child didn't fit neatly into one of those two gender binary boxes (Garcia-Navarro 2019). Gender reveal parties are often joyous celebrations for expecting parents and their loved ones. While most of these events are harmless fun, some unfortunate incidents have occurred that highlight our society's intense focus on binary gender norms. These rare but serious accidents serve as a reminder for us to reflect on the cultural importance we place on announcing a baby's biological sex.

It's worth considering why we feel such a strong need to categorize children before they're even born. What expectations and stereotypes might we be unconsciously placing on these babies? Our excitement about welcoming a new life is beautiful, but perhaps we could channel it in ways that don't reinforce rigid gender roles or potentially exclude those who don't fit neatly into the male/female binary.

As we celebrate new additions to our families and communities, we have an opportunity to create a more inclusive environment for all children. This doesn't mean we can't be excited about learning our baby's sex, but we can be mindful of how we express that excitement and what messages we might be sending.

By broadening our celebrations to focus on the joy of new life itself, rather than specific gender expectations, we can help create a world where all children feel free to be their authentic selves. This approach can be just as joyful and even more meaningful, as it embraces the full potential of each unique individual we're welcoming into the world.

Gender essentialism, in which gender is treated as a defining characteristic from which the rest of a person's identity flows, reinforces harmful stereotypes while excluding those who don't fit neatly into predefined categories. From an extremely young age, kids are introduced to a world that often sees gender in just two categories: boy or girl. Even more than half a century after the wide-scale feminist movements of the 1960s/1970s, TV shows and movies made for young children tend to adhere to and teach gender stereotypes, showing boys and girls in very specific lights. Girls are often portrayed as being concerned with their looks and needing assistance, while boys are depicted as bold, smart, and in charge. This reflects deeper societal norms, where boys are viewed as "more universal" in media. In other words, girls will watch shows or read books about boys, but boys are less likely to engage with content centered around girls.

Considering that women make up the largest demographic on earth, it's worth questioning why boys and men are seen as more "organic" or "universal," while girls and women are viewed as "specialized" and "niche." This perception extends into adulthood with terms like "chick flicks," "women's fiction," and other women-centered entertainment, which is often assumed to be of no interest to men simply because women are in the leading roles. Girls are often socialized to be more flexible and accommodating, which includes accepting and identifying with male characters in stories and media. Conversely, both boys and girls receive the message that embodying male traits is preferable, whereas female traits may be undervalued (Steyer 2014). This bias influences children's media preferences, leading to a predominance of male characters in popular children's shows, whether they are animals, magical creatures, or humans (Lemish 2019). This isn't just an outdated way of thinking; it can actually lead kids to believe in unfair stereotypes about what boys and girls can or should be like. When children believe that their options in life are constrained by their gender identity, they may limit their dreams and diminish their potential contribution to society, and we are all harmed as a result.

Parents are not immune to these pervasive stereotypes. We may find ourselves unconsciously reinforcing these norms in our daily interactions with our children, from the colors we choose for their clothes to the activities we encourage them to undertake. It's crucial to recognize that our own perceptions of gender have been shaped by societal norms that have shifted dramatically over time.

These stereotypes don't just affect children's perceptions; they have real-world consequences that extend into adulthood. Women, despite making significant strides in the workplace, still shoulder a disproportionate amount of unpaid domestic labor and childcare responsibilities. This "second shift" at home often goes unrecognized and undervalued, contributing to what's known as the "mental load" or the invisible work of household management that typically falls to women.

In recent years, concepts like "Fair Play" have emerged to address this imbalance. Fair Play, developed by Eve Rodsky, proposes a system for couples to more equitably divide household tasks and mental and emotional labor. It challenges traditional gender roles and encourages partners to view domestic responsibilities as shared, regardless of gender. This approach not only benefits women but also allows men to engage in family life and domestic responsibilities more fully (Rodsky 2021).

These stereotypes are slowly evolving. Men, once primarily viewed as emotionless breadwinners, are increasingly embracing more involved parenting roles and expressing a wider range of emotions. There's a growing acceptance of men seeking therapy, discussing mental health, and showing vulnerability—shifts that challenge traditional masculine stereotypes. This evolution is reflected in media portrayals of fathers as nurturing, emotionally available figures, a stark contrast to the distant or bumbling dad stereotypes of the past.

By becoming aware of these historically and culturally ingrained biases and stereotypes about gender roles, we can better understand the complex landscape our children are navigating. This awareness allows us to more effectively support our children, regardless of their gender identity, and work toward creating a more inclusive and equitable environment for all. Remember, challenging these norms isn't just about our children—it's about recognizing and addressing our own internalized biases as well so that we can all be more free and authentic versions of ourselves.

Imagine a world where pink is the epitome of masculinity, where heels echo with the steps of the powerful men who wear them, and where makeup is a symbol of male nobility. This isn't a fantasy—it's history. There was a time when pink was a color for boys, heels were a staple in men's fashion, and makeup was a sign of status among the male elite. Yet today, these items are often listed under "Gifts for Her," showcasing how our perceptions of gender are not only constructed but fluid over time. These shifts in norms remind us that what we see as inherent gender attributes are often just current societal agreements.

In fact, the idea that there are strictly two genders is actually fairly new, at least in the grand scheme of things. This may seem shocking, considering how deeply entrenched the view became across many cultures. But if we look back before the eighteenth century, folks used to think of gender in a much more expansive and fluid way. During this time, there was a prevailing belief that all humans shared essentially the same anatomical features, which were merely variations of a single underlying form. This notion implied a fluid and inclusive understanding of gender, viewing differences as minor variations rather than as strict dichotomies. However, as scientific understanding evolved, Western societies began to emphasize the physical differences between sexes, which overshadowed the similarities. This shift in focus contributed to more rigid definitions of gender roles that heightened distinctions between men and women, cementing a binary view of gender. As Western nations expanded their influence globally through colonialism, they imposed these narrow views on gender, often clashing with and overriding the local, more inclusive understandings of diverse communities. This colonization of gender norms spread these restrictive ideas worldwide, deeply affecting how gender was perceived and lived in various cultures (Heyam 2022).

As Western countries expanded their influence, their military forces often imposed their own narrow views on gender, clashing with local cultures that had a broader understanding. For instance, in India, British officers targeted the hijras, a group recognized for their gender diversity, forcing them to conform to Western gender norms (Hinchy 2019). Similarly, in the Americas, European settlers encountered Indigenous tribes who acknowledged multiple genders, and these colonizers subsequently sought to erase these traditions and identities. This forced assimilation and the erasure of expansive conceptions of gender contributed to the widespread adoption of a strict binary view of gender, defining people solely by the sex assigned at birth and corresponding gender roles.

Over time, this push toward a strict binary view of gender simplified how the world sees gender and sexuality, overshadowing the diverse ways people have understood themselves across different cultures. The influence of certain powerful nations enabled them not only to spread their views on gender but to enforce them, creating the illusion that the gender binary is a natural and universal aspect of every culture and has always existed in its current form. This enforced perception masked the diverse and fluid understandings of gender that existed in many societies before this imposition (Snorton 2017).

### MARK AND DAVID'S FEAR OF DIFFERENCE
#### Embracing Their Nonbinary Child

*Mark and David were a gay couple who had been together for fifteen years when they decided to adopt a child from China. After a lengthy process, they welcomed their dream baby—an Asian child they named Liam. From the moment they took Liam home, Mark and David showered them with unconditional love.*

*Yet as Liam grew older, Mark and David couldn't help but worry about the challenges Liam might face. As a same-sex couple raising a child in a world that could still be harsh toward LGBTQ+ families, they feared intense mockery, bullying, and discrimination. Their own childhoods had been marred by relentless cruelty from peers, teachers, and even their own families because of their sexuality.*

*Mark and David were determined to protect Liam from that pain at all costs. But they didn't know how to prepare Liam for the anti-Asian racism and xenophobic harassment they knew was still prevalent in many communities. They agonized over striking the right balance—building up*

*Liam's confidence and self-worth, while also cautioning them about the realities of being a child of gay parents and a racial minority.*

*So, when Liam began identifying as nonbinary in middle school, it triggered Mark and David's deepest fears about their child being mocked and ostracized for being "different." Though they loved Liam fiercely, they struggled to understand the new pronouns and identity. A part of them wondered if this was just confusion stemming from the pressures of having two dads and being one of the only Asian kids in their community.*

*Liam felt deeply unsupported and misunderstood by their parents. They loved Mark and David with every fiber of their being, but Mark and David's inability to affirm Liam's identity made them feel erased, unloved, and alone during a pivotal time. The rift grew until Liam withdrew from their parents, creating a painful divide in their once close family.*

*Through LGBTQ+ counseling, painstaking research, and connecting with other families of transgender and nonbinary children, Mark and David began to understand that gender existed on a spectrum. They had to unlearn generations of ingrained biases not just about sexuality but about rigid cultural norms around gender expression. While they had been part of the LGBTQ+ community for their adult lives, they still viewed gender as a binary and thus found it difficult to understand Liam's identity.*

*It was a difficult journey for them. Raised in a society that relentlessly enforced a strict gender binary, deconstructing those boundaries in their minds felt radical and terrifying. But their love for Liam remained unwavering. Mark and David realized that by rejecting any part of their child, they were rejecting the opportunity to know and love their full, authentic self.*

*Though the process was fraught with stumbles, tears, and regrets about past mistakes, they learned to truly listen and embrace Liam's identity. They came to understand that Liam's gender identity was not new or unusual, but part of a legacy of expansive conceptions of gender that have been oppressed by dominant culture and limiting beliefs. With this knowledge, they created an affirmative, supportive environment for their nonbinary child to thrive—mockery be damned. Their family was stronger than any cruelty the outside world could throw at them, united in their commitment to honoring Liam's authentic self.*

In my work with parents and caregivers, I've developed a tool that proves incredibly effective for broadening perspectives on gender identity—it's called the Gender Identity Challenge™. This exercise is designed to encourage thoughtful self-examination of one's own gender identity and experiences. It doesn't require any particular beliefs about gender but rather invites participants to explore their personal feelings and experiences related to gender through guided introspection.

The core of this challenge is two simple yet profound questions:

### GENDER IDENTITY CHALLENGE™

What is your gender?

How do you know you are that gender?

Rules: You can't reference body parts ("I know I'm a woman because I have ___________.")

You can't use gender terms/language ("I know I'm a man because I feel masculine.")

The Gender Identity Challenge prompts individuals to reflect on their own experiences of gender—whether it feels deeply personal and intrinsic or more like a role they were assigned without much say.

While engaging with these questions, if you find yourself feeling uncomfortable, that's perfectly natural, and we welcome that discomfort as part of the process. This exercise quickly reveals how gendered our language is and how heavily we rely on anatomy to define our identity. Without the usual references, you might have easily rattled off answers to the two questions, but when forced to move beyond body parts and gendered terminology, most cisgender people find themselves totally stuck. This is because most cisgender individuals are assigned a sex at birth and socialized to have a gender that aligns with that assignment, rarely questioning or reflecting on it.

People who engage with the Gender Identity Challenge in workshops, coaching sessions, or online communities, frequently provide responses that highlight the harm done by gender essentialism and societal norms that perpetuate "traditional" gender norms. Women often share insights about feeling defined by oppressive experiences—being spoken over in meetings or facing physical dangers—highlighting how societal views on femininity can impose limitations and hardships. The most common responses from cisgender women include "being belittled, feeling physically vulnerable, being groped, being overlooked in favor of male colleagues, being sexually harassed." They also expressed the exhaustion from the performance of femininity: "I need to engage in compensatory measures like hair removal, dressing feminine, using a nonconfrontational tone of voice," "I have faced oppression targeted against women, so I suppose I match the target," and "I know I'm a woman because I'm treated like one." These responses raise a troubling question: is being a woman defined by oppression? The exercise reveals the deep impact of societal expectations and stereotypes, prompting us to reconsider the broader implications of how gender identity is shaped and constrained by these external forces.

However, it is important to recognize that gender identity is not solely defined by negative experiences. Many women also feel a deep, authentic connection to their gender in positive ways. Some responses highlight this: "I feel like a woman because of the strength I draw from my female friendships," "I cherish the ability to nurture and care for others, which I feel is an integral part of my womanhood," and "Being a woman means embracing my creativity and emotional depth." These examples show that while oppression is a real and significant part of many women's experiences, it is not the sole defining factor of their identity.

The exercise reveals the deep impact of societal expectations and stereotypes, prompting us to reconsider the broader implications of how gender identity is shaped and constrained by these external forces. It also underscores the importance of recognizing and validating the diverse and multifaceted experiences of all individuals, whether their gender was assigned to them at birth or not. This holistic view allows us to appreciate the complex and varied ways people understand and inhabit their genders.

Many men who complete the Gender Identity Challenge express feeling boxed into protector roles, where showing strength is valued over vulnerability, reflecting societal expectations about masculinity. They often describe the pressure to conform to traditional notions of masculinity, such as "providing and protecting," "suppressing emotions to appear strong," and "facing criticism for showing sensitivity." One participant shared, "I feel like I have to be the rock in every situation, and admitting 'I need help' is seen as weak." Another man mentioned, "I know I'm a man because I'm expected to always be in control." These reflections highlight the intense pressure men face to uphold traditional masculine ideals, which can be emotionally exhausting and restrictive.

However, it's also important to acknowledge that many men feel a deep, positive connection to their masculinity. Some men express a sense of fulfillment and authenticity in their gender roles: "I feel like a man when I support and protect my loved ones," "I enjoy the camaraderie and bond I share with my male friends," and "Being a man means embracing my role as a father and the unique way I connect with my children." These positive experiences show that masculinity, like femininity, can be a source of pride and strength when not confined to rigid stereotypes.

By recognizing both the pressures and the positive aspects of masculinity, we can gain a more comprehensive understanding of men's experiences and challenge the stereotypes that constrain them. This balanced view encourages men to embrace a broader, more authentic expression of their identities.

Responses to the Gender Identity Challenge consistently cite relational context as a core component of how we conceptualize our gender identity. Social constructivist models of gender suggest that gendered attitudes and behaviors, such as femininity and masculinity, are context-dependent (Butler 2006, Lorber 2018). This implies that gender identity might be better conceptualized as variable states rather than stable traits. For instance, human giver syndrome is the false, contagious belief that women have a moral obligation to be pretty, happy, calm, generous, and attentive to the needs of others (Nagoski and Nagoski 2019). This idea reflects how deeply societal norms shape our understanding of gender roles and expectations.

Precarious manhood theory further illustrates this concept by positing that manhood, in contrast to womanhood, is seen as a precarious state requiring continual social proof and validation. Because of this precariousness, men often feel especially threatened by challenges to their masculinity (Vandello et al. 2008). This theory highlights how societal expectations pressure men to constantly demonstrate their masculinity, often through strength and dominance, while discouraging vulnerability and emotional expression.

Our rigid definitions of gender uphold toxic masculinity and restrict the full range of human expression for everyone. For example, societal norms often dictate who gets to be nurturing and who doesn't, typically reserving caregiving roles for women while discouraging men from expressing gentleness and care. To create a more inclusive and supportive society for the next generation, we must ask ourselves some critical questions: What cultural shifts are necessary so that we can all, regardless of gender, be human beings and human givers? How are we upholding toxic masculinity and precarious manhood by our rigid definitions of gender? Who gets to be nurturing and who doesn't?

In a society in which a person's gender identity can limit their access to opportunity, we must ask: in what ways is gender defined by the presence or absence of privilege? This question challenges us to think beyond the traditional binary and consider the broader implications of how we perceive gender. What if gender was defined by collective strength, by the ways we uplift each other, or by the pursuit of pleasure rather than by shared experiences of pain and oppression? Imagine a world where gender identity isn't confined by societal expectations and limitations but is celebrated as a diverse and dynamic facet of our shared humanity. Is your gender identity a variable state, shifting and evolving with your experiences, or is it a stable trait, a core aspect of who you are? Reflecting on these possibilities invites us to redefine gender in a way that honors each individual's unique journey and fosters a more inclusive and compassionate society. What do you want gender to be defined by?

By challenging restrictive norms and embracing a more fluid understanding of gender, we can foster an environment where everyone, regardless of gender, can express their true selves. This shift will enable individuals to move beyond the constraints of traditional gender roles and stereotypes, allowing for a more authentic and fulfilling expression of identity.

Trans folks often carry the additional burden of being expected to explain or justify their gender identity in ways that cis folks are not. This disparity highlights a fundamental issue: while cisgender individuals typically move through life without their gender being challenged or questioned, trans people are often subjected to invasive questioning and skepticism despite the fact that they likely have a far deeper and more thorough understanding of their gender identity than people whose assigned gender at birth corresponds with the way in which they are perceived.

These discussions reveal how traditional gender roles can be restrictive and not truly reflective of individual identities and personalities. When participants say, "Well, I just know," they are expressing an intrinsic understanding of their identity, what researcher Jack Turban calls "transcendent sense of gender." If we accept this explanation from cisgender individuals, then, in the spirit of equality, we must accept it from everyone, including trans and nonbinary individuals. This exercise underscores the importance of allowing people to define their own identities, paving the way for a future where everyone can express themselves more fully and authentically, free from the constraints of assigned roles and expectations. This shift can empower all of us to live as our true selves and honor when people tell us who they are.

As we began this chapter, you may not have fully recognized the ways binary thinking shapes and restricts our understanding of gender and identity. Now, as you reflect on what you've learned, I invite you to embrace this empowering belief instead:

---

"I embrace the belief that gender is expansive and fluid; I celebrate and support the diverse expressions of identity."

---

## KEY POINTS

**Binary Thinking Oversimplifies the Complexity of Human Experience:** The belief that everything must fit into two opposing categories—male/female, right/wrong, strong/weak—ignores the reality of diversity.

**Gender Roles Have Been Socially Constructed and Reinforced:** From childhood toys to workplace expectations, society dictates rigid ideas about how people "should" behave based on gender.

**Marketing and Media Perpetuate the Gender Binary:** Products, advertising, and entertainment reinforce gendered expectations that shape how people see themselves and others.

**The Binary is a Colonial Construct:** Many Indigenous and non-Western cultures historically recognized multiple genders, but colonialism imposed rigid classifications that erased or criminalized gender diversity.

**Expanding Beyond the Binary Benefits Everyone:** When gender norms are challenged, all people—not just trans and nonbinary individuals—gain more freedom to express themselves authentically.

**The Gender Identity Challenge™:** This tool helps individuals explore their own gender identity beyond physical characteristics and societal roles. It encourages introspection and reveals how traditional gender roles can be restrictive and not truly reflective of individual identities.

## REFLECTION QUESTIONS

1. How has binary thinking shaped the way you view gender, work, parenting, or relationships?
2. In what ways do gendered expectations affect your daily life, even if you don't always notice them? (think back to the Gender Identity Challenge™)
3. How does the language we use about gender reinforce or challenge the binary?
4. What aspects of your upbringing encouraged or discouraged gender nonconformity?
5. What are some ways you can help create a world where all children—regardless of gender—can thrive as their authentic selves?

3

# AREN'T THEY TOO YOUNG TO KNOW?

**When did you first know** your gender identity? Do you remember feeling sure of it? If you can't recall, don't beat yourself up, because you were likely around three years old. Often people don't vividly recall moments that confirm what they've always been told; it's the experiences that diverge from expected norms that stand out in our memories. For example, while many remember their first crush, few heterosexual people recall a specific moment when they realized they were heterosexual, in part because a heterosexual orientation aligned with societal expectations and required no internal conflict or reevaluation.

Similarly, moments when we realize our gender identity doesn't match societal expectations are more memorable because they challenge our sense of self and highlight our differences. This can evoke a strong sense of being "different" and can be unsettling. However, for those whose gender identity aligns with societal expectations, there often isn't a memorable "aha" moment—it simply fits seamlessly into the background of their life, unchallenged and accepted as the norm. Recognizing the diverse experiences of those with varied gender identities helps us to be empathetic to their journeys. It underscores the importance of providing support and understanding for all individuals, regardless of how they identify.

To best answer this question of when and how we first discover our gender identity, let's break down what we know about gender identity development in kids. Research suggests that by a child's third birthday, they are clearly able to label and identify their gender (Graham 2022). Often before school age, children begin to experience more gender stability; their basic gender identity doesn't change over time. This stability increases in children in early elementary school as they experience greater gender constancy (Martinez et al. 2020). Gender constancy means their gender remains the same across changes in gender expression (e.g., hair length, clothing, behavior) (Psychology.JRank.org n.d.). A great example of this is playing dress-up or other imaginary games in which a child can know their own gender regardless of the garments they are wearing or the role they are playing.

However, it is important to note that just because a child appears aligned with their sex assigned at birth during childhood, that does not mean they are not trans or gender nonconforming. For a variety of reasons, many people don't feel safe or confident disclosing their identity until later in life due to fears of discrimination, rejection, or loss. They may also lack the language to articulate their feelings, leading them to conform to expected gender roles because they believe they won't be understood or believed if they express their truth. Internally, they might feel a persistent discomfort, sensing that "something is not right," even if they aren't yet able to communicate it effectively.

### Jamie's Early Gender Dissonance and Affirmation

*From the moment Jamie (assigned male at birth) could communicate, there were signs that her inner sense of self didn't align with societal expectations. As a toddler, Jamie gravitated exclusively toward dolls, dresses, and anything traditionally coded as feminine. Jamie's parents, Samantha and Michael, initially brushed it off as a harmless phase, assuming Jamie would eventually embrace more masculine interests and expression.*

*However, as Jamie approached her third birthday, her insistence about being a girl intensified dramatically. "I'm not a boy, I'm a girl!" Jamie would protest adamantly whenever referred to with he/him pronouns or as someone's son. Samantha and Michael felt their concerns growing as Jamie became increasingly distressed about having a male body, refusing to use the boys' bathroom and crying over the prospect of growing up to look like a man.*

*By age five, Jamie was exhibiting signs of gender dysphoria—a persistent and significant dissonance between her inner gender identity as female and her assigned male sex at birth. After consulting with a gender therapist, Samantha and Michael came to understand that Jamie's feelings and identity as a transgender girl were deeply rooted, unwavering, and required affirmation rather than denial.*

*With parental support, Jamie was able to socially transition to live fully as her authentic self by age six. She felt immense relief at being able to use she/her pronouns, growing out her hair, wearing dresses, and being recognized by her chosen name, Jamie. Her self-esteem and confidence flourished in the affirmative environment her parents worked hard to create.*

*Though Samantha and Michael were fully supportive of Jamie's transition, Jamie's grandparents initially struggled, expressing concerns about her being "too young" and fearing she was "going through a phase." Through their religious community, Jamie's grandparents found an educational support group for grandparents of trans youth. As they learned more and talked with other grandparents about supporting transgender youth and creating a strong support network, they became Jamie's fiercest advocates. Now, ten years old, Jamie is thriving as her authentic self, and her grandparents are helping to support other grandparents who are also in the process of broadening their understanding of gender identity and sexual orientation.*

Gender development of transgender kids between the ages of three and twelve years old is, at the most basic level, the same as cisgender children's gender development (Gülgöz et al. 2019). More and more studies have shown that gender nonconforming and transgender children are just as confident and consistent in their own gender identity as cisgender children (Olson and Gülgöz 2017). Any identity confusion a caregiver witnesses is more likely due to societal expectations and a desire to conform than doubting their own identity. Researchers have found that preschool-aged transgender children who have socially transitioned are similar to their gender-typical peers in their preferences for toys, clothes, and friends. Similarly, children who had socially transitioned expressed greater feelings of similarity to peers of their own expressed gender than those of their sex assigned at birth (Rae et al. 2019).

Kids know themselves a whole lot more than adults tend to give them credit for, and we need to listen to them. It's entirely possible that your child will go through a phase of wanting to wear certain types of clothing or style their hair a certain way, and that does not mean that they are transgender. It means they are exploring their identity, and it's essential that they have the space and support to do so. Restricting a child's exploration of gender identity will not prevent the child from exploring. Instead, it teaches them that nonconformity is shameful and must be done in secrecy.

### KAI KNEW FIRST

#### A Child's Gender Identity and Parental Learning

*From the moment they could express preferences, Kai (assigned female at birth) gravitated toward a wide range of gender expressions. As a preschooler, Kai loved wearing dresses one day and superhero costumes the next. Some mornings they insisted on being called different pronouns or a masculine name like Jake; other days they went by she/her pronouns and feminine nicknames.*

*Kai's parents, Anna and Patrick, were initially wary of their child's fluid relationship with gender norms and tried to encourage them to dress and behave like girls their age. When Kai's exploratory gender expression was not immediately accepted or understood, they resorted to dressing up in their brother's clothes in secret when the family was asleep. This private act allowed Kai to play and express themself as who they truly were, but over time, doing it in secrecy began to cause a deep sense of shame. They knew their parents wanted them to be a girl, and this conflict between their authentic self and their parents' expectations weighed heavily on them, fostering feelings of guilt and isolation.*

*However, after consulting gender therapists, Anna and Patrick learned that Kai was simply exhibiting the natural gender creativity and exploration common in young children. Rather than enforce rigid roles, they decided to take an affirmative, supportive approach—allowing Kai freedom to explore without judgment. They used Kai's pronouns of the day, let them choose clothes and toys across the binary, and surrounded them with positive gender diversity role models.*

*As Kai entered elementary school, their tendency to move fluidly between masculine and feminine presentation persisted. Though some extended family members expressed concern that Kai was "confused," their parents created an environment where Kai felt safe to embrace their authentic self.*

*By the end of middle school, Kai had landed on using they/them pronouns and began identifying as nonbinary. Though the process of adolescence and puberty brought some new challenges, Kai's parents continued affirming their identity. Now eighteen, Kai is preparing to head off to college with a strong sense of self and confidence in their gender identity. They credit their parents' unconditional love and willingness to provide a judgment-free space to explore as a kid for allowing them to become a well-adjusted, thriving nonbinary adult.*

*While Kai's gender journey involved many twists and turns, their parents' commitment to listening and affirming their child's inner truth ultimately fostered trust, open communication, and Kai's ability to blossom into their authentic self.*

Parents will naturally ask, "How do I know if this is my kid exploring or if my kid is really transgender?" As much as it may feel like it's your job to know, it isn't. Your job is to provide unconditional love and support. When it comes to gender, there are no guaranteed outcomes. Your best bet is to listen to your child. I know this is scary, but it's important not to let that fear become an exercise in control. Preferences for colors or activities are different from a proclamation of identity such as "I am a girl," which is a much stronger indicator of gender identity. Studies show that the gender nonconforming children who identify as transgender later in life showed more extremity in their nonconformity than other children (Fast and Olson 2017). Simply put, the more a child identifies with and expresses a gender identity other than the one they've been assigned at birth, the more likely they are to transition (Rae et al. 2019). Results further suggest that children who socially transition at early ages are likely to continue to identify as transgender later in life (Fast and Olson 2017).

One thing in the research that's incredibly clear: kids who have parental support are happier, healthier, and have greater self-esteem. Ask yourself this: whether this is a phase or not, can you love and support your child anyway?

Learning that your child's gender identity is different from what you believed it to be can feel confusing and even frightening, and you may be concerned that they are too young to know. I encourage you to consider this empowering belief instead:

> "I trust my child's deep understanding of their own identity and respect their self-expression at all stages. I'm committed to supporting my child's unique journey, wherever it may lead."

## KEY POINTS

**Early Understanding of Gender Identity:** Children often know and label their gender by age three, with gender stability developing in early childhood. They experience greater gender constancy in early elementary school, understanding that their gender remains consistent regardless of external changes in appearance or activities.

**Memorable Realizations:** While cisgender individuals often don't remember specific moments of gender realization because it aligns with societal expectations, transgender individuals often remember these moments vividly as they challenge those norms.

**Research and Consistency:** Studies show that transgender and gender nonconforming children are as confident and consistent in their gender identity as cisgender children. Any perceived confusion is often due to societal pressures rather than an internal lack of understanding.

**Parental Support is Crucial:** Kids who receive parental support in their gender identity are happier, healthier, and have higher self-esteem. Young people who feel that their gender identity is affirmed by their parents are less likely to experience negative outcomes such as depression and anxiety.

**Case Studies:** Real-life examples of children like Jamie and Kai illustrate the importance of early support and affirmation from parents. These stories show how understanding and acceptance can lead to positive mental health and well-being for transgender and nonbinary youth.

## REFLECTION QUESTIONS

1. How did you come to understand your own gender identity? Do you remember any specific moments that were significant to you?

2. How can you create a supportive environment for your child to explore their gender identity without judgment or pressure to conform to societal norms?

3. What steps can you take to educate yourself about gender diversity and the experiences of transgender and nonbinary individuals?
4. How do you differentiate between your child's exploration of gender expression and their proclamation of gender identity? What signs might indicate a stronger alignment with a gender other than the one they were assigned at birth?
5. How can you ensure that your child feels loved and supported regardless of their gender identity or expression? What practices can you put in place to reinforce this unconditional support?

4

# WHY DIDN'T THEY SHOW SIGNS—OR DID I MISS THEM?

**Every parent's experience** of their child's coming out is unique, but many fall into two categories: the parents who feel like their kid never showed signs, and the parents who feel guilt and shame because they feel they should have known. The reality is that no one prepared you for this, and your initial response is likely a result of a wide range of emotions that are shaped by cultural norms that limit our understanding of identity. You can't change the past, but you can reflect on it and adjust how you'd like to parent your child moving forward.

> What emotions did I experience when I first learned about my child's gender identity?
>
> Did my reaction fall into one of these categories?

## BREAKING THROUGH DOUBT

### A Mother's Path to Unwavering Support

*When fourteen-year-old Taylor came out as nonbinary, their mother Claire experienced a whirlwind of emotions. On one hand, she felt blindsided—Taylor had never expressed any discomfort with their assigned sex and gender growing up. They loved dolls, dresses, and all things traditionally feminine. How could Claire have missed this?*

*At the same time, Claire's mind raced back through Taylor's childhood, analyzing every memory for potential signs or hints she may have overlooked. The way Taylor would get visibly uncomfortable when relatives commented on them "becoming a beautiful young lady." Their tendency to bristle at being called "pretty" or complimented on their looks. A general aversion to highly sexualized girls' clothing as they got older.*

*Guilt and shame washed over Claire as she wondered if she had somehow failed as a parent by not recognizing Taylor's nonbinary identity sooner. Had she inadvertently forced them into an ill-fitting gender box all these years? The thought made her ill.*

*Yet even as Claire berated herself, she knew her reaction stemmed from a place of love and concern for her child's well-being. Like most parents in her situation, she simply hadn't been equipped to anticipate this revelation. Nothing truly prepares you for how to navigate your child's gender journey. After the initial shock wore off, Claire resolved to focus not on what she could have done differently in the past, but on how to best support Taylor now that she understood their truth. She sought out a local support group and found an organization called PFLAG that provided weekly meetings for parents of transgender youth. She apologized to Taylor for any misgendering or invalidations and committed to using their correct name and pronouns from that day forward.*

*Though the process wasn't always easy, Claire made protecting Taylor's mental health and sense of self her top priority. She let go of her own vision of who she thought her child was and embraced them for who they really are. In doing so, their bond grew stronger than ever before.*

*Looking back, Claire realizes her initial reactions—whether feeling blindsided or racked with guilt—were merely human responses borne from love and fear of the unknown. The true test was how she chose to move forward. By leading with empathy, validation, and an open heart, Claire and Taylor were able to strengthen their relationship and thrive on this journey together.*

Shock and disbelief often accompany parents' reactions to their trans child coming out. "But there were never any signs! This can't be real." For all of their life, they were your little girl or baby boy—and now you are being asked to alter your perception of your own child. For many parents, this feels like a drastic change and comes as a painful surprise. If you have searched online for anything about transgender adolescents, it's likely you have come across the term "rapid onset gender dysphoria" (ROGD). As a gender specialist, I have received many frantic voicemails and sat with many distressed parents who have been exposed to false literature presenting ROGD as a real phenomenon and are now afraid to believe their adolescent telling them that they are trans or nonbinary.

*"It just doesn't make sense, we know our kid, there's no way."*

*"It seems like their whole friend group is trans, so that's probably what started this."*

*"How did this happen so fast?"*

The disbelief that often accompanies an adolescent coming out as trans has dangerously permeated the fringes of the medical community, distorting the larger cultural narrative around trans adolescents. The term ROGD was coined by Dr. Lisa Littman in a study she conducted and published through Brown University's academic journal PLOS ONE (Littman 2018).

Her assertion was that ROGD is a real phenomenon and that social influences, parent-child conflict, and maladaptive coping mechanisms may be contributing factors for some individuals. The term invigorated controversy in both the medical community and the broader queer community for both incendiary claims and flawed methodology.

*What was so wrong with the research?*

The research utilized a pathology framework: the method which doctors would use to study a viral contagion or influenza. Littman garnered data from transphobic sources only, so of the parents she surveyed, 76.5% believed that their child was incorrect in their belief that they were transgender. The article employed transphobic language and regarded gender dysphoria as a "psychological affliction" and "viral contagion." Littman wrongly compared gender dysphoria to eating disorders like anorexia and bulimia. She claimed that teenagers might say they're transgender just because their friends are doing it, similar to how some teens might develop eating disorders due to peer influence. This comparison is not accurate and oversimplifies the complex nature of gender identity. Gender dysphoria, an actual diagnosis in the Diagnostic and Statistical Manual of Mental Disorders (DSM-5), is defined as a "marked incongruence between their experienced or expressed gender and the one they were assigned at birth"; gender dysphoria isn't something you catch like a virus or pick up from a group of friends to fit in.

On August 27, 2018, Brown University removed their press release about the publication due to concerns over the "research designs and methods." That same day, PLOS ONE conducted a post-publication review and insisted that revisions be made. The academic journal's correction notice stated that the study was of parent observations and interpretations but failed to "collect data from the adolescents and young adults (AYAs) or clinicians and therefore does not validate the phenomenon" (Littman 2019). The flawed methods and erroneous conclusions of Littman's report have been widely debunked, but many anti-LGBTQ+ activists still cling to the idea of ROGD because it is politically useful to them as they prey on the fears and insecurities of parents of gender-expansive youth.

### DEBUNKING ROGD

#### How the Williams Family Found the Truth

*The Williams family considered themselves a progressive, LGBTQ+-supportive household. So, when their twelve-year-old child came out as transgender, identifying as a girl named Sarah, they were blindsided. Sarah had never expressed any discomfort with being a boy throughout childhood, and the announcement felt sudden and disorienting.*

*In their confusion, the Williams began scouring the internet for information and came across the concept of "rapid onset gender dysphoria" (ROGD). The theory claimed that some teens, especially those with pre-existing mental health issues or trauma, could become trans-identified due to social contagion and peer influence. The Williams felt the ROGD hypothesis fit their situation. Sarah did struggle with anxiety and had been bullied at school. Plus, two of her closest friends had also recently come out as trans or nonbinary. The parents worried Sarah was simply going through a phase or had been swayed by these influences to identify as a different gender.*

*Fueled by fears stoked from ROGD websites, the Williams initially refused to use Sarah's new name and pronouns. Sarah's father David was adamant that they should not "indulge" this new identity. He believed it was their responsibility as parents to help their child see reality and feared they would regret affirming Sarah's gender in the future. Sarah's mother Rachel, however, began to worry about the escalating conflicts and Sarah's deteriorating mental health.*

*Over time, Rachel quietly began researching beyond the ROGD theory. She discovered that the overwhelming majority of reputable medical organizations, including the American Psychological Association and the American Academy of Pediatrics, did not recognize ROGD as a valid diagnosis. She started attending support groups for parents of trans youth, where she heard other families' stories and began to question the narrative David was holding onto. Rachel started using Sarah's name and pronouns in private and tried to gently engage David in discussions about gender identity, though these conversations often ended in frustration.*

*For Sarah, the lack of full family support was devastating. While she found some solace in her mother's quiet affirmations, the ongoing rejection from her father deeply hurt her. She began withdrawing from family interactions, and her mental health suffered as she felt increasingly unseen and invalidated in her own home.*

*After several months of this conflict, the family sought out a gender therapist. The therapist helped Rachel and David explore their own fears and misconceptions about Sarah's identity. While Rachel was ready to embrace Sarah fully, David remained resistant. He continued to struggle with accepting Sarah's gender, believing that affirming her would cause long-term harm. He refused to use her chosen name and pronouns, creating an ongoing source of tension.*

*Despite this, Rachel and Sarah moved forward together. Rachel advocated for Sarah at school, helping her socially transition and ensuring that her teachers and peers used the correct name and pronouns. Sarah found support in friends and a local LGBTQ+ youth group, which became a vital lifeline. While her relationship with her father remained strained, she began to rebuild her confidence and sense of self through the affirmations she received elsewhere.*

*David's resistance remained, but over time, the family found a fragile equilibrium. Rachel and Sarah maintained a close bond, while Sarah and her father remained distant. Though Rachel continued to hope David would come around, she recognized that Sarah's well-being couldn't wait. She chose to support her daughter openly, even if their family dynamic would never be the same.*

The key takeaway from the Williamses' experience is that while initial confusion around a child's gender identity is understandable, parents should approach the situation with an open mind and prioritize their child's mental health over unsubstantiated theories like ROGD. With affirmation and love, families can navigate this journey together, ensuring the well-being and happiness of their transgender children.

It's important to revisit the statistic mentioned in the first chapter: 95% of people identify with the sex assigned to them at birth. This highlights that being transgender is far from a "fad" that the media sometimes portrays it to be. Adolescents and teens, who often strive to fit in, are not suddenly "jumping on the bandwagon" of being transgender. If your child has friends who have also come out as transgender, it's not indicative of a trend but rather a reflection of trans youth seeking each other out for support and understanding. Transgender individuals are in the minority, and naturally, they find solace in forming friendships with others who share similar experiences. Even when media narratives or biased reports suggest otherwise, it's crucial to consider simpler, more straightforward explanations grounded in empathy and reality.

Littman's so-called research creates a false "medical" foundation behind transphobia, prompting parents to question the truth in their child's trans identity under the guise of medical validity, and manipulates parental confusion and shock into full-on denial and rejection. To make matters worse, Littman's work is often one of the first publications that concerned parents will come across online. Many anti-trans organizations point to her work as an evidence base for their transphobic claims. Although drawing attention for its contentious nature, Littman's term ROGD is not a recognized clinical term or phenomenon and is not used medically.

To put it simply, ROGD does not exist and is not a diagnosis. Rather, the small truth to extract from Littman is that the perceived rapidness of coming out is actually a parental temporal misalignment. In essence, temporal misalignment asserts that your child has likely explored, researched, questioned, and educated themselves long before coming out to you. It is possible that your child was holding back sharing their identity with you, not because they didn't trust you to support them but because of the pathologizing of trans identities that results from shoddy pseudoscience that figures such as Littman disguise as true research.

While a young person's coming out may seem abrupt, it's crucial to remember that just because the revelation is new to you, does not mean it was a recent discovery for them as well. Coming out as trans is never a trivial decision, even in the most progressive communities. It is challenging and fraught with potential backlash; it's not something one does impulsively. Nearly everyone who comes out faces difficulties, including disapproval, transphobia, disbelief, and even the shock or sorrow of loved ones. Given these stakes, the decision by your child to share their truth with you is a significant act of trust and should be treated with the highest degree of seriousness and consideration, rather than being dismissed as a passing trend.

## WHEN GENDER DYSPHORIA EMERGES LATER

### The Roberts Family's Story

*For the first twelve years of Taylor's life, there were no overt signs that his inner gender identity didn't align with being assigned female at birth. Taylor had always been a "typically feminine child" who loved princesses, dance, and dresses. So, when Taylor began puberty and suddenly expressed feeling "like my body is betraying me," it completely blindsided his parents, Liz and Carlos.*

*Initially, Liz and Carlos thought Taylor's discomfort was simply a reaction to the normal changes of female puberty or perhaps influenced by social contagion after a classmate came out as trans. They tried to reassure Taylor that these feelings were just a phase and encouraged him to embrace the changes. However, Taylor's distress only intensified over the next year. He experienced a severe aversion to developing breasts, getting a period, and other female secondary sex characteristics. This discomfort quickly turned into deep emotional turmoil.*

*Taylor became withdrawn and started to isolate himself from friends and family. He experienced periods of intense depression and began engaging in self-harm behaviors like cutting. Liz and Carlos were beside themselves with worry, feeling helpless as they watched their child suffer. The situation reached a critical point when Taylor began expressing suicidal thoughts, desperate for any solution to alleviate his suffering.*

*In an attempt to find answers, Liz and Carlos sought the help of a family counselor who specialized in gender identity issues. Through counseling sessions, it became clear that Taylor's distress was not just about puberty or peer influence; it was a profound disconnect between his assigned gender and his true identity. The counselor explained that gender dysphoria can sometimes emerge more clearly during adolescence, especially with the onset of puberty.*

*With professional guidance, Liz and Carlos began to understand that Taylor's identity as a transgender boy was valid, persistent, and couldn't be ignored or repressed without devastating consequences. They were advised to support Taylor's exploration of his gender identity and to consider medical options that could help alleviate his dysphoria. The counselor emphasized the importance of listening to Taylor and trusting his deep understanding of himself.*

*Despite their initial shock and confusion, Liz and Carlos decided to take a leap of faith for the sake of their child's well-being. They began using Taylor's chosen name and pronouns and sought out a gender therapist to help guide the family through this transition. After thorough discussions with medical professionals, Taylor started puberty blockers to halt the unwanted physical changes and give him time to explore his gender identity without the added distress of puberty.*

*As Taylor began to present in a way congruent with his male identity, his mental health improved dramatically. He became more open, engaged, and his periods of depression and self-harm significantly decreased. Liz and Carlos saw their child smile and laugh again, something they hadn't seen in a long time.*

*The path was unexpected and involved a period of mourning for Liz and Carlos. They had to let go of the daughter they thought they had and the future they envisioned for her, and embrace their son, Taylor. This was not easy, but their love for their child and commitment to his happiness and well-being overrode any other concerns.*

*Taylor's journey also brought the family closer together. They learned the importance of open communication, empathy, and unconditional support. Liz and Carlos joined a support group for parents of transgender children, which provided them with a community of understanding and shared experiences.*

*In retrospect, Liz and Carlos realized that their initial fears and misconceptions had been unfounded. Taylor's identity as a transgender boy was not a phase or a result of social influence; it was his authentic self finally emerging. They understood that affirming Taylor's gender identity was crucial for his mental health and overall well-being.*

It is a jarring experience for a parent to feel as if their child isn't "who you thought they were." The truth is that your child is still the same person, they are just being more authentic with you now. That bears repeating. Your child's gender identity is not something "new," even if they did not realize or articulate it when they were three years old. This has always been a part of your child's identity, but they may not have had the language and framework to understand it themselves and explain it to those they're close to. Your child is still the same person you have always loved, only now they are less alone in being who they truly are. While the part of you that is shocked or even terrified may be present, I encourage you to allow the part of you that has the capacity to truly listen to and trust your child to take the lead. The fear you experience won't last forever, but the impact of your love and support of your child will.

When you think about your child's transition, what are you most afraid of?

*"When I look back now, I feel like I should have known!"*

Often parents express feeling a stew of emotions as they adjust to the evolving identity of their child. Some parents experience shame or guilt for not recognizing their child's gender identity sooner. Parents will often report wishing they had known what to look for, or that they had somehow "acted on" suspicions they may have had before their child was ready to come out. I have witnessed parents engage in such negative self-talk about their parenting because they feel they failed in some way. But there is no formula, and you didn't fail parenting! You were not "supposed to know," and if you suspected, you were not supposed to inundate your child with questions and suspicions when they were not ready and might have been confused and distressed. Maybe there is no 'right' timeline; there is only being there for your child when they are ready and loving and supporting them on their timeline.

*"I just want to know if I missed something—where did I go wrong?"*

You may have read articles that contain lists like "Ten Signs Your Kid Is Transgender" or "How to Tell If Your Child Might Be Trans." These lists speak to the parts of caregivers that desperately want reliable answers and highlight the internet's tendency to make complex topics seem far simpler than they are in ways that make us feel inadequate and reinforce our insecurities, especially in regard to parenting. When we feel out of our depth, we look for certainty, and this is understandable. We want answers, we want to know that what we're experiencing is normal, and we want to know that it's all going to be okay.

The internet can also be a source of valuable information. Still, it is important not to take a brief article or list more seriously than you take your own child. Nor should you narrow your understanding of a wide and complex issue down to something like "ten signs." Such lists of behaviors must be taken in context and not overanalyzed. No single behavior or combination of behaviors makes someone trans, and these lists are often compilations of behavioral trends that tend to overlap in trans children. There is an expansive variation of childhood behaviors—some of them fleeting and others reflective of larger truths, and it's often very difficult to tell them apart. You are not the first parent who has struggled to identify this distinction.

Here is a compilation of reported behaviors from clients, caregivers, educators, clinicians, and in research:

1. Wanting to pee the "other way"
2. Taking dress-up very seriously
3. Referring to themself as the opposite gender
4. Consistently choosing characters in video games and/or pretend play that differs from their gender assigned at birth
5. Lack of interest in activities that are conventionally related to their assigned gender
6. Resistance to getting or wanting haircuts
7. Avoidance of dress clothes and more gendered garments
8. Disliking their name
9. Frustration with their genitals or refusal to use the bathroom
10. Hypervigilance about privacy
11. Difficulty with or dislike of bathing/showering/personal hygiene
12. Positive reaction when people get confused over their gender
13. Reporting wanting a "do-over" or to wake up as a different gender
14. Happier when allowed to experiment with their gender

Some of the items on this list might resonate with you—whether it's in relation to your trans child, your cis child, or even yourself. This is because, while there are common experiences many trans individuals share, there is no definitive checklist that encompasses all trans experiences. Similarly, many cisgender people might exhibit traits or qualities often associated with trans identities without identifying as trans themselves. While these are commonly documented behavioral and emotional patterns in trans children, they are not to be used as a tool to prove (or disprove) one's trans identity. Each child's gender evolution charts a new path, so we cannot expect that a specific combination of behaviors points to some unequivocal truth. Some children as young as the age of three unwaveringly proclaim that they are a particular gender, while others may not show a single one of the aforementioned signs—and these children are not any less trans. In reality, 50% or more of trans people do not present until the start of puberty or later, and 50% or more have not shown the typical signs (Hassouri 2019).

*"I wish I didn't feel . . . betrayed."*

While mourning and grief are discussed frequently, the feeling of betrayal is not often a part of the discourse around parenting trans youth, but I see it often. It's important to remember that this feeling is not permanent and it does not dictate your ability to be a loving, supportive parent who feels close to their child. Parents will quietly mutter something about it in session, and when invited to say more, often report feeling silly or that it doesn't matter. After some validation, they will eventually share their feelings of betrayal like it's a secret they had planned to keep.

Often parents will share, "I can't help but feel like my kid has been keeping something from me. Do they not trust me? Do they think I'm a bad parent? I feel like I don't even know what to believe anymore." If you have had these thoughts, you are not alone. The decision to come out is often a lengthy and winding road full of juggling a variety of concerns (safety, social, cultural, etc.) beyond just a parental response. If you experience a feeling of betrayal, I encourage you to get curious about it.

Discovering your child's trans identity can also stir feelings that go beyond feeling betrayed and excluded; it might feel like the future you envisioned with your child has shifted, which can provoke a sense of loss or grief. For example, a mother who dreamed of sharing mother-daughter activities, from swapping clothes to discussing womanhood, may find it hard to adjust when she learns her child identifies as a boy and is eager to embrace manhood with gender-affirming care. It's crucial to acknowledge that these feelings are complex and valid, and they don't mean you're rejecting your child or are transphobic.

However, it's also important to recognize that your child might not be the best person to help you process these feelings. They should not feel responsible for changing your envisioned future. There are support groups for parents and therapists specializing in gender issues that can help you work through these emotions. As you navigate your feelings and move toward acceptance, you'll likely realize that even if your child had remained the gender you initially thought, the reality might not have matched the perfect scenario you had imagined. Children are their own individuals, not extensions of us or bound to fulfill our specific hopes and dreams.

This can be a moment to reflect on what makes parenting truly meaningful and rewarding. It's about supporting your child's journey into their authentic self, rather than molding them to fit preconceived notions of what their life should look like based on their gender. Coming to this realization can be freeing, and it can empower you to deepen your relationship and enhance your appreciation of your child's unique identity, far beyond the limits of traditional gender expectations.

*"How do other parents deal with this?"*

Many families I've worked with describe an unexpected journey when their child comes out as trans, echoing a challenge that even medical professionals find daunting. One pediatrician shared how, despite extensive training and years of experience, nothing had prepared her for her own child's revelation at thirteen. This child, previously perceived as socially awkward and struggling with depression, had not exhibited any clear signs of gender dysphoria, which led initially to disbelief and a delayed response to seeking gender-affirming care.

In many cases, parents may initially react with denial, thinking, "This must be a mistake." While this is a natural reaction, influenced by feelings of shame or fear that they may have missed something, it's important to understand that timely support and care can lead to positive and meaningful transformations for their child. Once acceptance is embraced, and appropriate support is provided, the positive changes are profound: children often become happier and more vibrant because they've finally been able to embrace their true selves.

This narrative is not unique to one family but is a common scenario that underscores the importance of looking beyond surface-level signs and supporting children in their self-expressed identities. It's a reminder of the power of acceptance and the vital role that support plays in the well-being of trans youth. The journey is not just about medical responses but about fostering an environment of understanding and reflection.

> Which of our personal biases, prejudices, and fears have we, or do we, project onto our children?
>
> Who are they serving?
>
> What harm may they have caused?

If this reflection was challenging, I encourage you to put this book down and come back to it—in two hours, two days, or two weeks. You are a human with your own history, and you cannot expect to do everything perfectly. At the same time, accountability matters. If there are things you wish you hadn't said or done, you can communicate them with your child. This is an opportunity to take accountability for your own behavior and demonstrate to them that, much like they are learning and growing and understanding their identity, you are also on a journey of becoming. Perhaps there are messages you were raised with or ways of knowing that make your adjustment to your child's identity particularly challenging. This doesn't need to be a bad thing—in fact, it is an opportunity to show your kid that you are imperfect but actively *trying*.

While initially learning about your child's identity may have left you feeling blindsided, guilty, fearful, betrayed, or mourning, I encourage you to consider this empowering belief instead:

"No matter what I have believed or thought I knew in the past, I can learn, shift my perspective, and support my child's identity."

## KEY POINTS

**Parental Experiences Differ:** Every parent's experience of their child's coming out is unique, but many fall into two categories: parents who are skeptical or disbelieving because their kid never showed "signs," and parents who feel guilt and shame as they look back on their child's early life and feel that they should have known. The reality is that no one prepared you for this and you can't change the past, but you can reflect on it and change how you parent your child moving forward.

**Rapid Onset Gender Dysphoria:** ROGD is not recognized as a valid diagnosis; research supporting ROGD is flawed and creates a false "medical" foundation for transphobia. ROGD has been adopted as a line of argument by anti-LGBTQ+ groups and therefore is often a part of the conversation about trans identities even though it has been thoroughly debunked and disavowed by organizations affiliated with the original study.

**Parents' Feelings of Betrayal and Grief:** These feelings are common but can be overcome. They may come from a sense of missed signals or the loss of an envisioned future. Processing these emotions with the help of support groups or therapists can be beneficial, and focusing on supporting your child's journey into their authentic self rather than preconceived notions can help strengthen the parent-child bond.

**Support and Affirmation:** These are crucial for the mental health and well-being of transgender children. Denial and rejection can lead to deteriorating mental health, whereas with support, children often become happier and more vibrant. There is no definitive checklist for identifying trans children; many behaviors can overlap in both trans and cis children, so it's important to listen to and support your child's self-expressed identity.

**Temporal Misalignment:** Your child may have explored their identity long before coming out to you; their coming out may seem sudden to you, but it is typically a well-considered decision for them. Coming out to one's parents is, for many young people, a significant risk. If your child has come out to you, it is a sign of trust and a belief that you have the capacity to support and love them regardless of their gender identity.

## REFLECTION QUESTIONS

1. What emotions did you experience when you first learned about your child's gender identity?
2. Did your reaction fall into one of these categories: disbelief or guilt/shame?
3. When you think about your child's transition, what are you most afraid of?
4. Which of your personal biases, prejudices, and fears have you, and do you, project onto your children?
5. What does it mean that your child was able to come out to you?
6. How can you show your child that you are actively trying to support them, even if you are struggling with understanding their identity?

# 5

# IS TRANS IDENTITY ANTI-FEMINIST?

**When a child comes out as transgender**, it can stir up a whirlwind of emotions and beliefs in parents. These responses can vary depending on their backgrounds, belief systems, and familiarity with the gender spectrum. There is, however, a particular challenge not often written about in the literature for otherwise highly progressive and forward-thinking mothers who proudly consider themselves to be feminists. These parents may have invested deeply in raising strong, empowered daughters, only to find out that the children they viewed as their daughters for many years have grown to identify as boys/men. In these cases, it can feel like their child's transition is a rejection of the womanhood and feminist values they hold dear. Sometimes feminist mothers fear that their trans sons are responding to a sexist or misogynistic culture by rejecting femininity and "wanting to be boys" because of the perceived superiority of men on a cultural and political level. Sometimes this fear is related to girls being "taught to hate their bodies," or because men are less at risk of sexual assault.

This reaction is natural and deeply personal considering the challenges that come with being a woman in a world that does not always value men and women equally on either a social or legislative level. But there is simply no research to support the theory that those assigned female at birth are looking for a way to "jump ship" by becoming transgender boys and men. In these cases, even with the best intentions, mothers are projecting their own views or fears onto their transgender sons and failing to accept that people do not become transgender because of sexism—as evidenced by the fact that transgender women have always existed across cultures regardless of the presence of patriarchal structures that have limited their access to opportunities, resources, and status.

The journey to understanding and accepting a trans identity is complex, but it's also an opportunity to expand our notions of gender and feminism, ultimately enriching our understanding of empowerment and equality. By exploring these feelings with compassion and openness, we can find new ways to support our children while honoring the values we cherish. It's important to understand, however, that a feminist mother struggling with these feelings is not automatically aligned with trans-exclusionary radical feminist (TERF) beliefs, even if it is important to acknowledge that TERF ideology is an extreme manifestation of these concerns. Most feminist mothers ultimately achieve a greater understanding of their trans children and do not see being transgender as mutually exclusive with feminism. In fact, intersectional feminism stands against all forms of oppression, including racial and trans oppression.

The term TERF describes a more fringe—but sometimes highly vocal—group within the feminist movement that does not accept transgender people (especially trans women) in feminist spaces and discussions. They believe that gender is determined solely by biological sex and view transgender identities as invalid or confused. This perspective often leads to opposition against medical treatments for gender transition and the implementation of policies that exclude transgender individuals from gender-specific spaces like women's shelters or sports teams. Trans-exclusionary beliefs started with second-wave feminism, a movement in the 1960s and 1970s that focused on fighting for women's rights based on biological sex. While this movement made important progress, it also reinforced the idea that there are only two genders: men and women. This view excludes people who do not fit neatly into these categories.

Such exclusionary beliefs can be very harmful to transgender people. Rejecting or not supporting a transgender child can lead to serious problems like depression, drug abuse, suicide attempts, and other health issues. Studies show that when parents support their transgender child's identity, it greatly improves their mental health and well-being (Wilson et al. 2016). Denying a trans identity can have devastating, even life-threatening consequences. The painful irony is that, in reacting with fear, these feminist mothers often end up devaluing, undermining, and disregarding their transgender sons—thus creating the very negative experiences they believe their child is avoiding by 'becoming trans.'

Medical experts, including the American Medical Association and the American Psychological Association, agree that being transgender is a natural part of human diversity. These organizations strongly support access to gender-affirming care like puberty blockers, hormones, and surgery, which they consider essential medical treatments (GLAAD 2023). In addition to contradicting the recommendations of the AMA and APA, exclusionary beliefs also contradict the core values of feminism, which aim to break down rigid gender roles and fight against discrimination. By excluding transgender women and denying their womanhood, these beliefs actually support the same sexist ideas that feminism opposes. True feminism supports everyone who faces gender-based oppression, including transgender people.

One argument made by those holding exclusionary views is that allowing transgender people to use bathrooms that match their gender identity will lead to sexual predators attacking women and children. However, there is no evidence to support this claim. Many places have had trans-inclusive bathroom policies for years without any increase in crimes or assaults. Sexual assault prevention experts and women's rights organizations alike assert that this "bathroom predator" myth is an excuse to discriminate against transgender people. The bathroom myth also wrongly suggests that trans people are dangerous, when in reality, they are more likely to be victims of violence inflicted by cisgender men (Hasenbush et al. 2018).

Feminism is about equality and the right of everyone to define their own identity and live without discrimination. It aims to dismantle the structures that tell people how they should act based on their gender. Trans identities challenge these rigid norms and push for a more inclusive understanding of gender. Recognizing and respecting the diversity of human experiences is a key part of true feminism.

Feminism at its core is about allowing individuals the autonomy to define and express their identities freely, without fear of discrimination or exclusion. Embracing a child's trans identity is not a rejection of feminist values but a true embodiment of them.

### EMILY AND MAX

#### A Parent's Evolution in Understanding Gender

*Emily had always prided herself on raising strong, empowered daughters free from oppressive gender stereotypes. She built her identity around being a woman and a mother dedicated to raising girls who would grow into confident, independent women. When her teenage child, Max, came out as a transgender boy, Emily's world was turned upside down. She had invested so much of her identity in the idea of womanhood and mothering girls that Max's transition felt like a rejection of everything she valued and had worked so hard to instill.*

*Naturally, she went online and found strong networks for women who felt just like she did. Initially consumed by TERF ideology, Emily feared that Max was simply confused or being influenced by "rapid onset gender dysphoria." She clung to the belief that Max was going through a phase and denied his identity, hoping it would pass. However, as time went on, Max's mental health deteriorated, and he needed support from his mom. Emily watched as her once vibrant child became withdrawn, depressed, and increasingly isolated.*

*The turning point came when Max began expressing suicidal thoughts, a stark reminder of the severity of the situation. Emily was forced to reckon with the reality that her refusal to accept Max's identity was causing significant harm. As Emily sought guidance from gender-affirming counselors and sought relationships with other parents of transgender children, she began to understand that Max's identity was legitimate and immutable. She realized that denying his identity was not only unethical but also potentially life-threatening.*

*It was an immense adjustment for Emily, but she came to see that supporting Max's transition was the true embodiment of her feminist values. She recognized that feminism was about allowing autonomy over one's body and identity, a principle that applied to all genders. By prioritizing Max's well-being over her own preconceptions, Emily was able to rebuild a healthy, affirming relationship with her transgender son while also reaffirming her identity as a proud feminist.*

*The path was not easy. Emily had to confront her own biases and unlearn deeply ingrained beliefs about gender. But as she supported Max through his transition, she saw him flourish. He became happier, more confident, and more engaged with life. Emily's journey didn't stop with Max's acceptance; she became an advocate for trans inclusion in feminist spaces. She recognized that the struggle for gender self-determination was a universal human rights issue at the core of the feminist movement.*

### RACHEL AND JORDAN

#### Exploring Identity on Parallel Tracks

*Rachel had always struggled with her body image, particularly during puberty. She remembered the discomfort and dissatisfaction she felt as her body changed in ways that made her feel awkward and self-conscious. So, when her child, Jordan, expressed similar discomfort with his body, Rachel assumed it was the same experience she had gone through—a natural aversion to puberty.*

*Jordan, assigned female at birth, began expressing a deep discomfort with developing breasts and other secondary sex characteristics as he entered puberty. Rachel, projecting her own experiences, thought Jordan's distress was a typical reaction to puberty and body changes. She reassured Jordan that these feelings would pass and that he just needed time to adjust.*

*However, as time went on, Jordan's discomfort only intensified. He expressed a persistent sense of wrongness about his body that went beyond typical puberty-related issues. Jordan began avoiding social situations, wearing baggy clothes to hide his body, and showing signs of depression. Rachel was at a loss, unable to understand why Jordan's distress was so severe.*

*Jordan eventually confided in Rachel that he felt like a boy trapped in a girl's body. Rachel was taken aback and initially dismissed Jordan's feelings as a phase or a result of peer influence. She couldn't fathom that Jordan's experience could be fundamentally different from her own struggles with body image.*

*But as Jordan's mental health continued to decline, Rachel talked to a trusted guidance counselor at Jordan's school who helped her find a gender therapist. Through therapy sessions, Rachel learned about gender dysphoria and began to understand that Jordan's feelings were not just about body image but about a deep-seated gender identity that didn't align with his assigned sex at birth.*

*With professional guidance, Rachel started to listen to Jordan without projecting her own experiences onto him. She realized that Jordan's identity as a transgender boy was valid and needed to be affirmed. Rachel began using Jordan's chosen name and pronouns and supported him in his desire to start puberty blockers to halt the changes that were causing him so much distress.*

*As Jordan transitioned, his mental health improved dramatically. He became more outgoing, confident, and happy. Rachel saw a new light in Jordan's eyes that had been missing for a long time. She realized that by letting go of her assumptions and truly listening to Jordan, she could support him in a way that honored his unique journey. Rachel's experience taught her the importance of separating her own past experiences from her child's present reality. By acknowledging Jordan's identity and supporting his transition, Rachel was able to foster a loving and supportive environment where Jordan could thrive. This journey also deepened Rachel's understanding of gender and the diverse ways it can be experienced, strengthening the bond between mother and son.*

Gender critical ideology, with its rigid views on gender and exclusionary practices, contradicts the true essence of feminism, which is about equality, autonomy, and dismantling oppressive systems. When parents affirm and support their transgender children's identities, they uphold these core feminist values, ensuring that their children can thrive as their authentic selves. Embracing a more inclusive and compassionate understanding of gender supports transgender individuals and enriches the feminist movement by challenging and expanding its scope to include everyone who faces gender-based oppression.

While you may have begun this chapter feeling like transition was at odds with your feminist values, I encourage you to consider this empowering belief instead:

> "By affirming my child's gender identity and embracing a more inclusive view of feminism, I uphold the true values of equality and autonomy, ensuring my child can thrive as their authentic self."

## KEY POINTS

**Navigating Emotional Responses:** When a child comes out as transgender, parents often experience a range of emotions, including feelings of loss and betrayal, especially if they have invested deeply in feminist values.

**Understanding TERF Ideology:** TERF (trans-exclusionary radical feminist) ideology rejects transgender identities, particularly trans women, and opposes gender-affirming care and inclusive policies.

**Medical Consensus on Transgender Identity:** Medical experts agree that being transgender is a natural part of human diversity, and access to gender-affirming care is essential for the mental health and well-being of transgender individuals.

**The Importance of Affirmation:** Affirming a child's transgender identity is crucial for their mental health and well-being, and rejecting it can lead to serious negative consequences.

**Inclusive Feminism:** True feminism supports everyone's right to define their own identity and live without discrimination, including transgender individuals.

## REFLECTION QUESTIONS

1. How can you reconcile your commitment to feminist values with supporting your child's transgender identity?
2. What steps can you take to educate yourself about transgender issues and the experiences of transgender individuals?
3. How can you create a supportive and affirming environment for your child while addressing your own feelings and beliefs?
4. What resources or support groups can you seek out to help you navigate your child's transition?
5. How can you challenge and move beyond any exclusionary beliefs or biases you may hold to fully support your child's identity?

PART TWO

# DECISION-MAKING AND SUPPORT

## 6

# WHAT IF THEY'RE WRONG AND CHANGE THEIR MIND?

**Navigating childhood is no small feat.** Kids can be wrong sometimes, confidently misnaming their teachers or scrambling the dates of their science fair projects. Yet, even amid these mix-ups, children often have a remarkably clear understanding of their own identities. They are incredibly perceptive about knowing when their gender assigned at birth doesn't quite match up with who they feel they truly are inside. As a parent, understanding this dissonance can be a challenging concept to grasp, but it's crucial to recognize and trust your child's sense of self.

If you are like many of the parents and caregivers I have worked with, you likely have some questions beginning with: If my child says they know what they want and what they're experiencing internally, this could be something they feel now, but what if they change their minds? Shouldn't we just wait until they're older to discuss medical treatment? What if they feel differently after puberty?

When your child shares that they don't identify with their assigned gender at birth, it's not just about identity, it's about trust. They're telling you because they trust you to listen to them, to accept them, and to love them. They believe in your role as their protector and supporter. What they need most from you in this moment is understanding and assurance. They trust that you want to keep them safe and support their well-being. Acknowledging this trust is crucial, especially in a society where being transgender or gender nonconforming can unfortunately still pose real challenges and dangers. Your support can make a profound difference in their ability to navigate these challenges confidently.

The desire to support and protect is good—you're doing great! Parental support, defined as the help, advice, and confidential support that parents offer their children, is significantly associated with higher life satisfaction, less hardship related to their transgender identity, and fewer depressive symptoms. A study found that parental support was associated with a 32.4% increase in life satisfaction and a 26.3% decrease in depressive symptoms among transgender adolescents. Parental support acts as a critical protective barrier against depression and suicidality. The same study showed parental support was linked to a 44.1% lower perceived burden of being transgender (Simons et al. 2013). According to the Trevor Project, a nonprofit suicide prevention organization that provides crisis support services, research, and advocacy for LGBTQ+ youth, transgender youth with supportive parents had 40% lower odds of attempting suicide in the past year compared to those without supportive parents (The Trevor Project 2022). Time and time again, the research confirms that parental support has monumentally positive effects on the mental health of transgender youth.

Studies have shown that transgender children show a consistent understanding of their own gender identity across all measures within the Implicit Association Test (IAT), a series of questions that test the speed with which children associated binary gender (boy or girl) with their concept of self. Specifically, data from the various measures indicated that transgender children's responses were indistinguishable from those of two groups of cisgender children. Kids know who they are. Their feelings about their gender come from deep inside them, not from being confused, pretending, or being influenced by others.

Understanding the developmental stages of children's psychology and identity formation offers valuable insight into why the separation of sex and gender identity is often met with resistance. Adults rarely remember what it's like to be three, four, or five years old—ages defined by rapid growth in self-awareness. Because sex and gender seem fused together so early, many assume they are inextricably linked. However, gender identity is shaped by cultural and societal influences, which play a significant role in how it develops. Since so much of this is learned behavior, children can learn early on when something aligns with their self-understanding and when it doesn't. If you give your child the opportunity to play and explore who they are without judgment, you'd be surprised by all they're capable of discovering.

Of course, sometimes kids are wrong. So, what are the chances that your child is wrong about being transgender? Turns out, pretty slim. Approximately 94% of the youth that socially transition maintain their social transition and gender identity rather than the gender they were assigned at birth (Olson et al. 2022). The remaining 6% accounts for children who explored even further, adopting self-understanding of gender neutrality or a step away from any gender identity whatsoever. Should you pursue the route of having your child take puberty blockers (a reversible intervention we will cover in later chapters), only 1.3% of trans adolescents make the decision to "detransition" after experiencing social transition. Overwhelmingly, children do not regret their decisions. It is ultimately your job, as their caregiver, to support their decisions. But transition can mean many different things. In our next chapter, we will talk more about the nuances between different aspects of gender transition.

### PETER'S SOCIAL TRANSITION

#### Finding Authenticity in Everyday Life

*Peter, a ten-year-old trans boy assigned female at birth, always felt different. From a young age, Peter preferred playing with trucks over dolls and always wanted to wear "boy" clothes. His parents, Mimi and Michael, initially thought it was just a phase. However, as Peter grew older, his insistence on being called by a male name and using he/him pronouns became more pronounced.*

*Mimi and Michael decided to find a therapist who specialized in gender for Peter to talk to. The specialist confirmed that Peter had a good sense of himself and recommended supporting his social transition. Mimi and Michael were apprehensive but ultimately decided to support Peter. They allowed him to choose his clothes, used his preferred name and pronouns, and informed his school about his transition.*

*The school was supportive, implementing policies to ensure Peter's peers respected his identity. With the support of his parents and school, Peter thrived. His grades improved, and he became more outgoing. Mimi and Michael were relieved to see their child happy and confident. However, not everyone was supportive. Some extended family members struggled to accept Peter's transition, causing tension during family gatherings. Mimi and Michael stood by Peter, educating their relatives and emphasizing the importance of respecting Peter's identity.*

*Peter's story highlights the importance of parental support and a nurturing environment. Mimi and Michael's decision to support Peter's social transition had a profound positive impact on his well-being and development.*

Puberty can be hard for transgender kids because the changes in their bodies can make them feel even more uncomfortable, often bringing up feelings they didn't have before. In the chapter "Isn't Transition Dangerous and Permanent?" we will provide more in-depth information and address misinformation about blockers. For transgender children, puberty blockers provide a delay of the physical changes associated with puberty that can cause significant distress and dysphoria. This delay gives children and their families time to explore their gender identity without the added pressure of irreversible physical changes. If, after a period of time, the child decides that transitioning is not the right path for them, they can simply stop taking the blockers, and puberty will resume normally. This reversible nature of puberty blockers makes them a safe and effective option for families navigating the complexities of gender identity (Guss and Gordon 2022).

Puberty blockers, originally developed for cisgender children experiencing precocious puberty, have been used safely for decades. Precocious puberty is puberty that occurs before age eight in children assigned female at birth (AFAB) and before age nine in children assigned male at birth (AMAB). These medications, known as gonadotropin-releasing hormone (GnRH) analogues, work by pausing the onset of puberty, allowing children to develop at a more typical pace alongside their peers. Pediatric endocrinologists have been using these medications for many years to treat precocious puberty safely and effectively. This long-established safety record and reversibility make puberty blockers a crucial option for parents concerned about their child's gender identity exploration, offering time to make informed decisions about future treatments (Mayo Clinic 2023).

Parents often feel apprehensive and nervous when considering the decision to start puberty blockers for their transgender children. However, recent insights from a groundbreaking study conducted by Harvard and Boston Children's Hospital provide both assurance and hope. This study involved 438 transgender and gender-diverse youth aged thirteen to seventeen, including forty participants who received puberty blockers at their early stages of puberty (Tanner stages two or three). The findings were remarkable and offer valuable insights into the benefits of puberty blockers.

The study revealed significant benefits for youth who received puberty blockers. These young individuals reported drastically lower rates of internalizing problems, anxiety, and depression compared to their transgender peers who did not receive puberty blockers. The data highlights how puberty blockers can play a crucial role in alleviating the psychological distress that often accompanies gender dysphoria during adolescence, as the incidence of suicidal thoughts was substantially lower among those on puberty blockers. Only 12.5% of the youth who received puberty blockers reported experiencing suicidal thoughts, compared to 27.2% in the non-blocker group (McGregor et al. 2023). This substantial reduction underscores the potentially lifesaving impact of puberty blockers for transgender youth. Moreover, the study indicated overall psychosocial well-being improvements among those who received puberty blockers. These youth experienced less stress and fewer total problems, suggesting an overall enhancement in their quality of life. The ability to delay puberty and prevent the development of unwanted secondary sex characteristics allows transgender youth to navigate their gender identity journey with less distress and more confidence.

The results of this study aren't just statistics; they represent real improvements in the daily lives of transgender and gender-expansive youth. As parents, it's natural to worry about your child's health, well-being, and future. This study provides compelling evidence that puberty blockers can significantly enhance the mental health and well-being of transgender youth by offering immediate mental health benefits and fostering a more positive and affirming path toward gender identity exploration and self-acceptance.

Incorporating puberty blockers as part of a child's journey can be a transformative step in supporting their overall well-being. This intervention allows them the space and time to explore their gender identity without the distress of unwanted physical changes. For parents concerned that their child might change their mind, puberty blockers offer reassurance: they are a temporary, reversible option that provides time for careful reflection. If the child later decides transitioning isn't the right path, they can simply stop the blockers, and puberty will continue as normal. This makes blockers a safe way to navigate the complexities of gender identity without fear of permanent decisions too early.

### PAUSING TO GROW

#### Tommy's Experience with Puberty Blockers

*Tommy, assigned female at birth, had always felt a disconnect between his inner self and the expectations placed upon him based on his assigned gender. As a child, Tommy gravitated toward activities and interests typically associated with boys, often expressing a desire to dress in "boy" clothes and play with toys like trucks and action figures. His parents, Sarah and David, initially thought it was just a phase, but they began to notice that Tommy's discomfort grew as he approached puberty.*

*When Tommy was eleven, the physical changes of puberty began to take a toll on his mental health. The development of breasts and the onset of menstruation caused severe anxiety and depression. Tommy felt like his body was betraying him, moving further away from who he knew himself to be. The once passionate and active child became withdrawn and anxious, struggling to find comfort in his own skin.*

*Sarah and David were deeply concerned for Tommy's well-being and decided to talk to a family friend who had a trans partner. The family friend suggested they go to their local hospital's gender clinic to meet with a team including an endocrinologist. After thorough discussions, the team recommended puberty blockers to delay the onset of further puberty and give Tommy the time he needed to explore his gender identity without the pressure of irreversible physical changes. The endocrinologist assured them that puberty blockers were a safe and reversible option, originally developed for children experiencing precocious puberty, and had been used successfully for many years.*

*Initially, Sarah and David were hesitant. They worried about potential long-term effects, social stigma, and the possibility that Tommy might regret the decision later. To ease their concerns, they delved into research from trusted sources, reading books for parents of transgender youth and memoirs from trans individuals to gain a deeper understanding of the experience. They also consulted medical professionals and reached out to other parents of transgender children who had faced similar choices, seeking guidance and reassurance from those who had already navigated this path.*

*After careful consideration, Sarah and David decided to proceed with the treatment. The puberty blockers provided immediate psychological relief for Tommy. His anxiety decreased significantly, and he began to feel more at ease in his body. With the unwanted physical changes paused, Tommy was able to focus on his personal growth and development, exploring his identity in a supportive and understanding environment.*

*Tommy's journey was not without challenges. Some extended family members struggled to understand and accept his transition, causing tension during family gatherings. Sarah and David stood by Tommy, advocating for him and educating their relatives about the importance of using his chosen name and pronouns. They emphasized the positive changes they had seen in Tommy's mental health and overall happiness since starting the puberty blockers.*

*At school, Tommy faced mixed reactions. While his close friends were supportive, some peers were less accepting. Sarah and David worked closely with school administrators to ensure that Tommy's identity was respected. They implemented specific policies to address bullying, such as establishing clear reporting procedures and designating a staff member as a point of contact for Tommy's safety. Additionally, they organized a workshop for teachers and parents to provide education on transgender issues, covering topics like respectful language, pronoun use, and how to create an inclusive classroom environment. This event aimed to increase understanding and support for Tommy and other transgender students within the school community.*

*As time passed, Tommy's confidence grew. He began to identify more strongly as male and took steps toward his social transition. With the unwavering support of his parents, he changed his name and pronouns at school and began to live more authentically. The supportive environment at home and school played a crucial role in Tommy's development, allowing him to thrive.*

*Sarah and David's decision to support Tommy's use of puberty blockers had a great impact on his life. It gave him the necessary time and space to understand his gender identity without the added distress of unwanted physical changes. Tommy's mental health improved, and he began to flourish academically and socially. His journey underscored the importance of timely medical intervention and parental support for transgender youth.*

*Through Tommy's experience, Sarah and David learned the value of trusting their child's understanding of his own identity. The parents' journey from initial hesitation to wholehearted support highlighted the transformative power of acceptance and affirmation in the lives of transgender children. By prioritizing Tommy's well-being and happiness, they created a nurturing environment that allowed him to grow into his true self.*

It's natural for parents to worry about their children's future, especially when it comes to something as significant as transitioning. That concern is a sign of love and care—wondering about the impact on their well-being, or even hoping that they might be mistaken, is an understandable response. Many parents want the best for their children and fear that the challenges of being transgender may complicate their lives.

However, if your child trusts you enough to disclose that they don't feel fully aligned with the gender they were assigned at birth, that trust is a gift. By believing them, you are reciprocating that trust and offering them the support they need. When a child expresses their discomfort or dysphoria, they are sharing a deep part of themselves. Even if it's hard to fully grasp or accept at first, acknowledging their feelings and taking them seriously is a powerful way to show your love. Transitioning decisions, whether social or medical, should come from a place of understanding and support, not fear.

While initially, learning about your child's identity may have raised fears of them being wrong or changing their mind, I encourage you to embrace this empowering perspective instead:

> "I support my child's journey by celebrating exploration and fostering their confidence, supporting their growth in whatever direction it takes."

## KEY POINTS

**Kids' Self-Understanding:** Children often have an impressive clarity about their own identities, even in the midst of the confusion and exploration that comes with growing up.

**Parental Concerns:** It's natural for parents to have concerns and questions about their child's expressed gender identity, especially about the possibility of them changing their minds.

**Trust and Assurance:** When a child shares their gender identity, they are communicating that they trust you and believe that you are a safe person to tell. They are seeking understanding and assurance from their parents.

**Benefits of Parental Support:** Parental support significantly improves the mental health and well-being of transgender youth.

It is associated with higher life satisfaction, lower perceived burden of being transgender, and fewer depressive symptoms.

**Consistency of Gender Identity:** Studies show that transgender children have a consistent understanding of their gender identity that is not a result of confusion or pretense.

**Exploring Gender Identity:** Sometimes kids are wrong, but the chances that a child is wrong about their gender identity are slim. Puberty blockers can serve as a precaution, providing time to explore gender identity without irreversible physical changes.

**Safety of Puberty Blockers:** Puberty blockers are a safe and reversible intervention originally developed for cisgender children experiencing "precocious puberty."

**Mental Health Benefits:** Recent studies indicate significant mental health benefits for youth who receive puberty blockers, including lower rates of internalizing problems, anxiety, depression, and suicidal thoughts.

**Enhancing Quality of Life:** Supporting your child's social transition and using puberty blockers can significantly enhance their quality of life and mental well-being.

## REFLECTION QUESTIONS

1. What emotions did you experience when your child first shared their gender identity with you?
2. How can you build trust and provide assurance to your child as they navigate their gender identity?
3. What specific actions can you take to support your child's mental health and well-being?

4. How can you educate yourself about the benefits and safety of puberty blockers to make informed decisions about your child's care?

5. What steps can you take to create a nurturing environment that respects and affirms your child's gender identity?

# 7

# IF THEY ARE NEURODIVERGENT, CAN THEY KNOW?

**Sometimes, parents of neurodivergent transgender youth** may wonder if their child's neurodivergence affects their ability to fully understand their own gender identity or make informed decisions about gender-affirming care. This belief can unintentionally underestimate the agency and self-awareness of neurodivergent individuals, while also overlooking the growing body of research and clinical practice that supports their capability and right to explore their gender identity.

Neurodivergence encompasses a variety of conditions that reflect differences in brain function and behavioral traits as compared to neurotypical development. Common forms of neurodivergence include autism spectrum disorder (ASD), attention deficit hyperactivity disorder (ADHD), dyslexia, mood disorders, obsessive compulsive disorder (OCD), and other conditions that affect how individuals process information, learn, and interact with the world around them. It is critical that parents and caregivers understand that being neurodivergent does not diminish a person's ability to know their gender identity. Research demonstrates that neurodivergent individuals, especially those with ADHD and autism, experience gender in ways that are just as complex and nuanced as their neurotypical peers. In many cases, neurodivergent individuals may feel less constrained by societal expectations, allowing them greater freedom to explore differences between their gender identity and the sex they were assigned at birth. In fact, recent studies show that individuals who do not identify with their assigned sex at birth are three to six times more likely to be autistic than their cisgender counterparts (Warrier et al. 2020).

According to the largest study yet to examine the connection, about 5% of cisgender participants have autism, whereas 24% of gender-diverse participants were autistic. It is crucial to note that this figure only includes those diagnosed with autism—many adults on the spectrum may be undiagnosed. This same study showed that 4.8%–26% of people who present at gender clinics had an autism diagnosis (compared to 1–2% of the general population). Globally, estimates suggest that between 3–9% of transgender and gender-diverse adults may be autistic (Warrier et al. 2020).

The intersection of neurodiversity and gender diversity has spawned new terminology that highlights the relationship between these components of identity and experience:

- "Autigender" is a term that some autistic people use to describe their unique relationship with gender. Lyric Holmans (they/them, xe/xem) defines autigender as "the relationship between being autistic and how that can influence and impact someone's relationship with their gender identity and their experience of gender" (Holmans 2021).
- "Neuroqueer" is a term that expresses the intersection of neurodivergence and queerness,

celebrating the unique ways individuals can experience and express neurodivergence, gender, and sexuality. The term was coined by Dr. Nick Walker (he/him) in 2008 and further developed through ongoing conversations with other neurodivergent and queer thinkers. Walker defines a neuroqueer individual as "any individual whose identity, selfhood, gender performance, and/or neurocognitive style have in some way been shaped by their engagement in practices of neuroqueering, regardless of what gender, sexual orientation, or style of neurocognitive functioning they may have been born with" (Walker 2021).

Just as a higher proportion of adults who have autism identify as LGBTQ+, studies also reveal significant rates of gender diversity among autistic youth. Research indicates that autistic children and adolescents are significantly more likely to identify as gender-diverse (Hisle-Gorman et al. 2019). A recent study found that autistic children/adolescents were four times more likely to be gender-diverse compared to their non-autistic peers. These findings echo those of previous studies, with percentages of autistic children potentially identifying as transgender or gender-diverse ranging between 4% and 5.4%, as opposed to 0.7% among non-autistic children (Warrier et al. 2020). This correlation does not imply confusion or incapacity but rather highlights that neurodivergent individuals can experience and express gender in diverse ways that are authentic and deeply felt.

The misconception that neurodivergent individuals are incapable of making informed decisions about their lives stems from outdated stereotypes about their cognitive and emotional capacities. However, current approaches in both psychology and neurodiversity affirm the competence of neurodivergent individuals in understanding their own identities and needs.

Autonomy and self-determination are fundamental rights that should be equally afforded to neurodivergent individuals. Denying them the opportunity to explore their gender identity or make decisions about gender-affirming care on the basis of neurodivergence alone is not only discriminatory but also harmful as doing so can lead to increased dysphoria and mental health challenges by forcing individuals to live inauthentically.

### HONORING IDENTITY

#### The Power of Autonomy and Self-Determination

*Twelve-year-old Audra was diagnosed with autism at age eight. As Audra entered adolescence, they began expressing discomfort with their assigned gender at birth and a desire to use they/them pronouns. Audra's parents, however, were hesitant to affirm their child's gender identity, believing that Audra's neurodivergence made them incapable of truly understanding their own gender.*

*Despite Audra's insistence that they felt more comfortable presenting in a gender-neutral way, their parents dismissed these feelings as a phase, a "special interest," or a manifestation of their autism. They refused to use Audra's chosen name and pronouns, citing concerns that Audra was "too neurodivergent to know" about their gender identity.*

*Frustrated by their parents' reluctance to trust their understanding of their own gender identity, Audra sought support from a school counselor who connected them with a gender-affirming therapist. Through this care, Audra learned to advocate for themself and their right to explore their gender identity. The therapist also worked with Audra's parents, educating them about the autonomy and self-determination of neurodivergent individuals, including those on the autism spectrum.*

*While Audra's parents initially struggled to accept Audra's identity, they gradually began to understand that Audra's neurodivergence didn't diminish their ability to know and express their own authentic gender. Though progress was slow and there were still moments of tension, Audra's parents joined a support group for parents of neurodivergent and gender-expansive youth. The group provided them with a space to learn from others who were navigating similar challenges and gave them the tools to better support Audra.*

*As the family began to offer more affirmation, Audra's mental health showed some improvement, though the journey was far from over. While they felt empowered to continue exploring their gender identity and consider future decisions about gender-affirming care, the path ahead still held challenges for both Audra and their parents as they navigated this evolving process together.*

## STRONGER TOGETHER

### How Collaborative Decision-Making Improves Support

*Sixteen-year-old Ari, who had been diagnosed with ADHD and dyslexia, came out as a transgender boy to his parents. Ari expressed a strong desire to start hormone therapy but struggled to process and retain all the information provided during medical appointments.*

*Ari's parents were initially hesitant, fearing that their child's neurodivergence might impair their ability to make informed decisions about medical care. However, they were committed to supporting Ari's gender identity and sought guidance from healthcare professionals experienced in working with neurodivergent transgender youth.*

*The gender-affirming healthcare team implemented a collaborative decision-making model that involved Ari, his parents, and a team of providers. They ensured that all information about hormone therapy and potential risks was presented in accessible formats, such as visual aids and written materials tailored to Ari's learning needs.*

*Additionally, the team provided Ari with extra counseling sessions to discuss his goals, concerns, and understanding of the treatment process at his own pace. Ari's parents were included in these sessions, fostering open communication and ensuring that everyone was on the same page.*

*Through this supportive and accommodating approach, Ari felt empowered to make an informed decision about starting hormone therapy. His parents, having witnessed the care taken to respect Ari's autonomy and ensure his understanding, felt confident in supporting his choice.*

*As Ari began his transition journey, his mental health and overall well-being improved significantly. His parents recognized the positive impact of affirming their child's gender identity and involving them in collaborative decision-making processes that respected their neurodivergent needs.*

Experiences such as Audra's and Ari's illustrate the importance of respecting the autonomy and self-determination of neurodivergent transgender individuals, as well as the benefits of providing accessible support and collaborative decision-making processes. By rejecting the myth that neurodivergent transgender youth are incapable and embracing a supportive approach, families and healthcare providers can help them explore their identities and make informed decisions about their care and well-being.

The intersection of neurodivergence and gender identity presents unique challenges that require trust, patience, flexibility, and understanding from parents. Sensory processing differences, for instance, can significantly impact a neurodivergent individual's comfort with gender-affirming practices such as binding or tucking (see glossary). These methods, while affirming for many, might introduce sensory discomfort, which necessitates finding adaptable alternatives that accommodate both gender identity and sensory preferences.

Communication can also pose a significant challenge, especially for those who experience alexithymia, a condition common among autistic individuals that affects their ability to identify and describe feelings. This difficulty in expressing emotions or discomfort can make it hard for them to articulate their feelings about gender identity or dysphoria. To ensure that their child's feelings and identity are understood and respected in both medical environments and at home, parents should consider facilitating alternative communication methods. Some effective strategies include using visual aids like picture cards or emotion wheels, augmentative and alternative communication (AAC) devices that generate speech, written communication through texts or journals, and art therapy for self-expression. Additionally, social stories, sign language, and role-playing can help bridge communication gaps. By implementing these methods, parents can create a supportive environment where their autistic child feels empowered to express their gender identity and related feelings.

It is very important for parents and caregivers to actively seek competent healthcare providers who understand the nuances of both neurodivergence and gender diversity. To assist you in this process, there is a list of questions to assess providers at the end of this chapter. Such professionals should be adept at adapting their care approaches to accommodate both identities, demonstrating patience, flexibility, and a willingness to engage with unique communication styles or sensory needs. Adjustments may also be necessary in standard gender-affirming treatments. For example, hormonal therapies might provoke different sensory and emotional responses in neurodivergent individuals, requiring modifications to standard treatment plans. Open discussions with healthcare providers about tailoring medical treatments can help ensure that they are suitable and effective for the individual's specific needs.

Parents can feel empowered to stand up against biases and misunderstandings that their neurodivergent child may encounter while exploring their gender identity. You have the ability to educate others—from healthcare providers to teachers—on the unique strengths and perspectives your child brings to their gender journey. By advocating for inclusive, respectful treatment, you're not only ensuring your child is seen for who they are but also creating a more supportive environment for all neurodivergent and gender-diverse individuals. Your voice is a powerful tool in making sure your child is treated with dignity and respect in every space they enter.

By understanding the challenges that come with raising a neurodivergent, gender-expansive child—such as navigating societal biases, misconceptions from professionals, and the pressure to fit into traditional norms—parents can actively prepare to address them. Through education, advocacy, and unwavering support, parents can help create an affirming environment that celebrates and respects all aspects of their child's identity, empowering them to thrive as their authentic selves. This comprehensive approach not only fosters a sense of belonging and acceptance but also supports the overall well-being of neurodivergent and transgender or gender-diverse individuals.

## EMMA'S EVOLUTION

### Finding Strength in Self-Acceptance

*Emma, now a young adult, came out to her parents shortly before her senior year of high school. Emma is neurodivergent, diagnosed with autism. Before coming out, Emma struggled with social interactions and emotional regulation, common difficulties for autistic individuals. At this time, she was isolated and experienced significant anxiety and depression. Emma's academic performance was inconsistent, reflecting her internal turmoil and lack of social support. She wanted to socially transition and come out at school but was preoccupied with worries about her safety and the potential negative reactions of her peers.*

*Emma's journey toward self-acceptance began with her parents, who created a safe and affirming home environment where she could explore her gender identity without fear of rejection. They encouraged Emma to express herself in different ways, whether it was experimenting with clothing, trying out new names and pronouns, or decorating her room in a way that felt authentic to her. They also had open conversations about gender, allowing Emma to ask questions and explore her feelings at her own pace. This supportive atmosphere gave Emma the freedom to discover her identity in a loving, nonjudgmental space.*

*Emma's coming out process was slow at first. She continued to use her legal name and pronouns that aligned with her assigned sex at birth and was anxious about altering her gender expression by wearing more feminine clothes or makeup—even at home or in session. Emma continued to worry that classmates would respond negatively. To further complicate things, she did not have school staff she trusted or felt comfortable around due to conflict involving requested academic support.*

*Emma was able to connect with a gender clinic and with her parent's approval began receiving puberty blocking medication as well as hormone replacement therapy (HRT). Emma was enthusiastic about the physical changes she experienced and began experimenting more with her gender expression in terms of hair and clothing. Midway through the school year, Emma felt comfortable coming out. Her peers and trusted school staff responded overwhelmingly positively. Emma started to socialize, connected with a new support team, and joined the LGBTQ+ group and the chess club after school which supported her identity as a neuroqueer individual.*

*Today, Emma is a more authentic version of herself. She is a confident and happy young woman who is actively planning for her future and moving into adulthood successfully. Throughout this entire process Emma's parents remained her biggest cheerleaders and advocates. Due to their support and encouragement, as well as their immediate work toward accessing gender-affirming medical and mental health care, Emma is thriving. Emma's story is a testament to the power of acceptance and support in the lives of neurodivergent and transgender individuals. Her journey from isolation and anxiety to confidence and social success highlights the importance of a nurturing environment both at home and in school.*

If you were initially concerned upon learning that your trans child was neurodivergent, or that your neurodivergent child was trans, because you were worried they would not have the capacity to make informed medical decisions for themselves, I invite you to try identifying with this empowering belief instead:

---

"As a parent of a neurodivergent transgender child, I recognize their profound capacity for self-awareness and honor their right to explore their identity fully."

---

## KEY POINTS

**Misconceptions About Neurodivergent Individuals:** The belief that neurodivergent individuals are incapable of understanding their own gender identity or making informed decisions about gender-affirming care is a misconception that underestimates their agency and self-awareness. Research and clinical practice support the capability and right of neurodivergent individuals to explore their gender identity.

**Understanding Neurodivergence and Gender Identity:** Neurodivergence includes conditions like autism spectrum disorder (ASD) and ADHD, reflecting differences in brain function and behavior compared to neurotypical development. Being neurodivergent does not diminish a person's ability to know their gender identity. Studies show that neurodivergent individuals can experience gender in complex and nuanced ways, similar to their neurotypical peers.

**"Autigender" and "Neuroqueer":** The term "autigender" describes the unique relationship between autism and gender identity for some autistic individuals, highlighting how neurodivergence may shape the way gender is understood or experienced. Similarly, "neuroqueer" describes the intersection of neurodivergence and queerness, and the ways individuals, regardless of neurotype, might experience and express gender, sexuality, and cognitive identity outside of dominant norms. Neuroqueering involves practices that challenge the expectations of both neurotypicality and cisheteronormativity, making room for expansive ways of being.

**Gender Diversity Among Autistic Youth:** Significant rates of gender diversity exist among autistic youth. Autistic children and adolescents are more likely to identify as gender-diverse compared to their non-autistic peers. This correlation reflects diverse, authentic gender experiences rather than confusion or incapacity.

**Challenging Outdated Stereotypes:** Outdated stereotypes about neurodivergent individuals' cognitive and emotional capacities contribute to misconceptions about their ability to make informed decisions. Current approaches in psychology and neurodiversity affirm the competence of neurodivergent individuals in understanding their own identities and needs.

**Fundamental Rights of Neurodivergent Individuals:** Autonomy and self-determination are fundamental rights for neurodivergent individuals. Denying them the opportunity to explore their gender identity or make decisions about gender-affirming care based solely on neurodivergence is discriminatory and harmful.

## REFLECTION QUESTIONS

1. How can you better understand the unique relationship between your child's neurodivergence and their gender identity?
2. What steps can you take to ensure that your neurodivergent transgender child feels respected and supported in their gender identity?
3. How can you advocate for your child's autonomy and self-determination in medical and social settings?
4. What resources and support networks can you connect with to help navigate the challenges at the intersection of neurodivergence and gender diversity?

5. How can you foster open communication with your child to ensure their feelings and identity are fully understood and respected?

## QUESTIONS TO ASK WHEN CHOOSING A HEALTHCARE PROVIDER FOR YOUR NEURODIVERSE, GENDER-EXPANSIVE CHILD

### Experience and Specialization

- Do you have experience working with neurodiverse children, particularly those on the autism spectrum, and their specific healthcare needs?
- How much experience do you have working with gender-expansive or transgender youth?

### Gender-Affirming Care

- Are you knowledgeable about and supportive of gender-affirming care, including social transitions, puberty blockers, and hormone therapy?
- How do you approach supporting children who are exploring their gender identity?

### Collaboration with Other Providers

- Do you work closely with mental health professionals, such as therapists, who specialize in gender identity and neurodiversity?
- Can you refer us to or work alongside other professionals (e.g., endocrinologists or gender therapists) as part of a comprehensive care plan?

**Communication and Accommodations**

- How do you tailor your communication style to accommodate neurodiverse children, especially those with sensory sensitivities or communication challenges?
- Are you open to using visual aids, AAC devices, or other communication tools to ensure my child feels comfortable and understood?

**Parental Involvement and Support**

- How do you involve parents in the care process while respecting the child's autonomy?
- What resources or support groups can you recommend for parents of neurodiverse and gender-expansive children?

**Approach to Decision-Making**

- How do you ensure that the child is involved in decisions about their care in a developmentally appropriate way?
- How do you handle situations where a child may be uncertain or change their mind about aspects of their gender identity or transition?

**Sensitivity to Neurodivergence and Gender**

- How do you address potential overlaps between neurodivergence and gender exploration, such as understanding that neurodivergent individuals may express gender differently?
- What steps do you take to avoid assuming that a child's neurodivergence is the cause of their gender identity exploration?

**Access to Gender-Affirming Resources**

- Are you aware of and able to provide referrals to gender-affirming resources and support groups for neurodiverse youth?
- Can you help navigate insurance coverage for gender-affirming care and services?

### Comfort and Environment

- How do you create a welcoming and affirming environment for neurodiverse and gender-expansive children in your practice?
- Are there any accommodations for sensory sensitivities, such as quiet waiting areas or shorter appointments, if needed?

### Ongoing Support

- How do you provide ongoing support as my child continues to explore their identity and transition over time?
- Can we schedule regular check-ins to ensure my child's emotional and physical well-being is being addressed?

# 8

# SHOULDN'T WE WAIT UNTIL THEY'RE EIGHTEEN?

**It's entirely understandable** for parents to feel apprehensive about making decisions regarding their child's gender identity, especially when those decisions might involve medical interventions. Many parents worry they might make the wrong choice or be responsible for their child's future unhappiness. The fear that comes with making significant decisions about a child's well-being is natural and deeply felt. While it's important to consider the potential harms of taking action, it is also important to consider the consequences of waiting until your child turns eighteen before taking proactive steps to acknowledge and affirm their gender identity.

Adolescence is a crucial period for identity formation, and for transgender youth, having their gender identity affirmed during these years leads to significantly better mental health outcomes. Research consistently shows that when transgender adolescents receive support and access to gender-affirming care, they experience reduced rates of depression, anxiety, and suicidal ideation (Olson and Gülgöz 2017). This support includes both social affirmation—such as using their chosen name and pronouns—and, when appropriate, medical interventions like puberty blockers and hormone therapy.

Waiting until your child is eighteen to begin any form of gender-affirming treatment is not a neutral option; it can prolong and intensify gender dysphoria. For many transgender teens, the onset of puberty brings about distressing physical changes that deepen their sense of disconnection from their bodies. Puberty blockers can delay the development of secondary sex characteristics that exacerbate this distress, allowing the young person more time to explore their gender identity without the added pressure of irreversible physical changes.

The belief that young people are too immature to make informed decisions about their gender identity is a common concern. However, evidence suggests that young people are quite capable of understanding their gender identity and making informed choices about their bodies (Graham 2022). For trans youth who feel ready, beginning hormone therapy and experiencing puberty alongside their cisgender peers can be incredibly beneficial. This timing can help them feel more aligned with their true selves and less isolated during a critical period of development. Regret rates among transgender individuals who transition are exceptionally low. When regret does occur, it is often due to external factors such as societal rejection and lack of support rather than the transition itself (Turban et al. 2021).

### JAYDEN'S PATH TO AUTHENTICITY

#### Overcoming Parental Doubt

*From an early age, Jayden knew he was a boy, despite being assigned female at birth. As a young child, he gravitated toward traditionally masculine interests and clothing. However, it wasn't until he was twelve years old that Jayden mustered the courage to come out as transgender to his family. His parents, while loving, had little prior experience with transgender identities. They struggled initially to understand Jayden's truth, fearing it was just a phase or confusion stemming from his youth.*

*"What if you change your mind later and regret making permanent changes to your body?" his mother would ask with trepidation.*

*Jayden patiently tried to educate them, explaining how he had felt disconnected from his assigned sex as long as he could remember. With the support of his school counselor, he was able to start seeing a gender therapist who could guide both Jayden and his parents through this journey.*

*The first major steps were socially transitioning by using he/him pronouns, changing his name legally, and expressing his male identity through his appearance and presentation. Jayden's parents had some adjusting to do but made efforts to respect his name and pronouns, even if they occasionally slipped up.*

*As Jayden approached sixteen, he became increasingly eager to begin masculinizing hormone therapy. His parents' fears resurfaced about him making such a significant medical decision before turning eighteen—worries about potential long-term effects, the possibility of regret, and whether Jayden was truly ready to make such a life-altering choice. However, after numerous conversations with Jayden's therapist and doctors, they recognized their son's maturity, his deep understanding of the process, and his resolute sense of self. These discussions reassured them that, while the decision was significant, Jayden was ready to take this step in his journey.*

*The provider reminded them, "As parents, we make the best decisions that we can for our children with the information that we have, and we never have all of the information, so we have to make the best decisions that we can with what we have." Jayden was extremely well informed about the effects and implications of testosterone.*

*More importantly, he expressed with conviction, "This is about aligning my body with my true identity. I've never felt more certain about anything in my life."*

*With guidance from providers experienced in transgender care, Jayden began hormone therapy shortly after his sixteenth birthday. The positive impact on his mental health and overall well-being was incredible. For the first time, he felt like his appearance truly reflected who he was inside.*

*"It finally feels like I'm comfortable in my own skin," Jayden said, smiling. "My parents realized that waiting any longer would have just made my dysphoria worse and kept me from feeling like myself."*

*While the age of eighteen had initially seemed like an arbitrary benchmark, Jayden's family recognized that respecting his personal readiness and trusting his self-determination was paramount. They created an affirming environment that empowered Jayden's authentic transition.*

*Jayden's parents expressed feeling "like a weight had been lifted" when they saw how Jayden's confidence bloomed. They took pride in raising a son who was true to himself. As Jayden looks to the future—attending college, building relationships, and thriving as his authentic self—he feels immense gratitude.*

*"My parents' affirmation and love helped me become who I'm meant to be."*

Withholding affirming care until the age of eighteen can have serious repercussions, including an increase in mental health challenges and a decrease in overall well-being. The distress associated with living in a body that doesn't align with one's gender identity can be profound, and delaying transition can intensify these feelings. By providing support and access to gender-affirming care during adolescence, parents can help their children navigate this critical period with a greater sense of security and affirmation.

For most trans youth, their gender journey often involves navigating not only their own identity but also the attitudes and beliefs of their parents or guardians. The next two case studies examine the experiences of two trans teens, Ryan and Jamie, whose attempts to access gender-affirming care were hindered by their parents' ever-changing requirements.

### MOVING THE GOALPOSTS

#### When Parental Expectations Keep Shifting

*Ryan knew he was a boy since he was five, though he did not come out to his parents until the age of thirteen. At the onset of puberty, Ryan expressed significant distress related to his body, as well as being perceived as female by others. At an annual physical at age fourteen, Ryan's pediatrician recommended connecting with a gender clinic with the goal of starting hormone replacement therapy (HRT), something Ryan had been thinking about and wanted to move forward with. It is often helpful for trans youth to begin receiving hormone therapy and go through puberty alongside their cisgender peers if they feel ready to do so.*

*Ryan's parents initially expressed concerns about the permanence of HRT and wanted him to undergo six months of therapy before they would consider it. After six months, his parents then requested that he achieve higher grades in school as a condition for their approval. Despite improving his grades, they later insisted he must first engage in more extracurricular activities to prove his mental stability and commitment.*

*The shifting expectations caused Ryan significant emotional distress and only exacerbated his feelings of dysphoria. Ryan described feeling invalidated and trapped, and no matter how much he complied with his parents' demands, their conditions kept changing. Ryan was not able to start HRT, experiencing a decline in his mental health and a rupture in his relationship with his parents as a result.*

It is important to understand that gender-affirming care is a gradual process. Social transition, which involves changes in gender expression and adjusting one's role within social settings, is often the first step and does not involve medical interventions. Social transition can include adopting a new name, pronouns, and clothing that reflect the young person's gender identity. Social transition alone has been shown to significantly improve the mental health and well-being of transgender youth.

For prepubescent and some pubescent youth, puberty blockers offer a reversible way to delay the physical changes of puberty, giving them more time to explore their gender identity without the added stress of developing unwanted secondary sexual characteristics. The effects of puberty blockers are reversible, and if the individual decides not to pursue further medical transition, puberty will proceed as it would have without intervention.

When considering hormone therapy, it's essential to approach it with careful thought and medical guidance. Gender-affirming hormone therapy can have profound positive effects, but it is typically introduced gradually and with the support of a medical team experienced in working with transgender youth (see Chapters 11 and 12 for more in-depth information on GAHT). These medical professionals can help ensure that the young person and their family understand the implications and benefits of the treatment.

Parents naturally want to protect their children and ensure their happiness. Providing affirmation and support during adolescence can help transgender youth thrive, reducing the risks associated with untreated gender dysphoria and allowing them to develop into confident, healthy adults.

### JAMIE'S TRANSITION

#### A Parent's Shift from Fear to Support

*When Jamie came out to her parents as a trans girl at the age of fourteen, her parents were initially open to the idea of gender-affirming care but wanted her to live as a girl for a full year before making any medical decisions. After a year had passed, they required her to undergo family therapy to ensure everyone was prepared for her transition. However, much like having a baby, they soon realized that there's no such thing as being fully "ready"—transitioning is a journey, and complete preparedness isn't a realistic goal for anyone. Once family therapy sessions concluded, they demanded Jamie wait until she was sixteen to start any medical treatment, claiming that she couldn't be mature enough to make an informed decision about her medical care until she was older.*

*The continuous postponement led Jamie to feel increasingly hopeless. Each time she met her parents' demands, they introduced new conditions, which made her feel that her needs and experiences were being dismissed. Like Ryan, this led to strained family relationships and a decline in Jamie's self-esteem and mental health.*

*Both Ryan and Jamie faced challenges in accessing necessary gender-affirming care due to their parents' hesitations. In Ryan's case, his parents continually shifted their requirements, hoping that delaying treatment would lead him to reconsider transitioning. Instead of protecting him, this caused Ryan significant emotional and psychological harm, as his dysphoria intensified during the delay. On the other hand, Jamie's parents weren't actively resistant but needed more education and information about gender-affirming care to feel confident in their decision. Once they became better informed, they were able to support Jamie in accessing the care she needed, showing how crucial it is for parents to educate themselves and address their concerns early on.*

When parents delay gender-affirming treatment that their child needs, it can lead to prolonged emotional distress and missed opportunities for early intervention—crucial moments that could greatly enhance their child's quality of life. Supporting your child through social affirmation and, when appropriate, medical interventions can help them navigate their adolescent years with greater ease and security, fostering a healthier, happier future.

It's common for parents to feel more comfortable with reversible or temporary interventions, such as puberty blockers, because they offer flexibility if a child's feelings change. However, when it comes to more permanent procedures, like top surgery, even the most supportive and affirming parents can find themselves feeling conflicted. It's natural to feel a sense of fear and hesitation when the intervention is more complex and harder to reverse. These feelings don't negate a parent's desire to support their child but rather highlight the weight of these decisions. The journey can be challenging, and it's okay to acknowledge the emotional complexity that comes with considering these next steps.

### TOP SURGERY AT SEVENTEEN

#### Navigating Barriers and Advocacy

*From a young age, Dallas knew they were transgender and used they/them pronouns. Growing up in a supportive environment, Dallas began gender-affirming hormone therapy at fifteen. As they approached their seventeenth birthday, Dallas felt increasingly eager to pursue top surgery to better align their body with their nonbinary identity. This decision, however, sparked a mixture of emotions and concerns within their family.*

*Dallas's parents, though supportive of their child's journey, harbored deep concerns about consenting to such a significant, irreversible procedure before Dallas turned eighteen. The weight of responsibility felt overwhelming. They worried that Dallas might later regret the decision, and the thought of their child undergoing major surgery was daunting.*

*"We want to support you, but this is such a big step. What if you change your mind?" they often found themselves asking.*

*However, Dallas's determination was unwavering. They had been working closely with a gender therapist for several years, who consistently affirmed Dallas's emotional maturity and well-established identity. Dallas was thorough in their approach, diligently researching the procedure, understanding the risks, and following all medical advice. They frequently engaged in open, heartfelt conversations with their parents, sharing their thoughts, fears, and the immense discomfort they felt living in a body that didn't align with their gender identity.*

*One evening, Dallas sat down with their parents, their eyes filled with both anxiety and hope.*

*"I know this is a lot to take in, but I've never been more certain about anything in my life. This surgery isn't just about my body—it's about my future, my happiness, and my ability to live authentically," they said, their voice steady but earnest.*

*Over the following months, Dallas's parents began to see the depth of their child's conviction. They saw how Dallas's face lit up when talking about the future, how their confidence had grown since starting hormone therapy, and how they meticulously planned every aspect of the surgical process. The family attended numerous therapy sessions together, where they explored their fears and hopes, slowly building a bridge of trust and understanding.*

*The pivotal moment came during a family therapy session when Dallas's therapist gently reminded them, "Bodily autonomy is crucial for everyone, especially for young people like Dallas who are navigating such significant aspects of their identity. They have shown remarkable maturity and insight. This isn't just a medical procedure; it's a vital step in Dallas's journey toward self-acceptance and happiness."*

*Gradually, Dallas's parents began to shift their perspective. They realized that the age of eighteen was an arbitrary benchmark and that maturity and readiness didn't necessarily align with legal adulthood. They recognized that respecting Dallas's bodily autonomy was an integral part of supporting their child's authentic self.*

*When the day of the surgery finally arrived, Dallas felt a mix of nerves and excitement. Their parents were right by their side, holding their hand, offering words of encouragement. The surgery was a complete success, and for the first time, Dallas felt a profound sense of relief and alignment with their body.*

*"I'm so grateful my parents respected my readiness," Dallas said, tears of joy in their eyes. "This was life-changing for me."*

Chronological age alone does not necessarily dictate preparedness for gender-affirming interventions like hormones or surgery. When given appropriate guidance and support, many transgender youth demonstrate the maturity and understanding necessary to participate in certain medical decisions before reaching adulthood. The key takeaway is that delaying gender-affirming care until an arbitrary age can prolong distress for transgender adolescents. By respecting each youth's personal readiness, families can provide vital support during this critical stage of identity development.

While initially, discovering your child's identity may cause you to want to postpone treatment until they are eighteen for any intervention, I encourage you to consider this empowering belief instead:

---

"I trust my child's deep understanding of their own identity and respect their ability to make informed decisions about their body."

---

## KEY POINTS

**Natural Parental Apprehension:** It's normal for parents to feel apprehensive about making decisions regarding their child's gender identity, especially when those decisions might involve medical interventions. Many parents worry that they might make the wrong choice or be responsible for their child's future unhappiness.

**Adolescence and Mental Health:** Adolescence is a crucial period for identity formation, and for transgender youth, having their gender identity affirmed during these years can lead to significantly better mental health outcomes. Research consistently shows that when transgender adolescents receive support and access to gender-affirming care, they experience reduced rates of depression, anxiety, and suicidal ideation.

**Consequences of Waiting:** Waiting can prolong and intensify gender dysphoria. For many transgender teens, the onset of puberty brings about distressing physical changes that deepen their sense of disconnection from their bodies.

**Capability of Young People:** The belief that young people are too immature to make informed decisions about their gender identity is a common concern. However, evidence suggests that young people are quite capable of understanding their gender identity and making informed choices about their bodies. Regret rates among transgender individuals who transition are exceptionally low.

**Gradual Process of Gender-Affirming Care:** Gender-affirming care is a gradual process. Social transition, which involves changes in gender expression and their role within social settings, is often the first step and does not involve medical interventions. This can include adopting a new name, pronouns, and clothing that reflect the young person's gender identity.

## REFLECTION QUESTIONS

1. What are your biggest concerns about allowing your child to begin gender-affirming treatment before the age of eighteen?
2. How do you think delaying treatment could impact your child's mental and emotional well-being?
3. What steps can you take to educate yourself about the benefits and risks of gender-affirming care for adolescents?
4. How can you support your child's social transition and create a more affirming environment at home and in their social circles?
5. What can you learn from the experiences of other parents and families who have navigated this journey with their transgender children?

9

# AM I GOING TO LOSE MY CHILD?

**When a child transitions**, many parents experience a sense of loss or grief as they realize that their child's future may be quite different from the one they imagined for them. The sense of "ambiguous loss" that parents of trans youth often experience isn't limited to memories of their child's past—it can deeply affect the hopes and dreams they had envisioned for their child's future as well (Bull and D'Arrigo-Patrick 2018). Oftentimes, even before a child is conceived, and then throughout pregnancy after learning the baby's assigned sex, parents begin envisioning and imagining a specific future for their child. Most parents have a specific vision of what they aspire for their child's life to look like, shaped by major social and cultural milestones such as religious ceremonies, career achievements, marriage, or eventual grandchildren. When your child comes out as transgender or begins their transition journey, you may feel as if you are somehow "losing" this long-imagined future, even though all these milestones remain possible after a young person transitions. Additionally, you may find yourself mourning the perceived role you had envisioned for your child within the family dynamic, and you worry that their transition will dramatically change their role and relationships. While your child is still present as their authentic self, the loss of an imagined future can trigger a complex grieving process.

What many parents are truly grieving when their child transitions, is their ingrained idea of who their child was or would become. Your child is still present, perhaps even more so as they become more comfortable expressing their identity, but your understanding of your child's identity has changed, and that can be a hard adjustment to make. It is also a difficult one to talk about: you may be accustomed to taking your child's gender for granted and may not have the language or communication patterns built up to discuss it openly, making the feeling of grief even stronger. This grief may also come with a perceived loss of control over your child's life, as well as a fear for their future and the difficulties they may face while living as a trans person. This fear is discussed more fully in the next section of the book, "Concerns About Well-Being and Safety."

As parents, it's natural to experience a wide range of emotions when your child comes out as trans or begins a gender transition. These feelings can be complex, and it's important to find outlets for them—whether through support groups, therapy, or conversations with trusted individuals—so you can process your emotions in a healthy way. Acknowledging your feelings doesn't mean they are wrong, but having a space to explore them helps ensure that they don't overshadow the love and connection you have with your child. Feelings of loss are meaningful parts of a parent's emotional reality, but the framing of ambiguous loss misses something crucial: *you have not actually lost your child or their future*. Your child may identify differently than you thought, but they are very much still both mentally and physically present, perhaps more so than ever before.

Some emotional response to the transition process is natural, but treating the situation as if you have "lost" your child can harm both their well-being and your relationship with them. For many trans youths, coming out brings a deep sense of relief or even joy. However, if you, as a parent, focus on feelings of loss or grief, it may convey that your child's feelings are not valid or legitimate. It can also suggest that your love is conditional on them being who you imagined or wanted them to be. This reaction, sometimes referred to as "gender mourning" by researcher Jess Constantine Miseo, stems from the disruption of cisnormative assumptions and the positioning of transgender identities as something to be mourned or grieved (Miseo 2022).

### WHEN SUPPORT FEELS HEAVY

#### The Complex Emotions of Parenting a Trans Child

*Riley loved their father deeply but struggled with the emotional labor he expected from them after Riley came out as transgender. Riley's father always reminded them, "You should be grateful I stuck by you when so many parents wouldn't accept a trans kid."*

*However, as Riley expressed in therapy, this implied they owed their father for his bare minimum acceptance and support.*

*"He acts like I should be thankful he didn't completely reject me, when that's the very least a parent should do," Riley said. "But I'm expected to constantly reassure him about his feelings around my identity."*

*Riley understood their father was going through an adjustment period. But they felt it was unfair to be the one consoling him over their own truth.*

*"My dad will get emotional saying he misses his 'daughter,' and then I have to comfort him about the fact that I'm trans. Like it's my fault he's grieving this idea of me."*

*What Riley's father didn't fully grasp was that both he and Riley were navigating challenging experiences, albeit in different ways.*

*Riley shared with their therapist in session, "Coming out was terrifying. I faced bullying, dysphoria, and the risk of rejection from my entire community." They acknowledged their father's adjustment process but added, "My dad had to adapt to new pronouns and my name, which I know isn't easy, but it's a different kind of challenge."*

*Riley expressed that their father's grief revealed a profound disconnect between the vision he had of Riley and their true identity. Initially, Riley took on the emotional burden of trying to reassure their father, but it became clear that this was taking a toll on their own mental health. Through our work together, Riley learned how to set boundaries and prioritize their well-being while still allowing space for their father to adjust. At the same time, their father sought support from a group for parents of transgender children, where he found understanding and guidance from others navigating similar experiences. With this support, he began to process his feelings in a healthier way, ultimately becoming a stronger advocate for Riley. By sharing the emotional load, both Riley and their father were able to focus on healing and building a relationship rooted in authenticity and mutual respect.*

Parental grief over the loss of their "daughter" or "son" involves real emotions that many parents must work through and cannot rush. However, working through these emotions with their trans/nonbinary/gender nonconforming child puts an inappropriate burden on the child, as Riley experienced above, to comfort their parent about their identity. This can exacerbate and compound shame that trans youths are trying to break away from by coming out, and that has likely already plagued their lives. Children deserve a safe and supportive place to land, so parents who are struggling with ambiguous grief are encouraged to seek support with therapists or support groups experienced in issues of gender identity, rather than bringing their grief to their children.

When parents can acknowledge and process their grief, an entirely new realm of possibility opens up. By disrupting the grief narrative, parents create space for deeper connection and understanding with their child. Instead of focusing on loss, they can embrace the opportunity to get to know their child more fully—perhaps for the first time—as their true, authentic self. This shift allows parents to offer more meaningful support, strengthen their relationship, and experience the joy and relief their child may feel in coming out. It transforms what could feel like an ending into a new beginning, filled with growth, trust, and shared discovery. Getting stuck in long-standing grief over your child's gender transition can send an extremely invalidating and harmful message. As transgender advocate Meredith Talusan states in a *New York Times* article, grief as a reaction to transition "reduces a person's very being to their gender and reveals that a loved one cares more about a phantom image than for the trans person they supposedly love, who is right in front of them" (Talusan 2019). For a transgender child, having their authentic identity be the subject of a parent's mourning can communicate that they are not fully accepted or affirmed for who they truly are. This places an unfair burden on the child to comfort and reassure the parent, rather than receiving the support they need during this vulnerable time. Parents should seek support and not expect their children to bear the brunt of their grief.

As parents process their emotional response to their child's gender identity, it's worthwhile to understand where these emotions come from. The "gender mourning" phenomenon arises from deeply ingrained cisnormative (the assumption that everyone is, or ought to be, cisgender) assumptions that view transgender identities as a "loss" or deviation from prescribed societal norms. As Mel Constantine Miseo explains in her research, it stems from "the positioning of trans identities and trans bodies as sites of danger" and the disruption of "gender-normative expectations of parent-child relationships" based on the cisnormative ideals embedded within many family systems (Miseo 2022). Miseo's work highlights how some societal views incorrectly frame transgender identities as potentially dangerous or disruptive to family structures, which is inherently flawed. Your child's authentic self is not a "loss" to be grieved but a truth to be celebrated. Remember, the child you loved when you first met them, perhaps even before you first met them, is still the same person sitting in front of you, just a more authentic version.

A young person's transition is a good time for parents to reexamine their own stereotypes about gender and what it means to have "a daughter" or "a son." Parents may have previously engaged in certain gender-coded activities with their children, such as coaching a single-gender sports team, shopping, cooking together, or watching specific types of movies as a family, based on what they believed they were "supposed to do" with a child of a particular gender. In reality, none of these activities are exclusive to any gender. Parents can (and do!) continue to enjoy the same activities with their child, even if it means visiting different departments in a store or cheering on a different sports team. If your child genuinely enjoyed these activities before, their gender identity is unlikely to change their interest in them. If your child participated in these activities due to gender stereotyping and felt pressured to "like" certain things, parents and children can work together to find new common ground and pastimes. Assuming all shared interests will change because your child has come out stems from harmful stereotypes that certain activities are only "for boys" or "for girls." This stereotype should be challenged, regardless of a child's gender identity or transition.

As you navigate the stages of adjusting to your child's transition, even though you should be patient with your own feelings, it remains important to remember that expressing grief in front of your child over their identity can have severely negative impacts on their mental health and well-being. Sharing your thoughts with a spouse, sibling, or trusted relative can provide valuable support and help you process your emotions. However, be cautious not to let grief become the dominant family narrative.

Transgender youth already face disproportionately high risks of suicide attempts and self-harm when lacking family support and affirmation of their identity. Communicating a sense of mourning or loss to your child compounds these risks at an already vulnerable time. It is crucial that parents who are experiencing emotional turmoil seek help and support so that their children do not end up bearing the burden of their emotions but instead receive the love and support at home that they need to become more resilient, authentic versions of themselves.

### WHEN GRIEF OVERSHADOWS TRUTH

#### A Parental Reckoning

*When Glenn and Sharon's sixteen-year-old child came out as transgender, they struggled to show the affirmation and support their child needed. Though they loved their child deeply, Glenn and Sharon became consumed by their own sense of grief over the idea of who they thought their child was.*

*"We told our child over and over, 'You have to understand how hard this is for us. We're trying our best, but we're grieving who you used to be,'" Sharon recalls. Glenn adds, "We'd say things like 'You're asking a lot of us to change how we see you after sixteen years.' Looking back, that was incredibly selfish."*

*Their child desperately wanted Glenn and Sharon's acceptance but constantly received the message that their identity was secondary to their parents' difficult emotions. "It made me feel like my parents' grief over an imagined version of me was more important than my actual self," the teen said. "Like they had lost a child when I was right there."*

*Glenn and Sharon's centering of their own grief prevented them from truly seeing the harm it caused their child. As Glenn admits, "We were so busy mourning this idea of who our child was, we failed to celebrate them coming into their full identity and truth."*

*This parental grief took a heavy mental health toll on the teen. "I already carried so much shame around my identity. Having my parents amplify that made me feel hopeless and depressed," they said. At one point, their despair became so severe that they attempted suicide.*

*It wasn't until this life-threatening crisis that Glenn and Sharon realized how damaging their grief narrative had been. "We thought we were being open by voicing our struggle," Sharon said, tears in her eyes. "But we never stopped to consider the struggle it placed on our child's shoulders."*

*Today, Glenn and Sharon are pursuing family therapy, parent coaching, and educating themselves as allies. As Glenn states, "Our grief was rooted in ignorance of what it means to be transgender. Our child has shown incredible courage, and the least we can do is match it by celebrating their true self, not mourning a false idea."*

*Glenn and Sharon hope others can learn from their mistakes. "Don't make your child's identity about your grief," Sharon advises. "It's not about you—it's about giving them the affirmation and life they deserve."*

The reality is, by not affirming your child's stated gender identity, you risk truly losing them—from your life, from feeling welcomed in your family, and in the most tragic cases, losing them forever. Research on parents of transgender youth found that when caregivers do not accept their child's identity, the child experiences a state of confusion and rejection about whether they still belong or have a place in their family at all. More than confusion, the risk of rejection represents an existential threat (Catalpa and McGuire 2018). Most trans youth still want to be a part of their families of origin and will attempt to find ways to negotiate those relationships if possible. By not accepting their identity, you put the onus on them to figure out how to navigate this conflict. For many trans youth, family rejection is life-threatening. Numerous studies, including the US Transgender Survey and the Trevor Project 2024 US National Survey on the Mental Health of LGBTQ+ Young People have shown that transgender young people who lack family acceptance and affirmation face drastically higher rates of suicide attempts, self-harm, homelessness, and other adverse outcomes (James et al. 2024; The Trevor Project 2024). Affirming your child's gender identity is quite literally a matter of keeping them safe and alive. Youth whose families support and celebrate their authentic selves are far less likely to suffer these devastating consequences. By embracing your child's truth, you not only gain a closer relationship—you may very well save their life.

Rather than mourning an imagined version of who you believed your child to be, the healthiest path forward is to reframe your perspective. Your child's transition is not a loss but an opportunity—a chance for them to blossom into their authentic, true self. Open yourself to adjusting your vision of their future while still celebrating the journey you've been on together. Seek out resources and support from other parents of transgender youth who can share how they've navigated major change, as Jeni Wahlig suggests in the *Journal of GLBT Family Studies* (Wahlig 2014). Most importantly, have open and affirming conversations with your child about their identity and experience. Let them know you see them, you hear them, and you are committed to learning and growing alongside them. The person you love is still there, perhaps more fully realized than ever before. By disrupting the grief narrative and choosing to champion your child's truth, you can strengthen your family bond and help your child thrive.

### A NOTE ON DISRUPTING THE GRIEF NARRATIVE

**by Lizette Trujillo,**

**advocate and proud parent of a trans son**

Reframing how we talk about things is how we move toward progress! We should always be reexamining language, ideas, societal norms, and our own unconscious bias and beliefs! I feel this is important when we talk about using the term "grief." When parents talk about having a LGBTQIA+ child (especially a trans/nonbinary child), they will often talk about this feeling of loss that is often tied up in their own misconceptions and fears for their child.

Grief was spoken about a lot by parents of lesbian, gay, and bisexual children in the '80s—and even done so now regarding the loss of not having "biological grandchildren," as well as fears regarding their child's safety due to discrimination and societal rejection. While the fears of impacts regarding discrimination and societal rejection are valid, we are now able to see how misguided this concept around grandchildren and LGB parenting can be. Especially over the last few decades, as we have seen adoption and other fertility options become more available to people who wish to become parents.

Now some will say that this is a valid term because there is a loss of expectation, and while that may be real, it still isn't grief. Our kids make choices outside of our expectations often, and we are not grief-stricken every time they do! So, what does this use of the word grief really mean? What are parents trying to communicate? Having an LGBTQIA+ child is often what many parents first encounter with the deeper experience of societal rejection and marginalization. Loss of privilege (worry about what family and friends will think, etc.) and fear of safety and marginalization is truly what is motivating this feeling . . . the loss of "normal" (a term I hate), the loss of status quo, and the unconscious understanding that your life and the life of your child will be met with resistance, rejection, and discrimination. These are all valid fears and worries, but if we want to be allies to trans/nonbinary people, we really need to stop talking about how sad we are that they are trans/nonbinary. Saying we are experiencing "grief" because of our child's identity puts the onus on the child, instead of placing the blame on long-held societal biases held against trans/nonbinary people. Reframing is necessary if we are going to truly gain equality. Blame this fear and loss on lawmakers, churches, and anyone else who will choose to discriminate and reject your child instead of loving them. Blame hateful rhetoric and harmful ideologies. It's time for us to do the inside work to break down transphobic beliefs, so that we can build a better tomorrow for the trans/nonbinary people in our lives. They deserve more from us!

As we started this chapter, you might have been feeling in the depths of grief or feeling sorry for yourself. It's important to acknowledge these feelings and address them with other adults, including mental health professionals, who can help you understand and process your experiences. In doing so, you become better equipped to meet your child's emotional needs by providing the love and support that they need to thrive. Should you find yourself sitting in the depths of grief, I encourage you to consider this empowering belief instead:

"Embracing my child's transition is not about losing who they once were but celebrating the blossoming of their true, authentic self.

## KEY POINTS

**Understanding Ambiguous Loss:** Parents may experience a sense of loss not over the physical presence of their child but over the anticipated future and roles they imagined for them, known as ambiguous loss.

**Shift in Family Dynamics:** A child's transition can lead to changes in family roles and relationships, which requires adjustments in how family members interact and support each other.

**Grieving an Idea, Not a Person:** The grief felt by parents often centers on the loss of the idea of who they thought their child was or who they expected them to become, rather than the actual child, who is still very much present.

**Impact of Societal Expectations:** Societal norms and expectations heavily influence parental reactions and feelings toward their child's transition, often exacerbating feelings of loss.

**The Importance of Supportive Parenting:** Supporting a child's authentic self is crucial for their mental health and well-being, and focusing on grief can undermine the child's sense of acceptance and self-worth.

**Reframing the Narrative:** when parents process their feelings of loss or grief in healthy ways, they become better equipped to celebrate their child's true identity, which can strengthen the parent-child relationship and support the child's overall happiness.

## REFLECTION QUESTIONS

1. Have you experienced grief relating to your child's transition, what do you think you're mourning?
2. What supports can you lean on to ensure that your processing of these feelings does not impose additional emotional burdens on your child?
3. In what ways can you actively celebrate your child's transition as a positive development in their life?
4. What are the non-gendered things you love about your child?
5. How can understanding the concept of ambiguous loss help you navigate your feelings and improve your relationship with your child?

PART THREE

# CONCERNS ABOUT WELL-BEING AND SAFETY

# 10

# WILL THEY HAVE A HARD LIFE?

**It is normal and even rational** to worry that life will be more challenging for your child because they are trans or gender nonconforming. While it is easier and safer for young LGBTQ+ people to find community and to pursue their hopes and dreams free from formal discrimination, there are also strong social and political currents that seek to diminish their right to freely express their identity and live as their authentic selves. This reality can make even the most supportive parents worry about their child's future. It's natural for any parent to want to shield their child from pain and hardship; for parents of trans children, there's a fear that supporting their child's true self might inadvertently lead to their child having a difficult life. This concern can sometimes cause parents to hesitate, worried that affirming their child's identity could expose them to greater challenges.

On a superficial level, these fears might manifest in concerns about how their child presents themselves to the world. Parents might wonder, "How can she expect people to use the right pronouns if she keeps wearing the same old clothes? Maybe if she wore a dress, people would get it!" This question highlights a common misconception: that for someone's gender identity to be valid or respected, it must match societal expectations of gender expression.

Gender identity is an individual's deeply held sense of being a boy/man, girl/woman, a blend of both, or neither—independent of the sex assigned at birth. It's an internal, personal experience of gender. Gender expression is an extension of identity, but it is different from gender. Gender expression is the external display of one's gender through behavior, clothing, haircut, voice, and other forms of presentation. Society often expects these two aspects to align in a conventional way: for example, someone identifying as female should express themselves through traditionally feminine clothing and behavior. But gender identity and gender expression do not always match these conventional expectations. A person may identify as female and choose to wear traditionally masculine attire or hairstyles, or identify as male but continue to wear dresses and high heels. Embracing identities that don't conform to traditional gender norms is not only valid but essential. It's a crucial part of recognizing and respecting each person's right to define their own identity.

However, the stakes are much higher than simply risking being misunderstood. Trans and gender nonconforming individuals often have to navigate their gender expression differently depending on their environment to ensure their safety. For instance, they might dress differently around certain relatives or in public spaces where they fear they won't be safe or accepted, and they might avoid certain places in which they feel like they would not be accepted or may be subject to ridicule or even violence. This constant vigilance is exhausting and highlights the undue burden and dangers that come with nonconforming gender expressions in a world that can be hostile.

The belief that a child must "perform" their gender in a certain way to be understood and respected by others often stems from cisnormativity—the assumption that being cisgender (identifying with the gender assigned at birth) is universal, and that gender is binary and should be visually identifiable. This societal expectation places undue pressure on individuals, particularly transgender and gender nonconforming people, to conform to specific gender expressions to gain acceptance, be treated with respect, or even ensure that they will be safe in a particular environment. Many trans folks feel more comfortable exploring gender expression after they have received some kind of gender-affirming care, such as someone who gets top surgery and then feels empowered to wear feminine clothes, because the physical alignment achieved through medical transition can alleviate dysphoria and boost confidence, allowing individuals to express their gender more freely without fear of misgendering or social discomfort.

Parents' fears are valid in that they stem from genuine concern for their child's well-being and safety. The world can indeed be harsh and judgmental, and the desire to protect one's child from harm and disrespect is a natural parental instinct. However, it's important to challenge the notion that respect and recognition should be contingent upon adherence to narrow norms. It's important to understand that while your fears are rooted in love and protection, demanding that your child conform to societal expectations of gender expression can cause them harm by forcing them to suppress their true selves. A child's safety should not be contingent on adhering to societal norms or conforming to a gender presentation that is familiar to other people. It's crucial to balance your fears with the recognition that your child's safety also depends on being able to express their identity authentically without constant fear or the need to hide who they are. We will dive deeper into safety concerns in a later chapter "Will They Ever Be Safe?" For now, it's important to start by recognizing that navigating these challenges is not about conforming to narrow norms but about supporting your child's journey toward living as their authentic self.

Fear for your child's safety and quality of life is a rational response to recent efforts by many state legislatures to restrict access to gender-affirming care and limit the rights and protections to which LGBTQ+ people are entitled. Many states have enacted or are attempting to enact laws that limit access to essential medical care for trans youth and employing harsh rhetoric in these efforts (Movement Advancement Project 2024). This state-sanctioned discrimination poses real threats not just to the well-being of these young individuals but to trans people of all ages, and this climate of fear and hostility makes it even more crucial for families and communities to stand firmly in support of the LGBTQ+ youth, adults, and families in their community and beyond to ensure that they are both safe and free to live as their authentic selves.

Navigating the complex challenges of supporting a trans child can be particularly daunting for parents who are not aligned with each other on this journey, especially in families affected by divorce or in regions where gender-affirming care is restricted by law. When one parent is supportive but the other is not, or when local laws hinder access to necessary medical treatments like puberty blockers, the situation becomes a high-stakes emotional and logistic minefield. Parents may find themselves navigating complex legal battles, risking family rifts, or even contemplating relocation to more accepting areas. This scenario demands extraordinary courage, unwavering commitment, and often personal sacrifice from the supportive parent. They might need to stand firm against a spouse's opposition, potentially jeopardizing their marriage, while becoming impromptu activists to challenge discriminatory laws and policies.

In such environments, where schools might refuse to recognize a child's pronouns and the state exacerbates gender dysphoria by forcing them through an undesired puberty, supportive parents face a heartbreaking reality in which they feel forced to choose between supporting their child and adhering to local laws. They must travel long distances or across state lines to access appropriate healthcare, all while shielding their child from family conflicts and providing constant emotional support. This journey requires them to educate themselves rapidly on complex medical and legal issues and make difficult financial decisions to fund necessary treatments or legal actions. Supportive parents often face social ostracism in less accepting communities, transforming into not just caregivers but fierce advocates, legal strategists, and emotional anchors for their children. Ultimately, this path requires immense resilience, adaptability, and a willingness to prioritize their child's well-being above all else, even in the face of significant personal and societal obstacles.

## FIGHTING FOR AFFIRMATION

### A Custody Battle Over a Child's Rights

*The Parkers were a married couple with two children, including a twelve-year-old transgender son named Dylan. When Dylan came out as trans, his mother Rachel was fully supportive and affirming, while his father Mark initially struggled to accept it.*

*Their relationship had been strained for years, but Dylan's coming out as transgender became the catalyst for their marriage's final breakdown.*

*A bitter custody dispute arose over Dylan's gender identity and medical treatment. Rachel wanted to proceed with puberty blockers and hormone therapy recommended by Dylan's doctors to align his body with his male identity. However, Mark vehemently objected to any gender-affirming medical interventions, citing concerns over the permanence and appropriateness of such treatments for someone so young.*

*As the legal battle intensified, Dylan's relationship with his father became increasingly strained. Mark's refusal to use Dylan's chosen name and pronouns created a rift between them, leading to Dylan's reluctance to spend time with his father. Despite court-ordered visitation, Dylan often felt uncomfortable and misunderstood during these encounters, further damaging their bond.*

*Rachel found herself navigating a challenging path as the supportive parent. She focused on what she could control: providing a loving, affirming environment for Dylan at home, connecting him with supportive therapists and LGBTQ+ youth groups, and educating herself about transgender issues. Rachel also worked on accepting what she couldn't control, such as Mark's views or the pace of the legal process.*

*To help Dylan cope with the situation, Rachel:*

1. *Consistently affirmed Dylan's identity and supported his choices.*
2. *Encouraged open communication about his feelings regarding his father.*
3. *Sought family therapy to help Dylan process his emotions.*
4. *Advocated for Dylan's needs in school and medical settings.*
5. *Connected with support groups for parents of transgender children.*

*Rachel reminded herself that while she couldn't change Mark's mind, she could provide Dylan with the unconditional love and support he needed. She focused on creating a strong support network for Dylan, including understanding family members, affirming friends, and knowledgeable healthcare providers.*

*The judge ultimately granted Rachel's request to move forward with gender-affirming care for Dylan over Mark's objections. The ruling cited ample evidence that withholding this treatment from transgender youth significantly elevates risks like depression and suicide. The judge highlighted the critical need for Dylan to receive the care necessary to live as his authentic self and to support his mental and emotional well-being.*

*After the ruling, Rachel and Dylan began the process of obtaining the necessary medical treatments. Dylan's mental health improved noticeably as he started puberty blockers and hormone therapy. With his mother's unwavering support and the court's validation of his identity, Dylan was able to move forward with greater confidence and hope for the future.*

*This case underscores the importance of affirming and supporting transgender youth, highlighting the potentially lifesaving impact of gender-affirming care and the critical role of understanding and empathy in navigating these complex family dynamics. It also demonstrates the challenges faced by supportive parents and the importance of focusing on what they can control while accepting what they cannot.*

In circumstances like Rachel's, it's vital for supportive parents to explore and understand the full scope of care that affirms their child's identity. Parents can seek support from community organizations, local and online support groups, therapists who specialize in gender identity issues, educational resources, mental health professionals, books on transgender topics, and advocacy networks focused on LGBTQ+ rights. Parents may also need to enlist an attorney to help them navigate parental rights in split families or restrictive regions. As a parent, there are limits to what you can control. Beyond seeking expert guidance and support, the most important contribution you can make to ensuring your child has a happy life is to focus on creating a nurturing home environment where the child feels seen and validated, which can help mitigate the pain of external rejections.

All parents want their kids to be happy, so it is reasonable that parents of trans and gender-expansive kids are concerned by studies that have found that on average transgender people report a lower quality of life than their cisgender counterparts, largely as a result of increased challenges for their mental health and well-being (US Trans Survey 2024). These challenges come with an increased risk of mental illness, self-harm, and suicidal ideation. Trans youth also face higher rates of social isolation due to bullying, as well as the potential for loneliness caused by the loss of relationships when they come out, as partially discussed in previous chapters (The Trevor Project 2024). It's important to recognize that the *difficulties faced by transgender youth do not stem from their identity itself.* The challenges trans youth face result from how society responds to their authentic expression of self.

Discrimination, bigotry, and stigma are the real reasons for the challenges that lower the quality of life for trans children and adolescents. While it's natural to fear these negative forces, we must not give that fear the power to limit our capacity to love, support, and affirm trans youth. Standing by your child's side and supporting their true self is not just an act of love, it is also an act of resistance to stand against the societal pressures that seek to undermine their well-being.

It might feel like you have little control over the challenges your trans child faces, but in reality, parents and caregivers have a significant influence on how difficult it is for their child to navigate being trans. By actively supporting their identity, even in places where affirming care is limited or opposed, you can profoundly impact their well-being. When your child knows that you love and support them, you enhance their mental and emotional health and provide a foundation of support that counteracts external adversities.

The challenges faced by transgender children and their families in states hostile to gender-affirming care and trans rights are real and significant. All major medical and psychiatric associations agree that gender-affirming care is not only beneficial but also medically necessary and lifesaving (GLAAD 2024). Research consistently shows that both medical and social transitions significantly enhance a trans person's quality of life, particularly in terms of mental health (Olson et al. 2016). While financial or legal constraints may limit access to medical treatments, parents can still have a vital and positive impact on their child's well-being by supporting their social transition and affirming their identity. It's important for parents to understand and respect that their child may ultimately seek to live in an environment where they don't fear that their safety or access to care is in jeopardy. However, it's crucial to note that if a child chooses to move to a more accepting area, it doesn't necessarily mean that their current home environment isn't validating or supportive enough. Many factors, including broader societal and legal considerations, can influence such decisions. Parents should continue to offer unwavering support and work toward creating the most affirming environment possible, regardless of geographical location. Extensive evidence demonstrates that family acceptance and support are crucial and provide clear mental health benefits, regardless of other factors (The Trevor Project 2024).

It is crucial for families to have open discussions with their children about the kind of environment they wish to live in as they come of age. Parents in states with restrictive and discriminatory policies against transgender youth should recognize that these environments are often unfriendly to transgender adults as well. If your child plans to attend college, you might face the challenge of considering only schools in states that strongly protect trans rights. If college is not in their plans, your child may desire to move to states or cities that have laws that protect their freedom of expression and access to gender-affirming care. While this may be difficult for some families, it is important to listen to your child and not assume they should remain in a restrictive and anti-trans environment simply because it is where their parents live. Discussing these possibilities openly is important in helping families understand that their children are not trying to "get away from them" but are seeking a place where they can safely and comfortably be themselves without constant self-advocacy and risks to their emotional well-being.

## NAVIGATING HOSTILITY

### The Struggle for School and Community Support

*When Emily Johnson's fourteen-year-old child, Jordan, came out as transgender and began identifying as male, Emily and her husband David were determined to support him wholeheartedly. They immediately started using his chosen name and pronouns, encouraging Jordan to express his true self at home and within their family.*

*Despite the Johnsons' unwavering support, they quickly encountered resistance from Jordan's school and the broader community. The school administration refused to acknowledge Jordan's name and gender, insisting on using his birth name and female pronouns in official records and communications. Teachers were hesitant to adapt, some out of confusion and others due to personal beliefs. Jordan was not allowed to use the boys' restroom or participate in boys' sports teams, causing him to feel isolated and marginalized.*

*The local community mirrored the school's resistance. Jordan faced bullying from peers, and several parents voiced their disapproval, believing that Jordan's identity was a phase or a result of bad parenting. Emily and David found themselves in the crosshairs of community gossip and judgment, adding to their stress and concern for Jordan's well-being.*

*Despite these external challenges, the Johnsons remained steadfast in their support. They held regular family meetings to ensure Jordan felt heard and valued, and they sought out local LGBTQ+ support groups to connect with other families and advocates. Emily and David became vocal advocates for their son, meeting with school officials repeatedly to push for changes in school policy, though progress was slow and frustrating.*

*The emotional toll on Jordan was evident. He struggled with panic attacks and depression due to the lack of acceptance at school and in the community. However, the strong foundation of love and affirmation at home helped mitigate some of the damage. Jordan knew he could always rely on his parents for understanding and support, which provided a crucial emotional anchor.*

*Emily and David also sought professional help for themselves and Jordan, finding a therapist who specialized in working with transgender youth (for families in states where gender-affirming therapy is banned, consider working with a qualified clinician in another state as "coaching"). This therapist provided Jordan with coping strategies and a safe space to express his feelings. The Johnsons' commitment to Jordan's mental health and well-being helped him navigate the difficult landscape of a non-affirming school and community.*

*In time, Jordan's resilience began to shine through. With the encouragement of his parents, he started a GSA (Gender and Sexuality Alliance) club at his school, which slowly began to change the attitudes of some students and teachers. The Johnsons' advocacy efforts also garnered attention from local LGBTQ+ organizations, which provided additional resources and support to challenge the school's policies.*

*Though the journey was fraught with challenges, the Johnson family's unwavering support enabled Jordan to persevere. They demonstrated that while parents cannot control every aspect of their child's environment, their unconditional love and affirmation can make a significant difference. Jordan's story highlights the critical role parents play in supporting their transgender children, even when faced with adversity from schools and communities. By prioritizing their child's well-being and advocating for change, parents can help their transgender children thrive despite external opposition and even exercise the power to change attitudes and perceptions within their community, ultimately creating the opportunity for other LGBTQ+ people in their community to thrive too.*

You can stand with your child by engaging in advocacy to challenge the negative forces targeting the trans community (see chapter "How Can I Make a Broader Impact?"). Together, you can work toward creating a more inclusive and supportive world. Showing your support and actively participating in efforts to combat bigotry and discrimination send a powerful message to your child: you are there for them, fully committed to their well-being and rights.

### FROM AWARENESS TO ACTION
#### Jessica's Path to Activism

*Jessica's twelve-year-old daughter Maya, who was assigned male at birth, had a gradual journey to discovering her transgender identity. From an early age, Maya exhibited signs of gender nonconformity; as a toddler, she preferred princess dolls over traditionally masculine toys and expressed herself in ways that didn't align with typical male gender expectations. Throughout her early childhood, Maya went through an extended period of identifying as nonbinary, using they/them pronouns. Over time, she began to express her identity more clearly as a girl, with her family supporting each step of her journey. Living in a quietly progressive community provided a supportive environment for Maya's exploration of gender identity, allowing her to transition socially without facing significant external pressure or discrimination. They faced no barriers to gender-affirming care, and the day Maya came out at school, the principal called Jessica to let her know they'd be there for her during her transition. In other words, they had been very fortunate.*

*While they were so fortunate, Maya's transition was also hard. Jessica experienced the terror of an uncertain future for her daughter. She grieved the idea of the son she thought her daughter had been and lost sleep (and still loses sleep) over medical transition decisions Maya wouldn't have to make for many years to come. But as time went on, their comfort with the uncertainty of Maya's transition grew, and so did their faith in their family's ability to navigate Maya's gender journey, no matter where it took them.*

*Six years after Maya socially transitioned, and she and her family felt sturdy in their understanding and support for her evolving identity, things changed in the political landscape, and the country around them was beginning to not just fail transgender kids but actively become more hostile toward them. Today, Maya's rights and freedoms as a trans person would be severely restricted in half the states in this country. In six short years, Jessica feared Maya would one day find herself living in a country that did not recognize her rights, a country in which she could be legally denied her housing, employment, service, and healthcare based on her gender identity.*

*Jessica refused to passively accept this possibility. Jessica co-founded the Employee Resource Group for Parents and Caregivers of Gender-Diverse Kids at work. She hosted a fireside chat for her workplace to provide education on active allyship and started a local Facebook group for other parents. In 2023 she found herself connected to a small group of other parents motivated and enthusiastic to organize in support of LGBTQ+ people's rights and freedoms. In consultation with members of the trans community and political advisers, they launched a nonprofit.*

*Representation matters, and they believed a key way of stopping the flood of anti-trans legislation is to have more trans people in those rooms where the laws are getting made. With the knowledge that trans representation is lifesaving, Jessica and her fellow activists joined a growing movement of philanthropic, communication, and artistic work happening to support trans people during this time. They decided to work with a laser focus on identifying, recruiting, and electing highly qualified transgender candidates to public office.*

*This work helped Jessica cope in a scary political environment and helped her to feel empowered rather than helpless—it was something she could do that brought her comfort, something she could do to pave a better way for her daughter. But the most surprising outcome of her advocacy was that her community grew in meaningful ways. For the first time since college, she was forming new friendships that she knew would be a central part of her life for years to come. They were durable friendships with people of various professions, ages, locations, and gender identities. They shared a sense of purpose that brought them all together, that made these friendships so essentially supportive and enriching. The driving motivation for them connecting was a deep love for their children and their community.*

As a parent, you cannot shield your child from all of life's challenges, regardless of their gender identity. However, this doesn't mean you're powerless in the face of adversity. By actively supporting your transgender child and advocating for their rights, you can contribute to creating a more inclusive and accepting world. While initially, the revelation of your child's identity may have sparked fears about their future and concerns over potential hardships, I encourage you to embrace this empowering perspective instead:

> "When I face my fears and support my child unconditionally, we strengthen our bond and make the world a better, safer place for LGBTQ+ folks."

## KEY POINTS

**Challenging Environment for Trans Youth:** The current environment is increasingly challenging and unsafe for trans and gender nonconforming young people, leading to significant parental worry about their child's future. It's natural for parents to fear that supporting their child's true self might inadvertently cause them to have a more difficult life.

**Legislative Threats to Well-Being:** Many state legislatures are enacting laws that limit access to essential medical care for trans youth, posing real threats to their well-being and the well-being of trans people of all ages. This climate of fear and hostility makes it crucial for families and communities to support trans youth, ensuring they feel validated and protected in their journey to live authentically.

**Complex Parental Challenges:** Navigating the complex challenges of supporting a trans child can be especially difficult for parents who are not aligned with each other, particularly in split families or regions with restrictive laws on gender-affirming care. When one parent is supportive but the other is not, it can create significant hurdles for the child's well-being.

**Quality of Life Concerns:** It is true that transgender people often report a lower quality of life than their cisgender counterparts, largely due to increased challenges to their mental health and well-being, including higher risks of mental illness, self-harm, and suicidal ideation. This is because of external societal factors rather than inner turmoil unique to trans identities.

**Parental Acceptance Is Crucial:** Parental acceptance can greatly enhance a trans child's mental and emotional health. By actively supporting their identity, parents can significantly influence how difficult it is for their child to navigate being trans, even in environments where affirming care is limited or opposed.

**Gender-Affirming Care Is Beneficial:** The consensus among major medical and psychiatric associations is that gender-affirming care is beneficial, medically necessary, and lifesaving. Research supports that both medical and social transitions significantly enhance a trans person's quality of life, especially in terms of mental health.

**Creating a Supportive Environment and More Inclusive Future:** Family acceptance and support are crucial for the mental health of trans youth. Parents can create a nurturing home environment, seek community support groups, and engage in advocacy to support their child and challenge societal discrimination.

## REFLECTION QUESTIONS

1. What are your primary fears about your trans child's future, and how can you address them constructively?
2. How can you create a safe and supportive home environment for your child, especially if external support is lacking?
3. What people or organizations in your community are working to advance trans rights; how can you contribute to their efforts?
4. How can you work to align with your co-parent or other family members to ensure consistent support for your child, even in the face of differing views or legal challenges?
5. What steps can you take to connect with community resources and support groups to better support your child and yourself in this journey?

11

# ARE THEY RISKING THEIR HEALTH?

**As parents and caregivers,** we naturally want to ensure our children's health and safety above all else. However, when it comes to concerns about transgender youth and sexual health, it's crucial to separate facts from stigma-driven fears. There is a harmful and inaccurate stereotype that being transgender inherently leads to contracting diseases or premature death. Sexual health risks exist for all people regardless of gender identity, and modern medicine provides ample resources to mitigate those risks through education and preventive care.

Rather than operating from a place of unfounded fear, take a moment to reflect on where these anxieties truly stem from. Much of what parents fear for their transgender child's well-being is rooted in misconceptions or false narratives perpetuated by others. Given the volume of misinformation about trans identities, parents and caregivers of trans youth must develop a keen ability to discern fact from stigma. Be a fierce advocate for your child by arming yourself with accurate information from credible sources. Approach their health needs through the lens of compassion and empowerment, not misguided trepidation. With the right knowledge and support, you can help your child navigate sexual health responsibly while allowing them to embrace their authentic identity.

### WHEN FEAR FADES

#### The Path to Acceptance and Affirmation

*Michelle was a nurse working in San Francisco during the height of the AIDS crisis in the 1980s. She witnessed firsthand the devastating impacts of the epidemic, caring for many young gay men as the disease ravaged the LGBTQ+ community. The widespread homophobia and misinformation of the era embedded deep associations in Michelle's mind between being LGBTQ+ and illness.*

*Decades later, when Michelle's teenage child came out as transgender, she found herself gripped by fears rooted in those experiences. "All I could think about were my former patients withering away from HIV/AIDS when they should have been in the prime of their lives," Michelle says. "I became terrified that my child's identity meant they were destined for disease and an early death."*

*Michelle acknowledges her fears didn't align with modern medical science, but they felt visceral nonetheless. "Logically, I knew being transgender isn't what caused AIDS, but those images from my nursing days were seared into my brain. I panicked that my child was now at heightened risk."*

*What helped Michelle overcome this ingrained narrative was educating herself through LGBTQ+ family resources and connecting with other parents of transgender youth. She learned that the true health risks facing her child stemmed from societal stigma and barriers to gender-affirming care—not their identity itself or the medical components of gender-affirming care.*

*Michelle had to confront her own biases that being LGBTQ+ inherently meant illness and death. Michelle admits that she learned these damaging myths in the '80s but learned they're simply not true and that with affirmation and proper medical support, her child can thrive.*

*Michelle now recognizes that her role is to facilitate an affirmative environment and access to care informed by current standards—not to project antiquated fears onto her child. "The health risks come from being denied affirmation, not from being transgender," she says. "My job isn't to expect the worst but to fiercely love and advocate for my child's well-being."*

*By examining the roots of her fears and replacing discriminatory narratives with facts, Michelle overcame ingrained biases to become the affirmative parent her transgender child needs for a healthy future.*

Being an informed parent or caregiver means more than just offering love and support—it also requires understanding the data and what it tells us about the specific health risks that disproportionately affect trans and gender-diverse youth compared to their cisgender counterparts.

The primary health concerns that trans people experience at higher rates than the general population can be categorized into three main areas: minority stress, lack of appropriate and comprehensive healthcare access, and mental health challenges. The most pervasive of these is minority stress. As defined by the Mayo Clinic (2024), minority stress refers to the negative outcomes stemming from societal stigma, discrimination, abuse, harassment, rejection, and internalized negative attitudes faced by marginalized groups. For transgender individuals, minority stress heightens their risk for emotional/psychological abuse, physical/sexual violence, sexually transmitted infections, viral hepatitis, HIV, substance abuse issues, and mental health problems like anxiety, depression, and suicidal ideation. Minority stress is not inherent to trans identities but rather it is a health response to social and political climates in which trans identities are not accepted or embraced.

### LAYERED STRUGGLES

#### Understanding the Impact of Minority Stress

*Miles, a seventeen-year-old transgender boy, has faced immense minority stress throughout his life. Growing up in a conservative rural town, he was routinely misgendered, bullied, and ostracized by peers for not conforming to gender norms. At home, while Miles's parents were supportive of his identity, they struggled to create a fully affirmative environment due to their own internalized biases and lack of knowledge about transgender issues. Miles frequently had to educate and correct them on proper name and pronoun usage and appropriate terminology.*

*This chronic stress from microaggressions and invalidation, combined with overt discrimination, took a heavy toll on Miles's mental health. He experienced severe anxiety, depression, and suicidal ideation stemming from the societal stigma he faced as a transgender person. His gender identity also made him a target for physical and sexual harassment; Miles was once violently assaulted by a group of classmates, leaving him with injuries and post-traumatic stress symptoms.*

*The compounding minority stressors led Miles to develop unhealthy coping mechanisms like self-harm and substance abuse. He turned to alcohol and marijuana to numb his psychological pain and societal rejection. Despite these challenges, Miles's resilience allowed him to graduate and pursue higher education. However, the legacy of minority stress persisted, making it difficult for him to access appropriate healthcare on campus due to discrimination and lack of provider competency.*

*Miles's story highlights how minority stressors can converge from multiple systemic and interpersonal sources, producing cyclical negative impacts on the mental, physical, and social-emotional well-being of transgender individuals. Addressing these minority stressors requires not only removing the stressors or leaving the environment in which they exist but also processing the experience and developing new habits and coping mechanisms. Even after the original perceived threats have dissipated or been removed, the effects of chronic minority stress can linger, necessitating ongoing support and healing.*

The rise in anti-trans legislation and systemic discrimination in the healthcare system hinders access to appropriate, gender-affirming healthcare that is crucial for transgender youth. These barriers compound the already challenging experience for families seeking to support their transgender children.

Even in regions where gender-affirming care is legally protected, accessing it can be a complex and frustrating process, often complicated by insurance limitations. Many transgender youth and their families are hesitant to seek medical attention due to fears of mistreatment, such as misgendering, deadnaming, outright refusal of care, or even verbal and physical abuse.

Healthcare providers may lack cultural competency, ask unnecessary or invasive questions, dismiss symptoms unrelated to gender identity, or fail to ensure adequate privacy protections. In some cases, transgender individuals experience what's colloquially known as "trans broken arm syndrome," where providers wrongly attribute all medical concerns—no matter how unrelated—to the patient's transgender status or hormone therapy. The fear of being outed or exposed can also pose serious risks to a young person's privacy and social well-being. Unfortunately, these negative experiences with healthcare providers, who may lack proper training in transgender health, often deter families from pursuing essential care. For parents navigating a healthcare system that doesn't fully understand or embrace gender diversity, this can be especially overwhelming and distressing.

Unfortunately, even though gender-affirming care is often covered by insurance, unexpected out-of-pocket costs can arise. Many prescription medication savings plans may not fully cover the cost of puberty blockers unless the child is diagnosed with "premature puberty," leaving gaps for those using them for gender-affirming care. Under some insurance plans that do not cover 100% of costs, injectable puberty blockers can range from several hundred dollars every three months to several thousand dollars for an eighteen-month implant. Similarly, fertility banking can also be expensive, but it's an important part of gender-affirming care for many trans individuals. Some hormone therapies and surgeries involved in gender transitions can impact fertility, so having the option to preserve sperm or eggs allows trans youth to make future decisions about having biological children. This preservation ensures they don't have to choose between affirming their gender and maintaining the possibility of parenthood. However, the costs don't end with the procedure—there are often monthly storage fees, which can further strain families already managing other healthcare expenses.

No matter how emotionally supportive a family may be, many families simply cannot afford the most advanced medical care for their children, which can be heartbreaking for parents who want to support and affirm their child's identity. It can also be challenging to find a healthcare provider who can provide effective guidance to you and your child as you navigate the process of accessing care. Many families ultimately consult with a specialized gender clinic, which has expertise in gender-affirming care. These professionals can provide letters of necessity that demonstrate the critical need for procedures, countering claims that such care is "elective." Additionally, they can help with appeals if insurance companies deny coverage, ensuring that your child receives the care they need. These clinics have providers who are experienced in navigating the complexities of gender-affirming care and can offer comprehensive guidance on available treatments and financial assistance programs. For example, if puberty blockers are prohibitively expensive under your insurance plan, a gender clinic may guide you to other oral medications that may offer similar results at a fraction of the cost.

If you encounter financial roadblocks, don't lose hope. Healthcare costs can be overwhelming, but there are often creative solutions and resources that can help you get the care your child needs. Meeting your child's needs may require patience, persistence, and a proactive approach. While navigating the medical system can be time-consuming and stressful, especially for those unfamiliar with it, persistence in securing quality care is crucial for your child's well-being. The effort is worth it, even in the face of the broader challenges of our healthcare system.

Supporting transgender youth effectively involves creating an environment where they can thrive, even within the limitations of the current world. While systemic changes, such as training healthcare providers in cultural competency and transgender health, are important, parents and families can still make a significant impact on their child's well-being within these constraints.

When families build robust support networks, seek out knowledgeable and affirming healthcare providers, and advocate for their children's rights, they not only help their own child receive quality care but also pave the way for other families to access the care their children need. By pushing for better systems and advocating for change, these families make it easier for others to navigate the healthcare system and receive affirming, comprehensive care. Though parents may not have the power to change state laws or influence distant college campuses directly, they have a significant impact within their communities by providing unwavering support, seeking accurate information, and finding (or even creating) community resources that promote inclusivity and affirmation.

By focusing on these actionable steps, parents can help ensure their transgender youth receive the care and respect they deserve, fostering an environment that supports their development and well-being despite broader societal challenges. This approach empowers both the youth and their families to navigate these obstacles with strength and resilience, demonstrating that positive, meaningful change is possible even in an imperfect world.

## GATEKEEPING AND DENIAL

### The Roadblocks to Gender-Affirming Healthcare

*At age fourteen, Lia came out as a transgender girl to her supportive parents. She expressed interest in exploring hormone therapy options to begin her medical transition. However, Lia's family faced immense barriers in accessing gender-affirming healthcare.*

*Their local providers lacked experience with transgender patients, making Lia feel uncomfortable. She was frequently misgendered and forced to explain her lived experience constantly. One doctor insisted on asking invasive questions about Lia's body and sexuality that felt dehumanizing and irrelevant. The few providers who did offer hormone therapy had prohibitively long wait lists, and Lia's parents struggled to find any comprehensive care under their insurance network that could support all of Lia's needs as a transgender adolescent.*

*The bureaucratic hurdles and lack of competent care took an emotional toll. Lia became so anxious about these negative healthcare experiences that she disengaged from the process entirely for over a year. Her gender dysphoria worsened, compounded by depression and feelings that her identity was not being validated. Lia began withdrawing from friends and family. It wasn't until her parents found an affirming clinic through a national LGBTQ+ resource database that Lia regained hope. Though the three-hour drive they had to make regularly for follow-up appointments was a challenge, she finally felt safe and understood by providers who could meet her needs holistically as a transgender patient.*

*Lia's case underscores how systemic barriers and discrimination within the healthcare system can delay or completely obstruct access to vital, gender-affirming services for transgender youth. Having an affirming support system helped her persevere, but many transgender individuals face these obstacles alone.*

As a parent, you have the power to mitigate these risks through proactive measures. First, thoroughly review your health insurance policies to understand what gender-affirming services are covered. Next, identify providers with expertise in transgender healthcare by consulting resources like the World Professional Association for Transgender Health (WPATH) and GLMA. When your child does receive care, encourage them to openly communicate their needs and concerns, and respect their privacy by allowing them to speak with the provider alone.

As part of the process of receiving gender-affirming care, ensure your child also receives age-appropriate screenings and preventive care, including cancer screenings, HIV/STI testing, vaccinations, and access to mental health support. While the process of gender-affirming care may seem daunting, remember that gender-affirming care is part of a broader spectrum of good healthcare, and parental support and affirmation are key protective factors against negative health outcomes. Data and anecdotal evidence consistently show that transgender youth with supportive families experience higher quality of life, resilience, and improved school performance (The Trevor Project 2024).

Ultimately, your child needs you to be their advocate, build a network of affirming providers, create a safe environment for discussing physical and mental health, show up without judgment, and prioritize their holistic well-being to empower them to thrive as their authentic self.

While initially learning about your child's identity may have sparked fears about their health and safety, I encourage you to embrace this empowering perspective instead:

> "Resources and care are available, and I will find competent providers who can equip my child with the education and services they need to thrive."

## KEY POINTS

**Debunking Myths:** Debunking common myths clarifies that being transgender does not inherently lead to diseases or premature death. Instead, this understanding emphasizes that sexual health risks are universal and not exclusive to transgender individuals. This perspective helps combat harmful stereotypes and promotes a more accurate, inclusive view of transgender health.

- Being transgender does not inherently lead to diseases or premature death.
- Sexual health risks are universal and not exclusive to transgender individuals.
- Proper healthcare and education can address health concerns for all, including trans people.
- Many health risks often associated with being trans are actually due to societal stigma and lack of access to affirming care.
- With appropriate support and healthcare, transgender individuals can lead healthy, fulfilling lives.
- It's important to focus on overall well-being rather than unfounded fears about health risks.

**Separating Fact from Stigma:** Parents need to learn to distinguish between facts and stigma-driven fears regarding their transgender child's health.

**Proactive Health Management:** Engage in proactive health management through education and preventive care to ensure the well-being of transgender youth.

**Parental Role:** Parents play a critical role as advocates who should arm themselves with credible information and approach their child's health needs with compassion and empowerment.

## REFLECTION QUESTIONS

1. What misconceptions did/do you have about the health of transgender individuals? Where did these misconceptions come from?
2. How can you advocate for your transgender child's health needs effectively in a system that may not always be accommodating or understanding?
3. Reflect on your initial reactions when you learned about your child's identity. How did concerns about their health and safety play into your feelings, and how have these concerns changed with more knowledge?
4. What steps can you take to build a support system that includes healthcare providers who are knowledgeable and affirming of transgender health needs?
5. How can you use your understanding and resources to help your child navigate their health journey positively and proactively?

12

# ISN'T TRANSITION DANGEROUS AND PERMANENT?

**The idea of transitioning** can be overwhelming for parents, especially in the absence of high-quality resources, and many parents worry that gender-affirming care is dangerous, untested, and permanent. Additionally, many people think of transition in binary terms—such as transitioning from male to female or from girl to boy. However, the reality is much more nuanced. Transitioning can involve social and/or medical steps, which are influenced by factors like the gender identity and goals of the person transitioning, age, maturity, emotional readiness, and financial situation of your child and family.

Transitioning is typically categorized into three main areas: social transition, medical transition, and legal transition. Social transition involves changes in how a person presents their gender within their everyday life. This might include adopting a new name, using different pronouns, and dressing in ways that align with their gender identity. Medical transition can include interventions like puberty blockers, hormone therapy, and gender-affirming surgeries. Legal transition focuses on updating important legal documents—such as a driver's license, social security card, and birth certificate—to reflect one's true name and gender identity. (See the chart at the end of this chapter, "Gender-Affirming Interventions," for more details.)

Social, medical, and legal transitions are different aspects of affirming one's gender identity, but not every trans or nonbinary person will undergo or need all these steps. Each person's journey is unique, and their transition may involve any combination of these elements based on their individual needs and circumstances. The transition journey is highly individual and must be approached with sensitivity to the specific needs and circumstances of each child and family.

In prepubescent youth, transitioning typically refers to social transition—adopting a presentation and lifestyle that align with the gender they identify with. This can involve adopting new pronouns, changing to clothes that reflect their gender identity, or choosing a new name. Social transition is purely about expressing one's gender identity through social means, without involving medical interventions such as cross-sex hormones or surgeries.

Social transition is often supported by therapy and conversations with medical professionals, ensuring the gender-affirming approach is tailored and comprehensive. The benefits of social transition for transgender youth are significant. Research indicates that children who undergo social transition report markedly better mental and physical health and enhanced self-esteem compared to transgender children who do not socially transition (Russell et al. 2018). Moreover, these children show similar rates of depression to their cisgender peers and only slightly elevated rates of anxiety (Olson et al. 2022).

Social transition is accessible, safe, inexpensive, and reversible. This freedom to explore and experiment helps reduce much of the psychological strain that many transgender youths face. While children who socially transition still experience the challenges of being in a minority, the evidence suggests that they are likely to maintain better resilience throughout these challenges (Durwood et al. 2016).

Prepubescent children who identify as transgender experience both unique opportunities and challenges. Many of these challenges involve questions of emotional, physical, and psychological maturity, each of which plays a critical role in navigating a healthful transition. Typically, there's a strong focus on the physical aspects when considering transition-related medical care. The medical consensus recommends that prepubescent children wait until adolescence to make decisions about medical interventions, with the support of a trans-informed medical team.

However, when children show early signs of puberty, gender-affirming care providers often recommend pubertal suppression hormones, commonly known as gonadotropin-releasing hormone analogues (GnRHas). GnRHas temporarily halt the progression of puberty, such as facial hair growth or breast development, thereby providing the child with more time to explore their gender identity without the added pressure of advancing physical changes that may not align with their gender identity. These are typically suggested around ages ten to eleven for sex-assigned girls and eleven to twelve for sex-assigned boys, coinciding with Tanner stage two when initial physical signs of puberty, like pubic hair and breast buds, appear. However, depending on the child's rate of maturation, puberty blockers can also be taken by teens who have already begun but not yet fully completed puberty and are frequently prescribed even for those in their late teens. Your child's care team will make an informed recommendation based on a variety of factors, including your child's genetics.

Despite what you may have heard in the media, puberty blockers are not an experimental treatment for transgender youth. In fact, they were originally developed and have been prescribed for about five decades to cisgender children (and two decades to trans youth) experiencing precocious puberty (the premature onset of puberty much earlier than typical developmental stages) (Smothers 2024).

Puberty blockers, commonly used for cisgender children experiencing precocious puberty, delay development until an age-appropriate timeline. Similarly, they provide transgender youth with time to explore their identity before undergoing irreversible puberty changes misaligned with their gender. Research highlights the well-established history and data on the safe, reversible usage of puberty blockers as an interim treatment to delay puberty onset, with clinical guidelines from reputable medical organizations like the Endocrine Society supporting their use for years.

## NAVIGATING FEAR AND FACTS

### Addressing Concerns About Puberty Blockers

*When their twelve-year-old child Sam came out as transgender, Sam's family had many questions and concerns about the next steps. While supportive of Sam's identity, they worried about the potential risks of medical interventions, especially the use of puberty blockers.*

*"We were scared that these drugs were experimental or could have long-term effects we didn't understand," Sam's mother Janine explained. "As parents, we wanted to proceed cautiously with Sam's transition."*

*Addressing their concerns directly, it was explained that puberty blockers are reversible and do not permanently affect fertility. If discontinued, a child's puberty simply resumes where it left off. The blockers buy time to figure out if a youth's identity is persistent before taking further medical steps.*

*For Sam, the puberty blockers provided relief from the extreme gender dysphoria he experienced as his body began developing in ways that felt incongruent with his identity as a transgender boy.*

*"We didn't know puberty blockers had been around so long and were such an established way to pause development," Sam's father Robert said. "Learning the facts really eased our minds about taking this low-risk, reversible step to support Sam."*

*By seeking guidance from a reliable, reputable source with expertise, and receiving affirmative care from a gender-specialized provider, Sam's family moved forward with puberty blockers. Having their fears addressed allowed them to embrace this treatment option, which is proven to reduce dysphoria and suicidality in transgender youth.*

The use of puberty blockers is a helpful option for many families as it delays irreversible physical changes, allowing for a more thoughtful consideration of one's gender identity. Importantly, the effects of GnRHas are reversible, offering a safeguard should the child choose a different path. As one expert gender-affirming care provider noted, "If we're doing this right, we're going to put some youth on blockers that are going to decide to go off blockers—that means we're doing our job right and giving them time to decide, not that anyone was wrong in the first place."

In addition to pausing physical changes that may be distressing while not causing any permanent damage, research indicates that the use of pubertal suppression hormones can have a profoundly positive impact on mental health. Adolescents who desire to suppress puberty and are able to do so generally report better mental health outcomes throughout their lives. This includes a notable decrease in suicidal ideation among these youths, underscoring the critical nature of timely access to gender-affirming treatments in promoting the well-being and safety of transgender children (Turban et al. 2020). This approach not only respects the child's emerging self-awareness and right to make decisions about their bodies (bodily autonomy) but also significantly contributes to their long-term happiness and mental health stability.

### MORE THAN JUST HEIGHT

#### Navigating Growth and Gender Identity

*When Jacob first expressed interest in medically transitioning at age twelve, his parents Emily and David had some trepidations. They felt embarrassed to admit their concerns about how puberty blockers and testosterone therapy might affect Jacob's future height, but the uncertainty weighed on them.*

*"As a kid, Jacob was always on the shorter side. We didn't want any treatments to stunt his growth even more," Emily explained. "Height was something he was self-conscious about." Their concerns arose from the limited research on the effects of gender-affirming medical interventions on factors like height and body composition, particularly when started at younger ages. Some studies suggested that transgender boys could experience reduced height due to estrogen exposure prior to puberty blockers while others found that pretreatment estrogen exposure on transgender boys' height is likely minimal compared to other factors like genetics and timing of treatment initiation.*

*However, after consulting with the gender-affirming care team and reviewing the available evidence, Emily and David realized that Jacob's mental health was far more important. They understood that delaying treatment could increase the risks of depression, anxiety, and other serious consequences for transgender youth who are unable to align their bodies with their identity. Ultimately, they chose to prioritize Jacob's mental well-being over concerns about potential height differences.*

*"The more we educated ourselves, the more we understood that Jacob's overall well-being had to be the priority," David said. "While height was a consideration, his gender dysphoria posed a much greater threat to his health if left unaddressed." With guidance from providers experienced in transgender care, Jacob began puberty blockers at twelve to pause any further premature development. At sixteen, he started masculinizing hormone therapy, allowing him to undergo a typically male puberty trajectory.*

*"I can't overstate how life-changing it was to go through puberty as myself, not trapped in a body and identity that felt completely wrong," Jacob stated. "My mental health improved drastically." While Jacob ended up around 5'6"—a couple inches shorter than average for an adult male—he and his parents agree it was well worth accommodating his gender through medical transition. "Jacob is healthy, happy, and comfortable in his own skin in a way he never could have been otherwise," Emily said. "Any concerns about height seem so trivial compared to supporting our son's authentic self."*

*The family's experience underscores how gender-affirming care, initiated at the appropriate age under medical supervision, can be crucial for the well-being of transgender youth even if specific impacts like height remain unclear. Jacob's parents made the choice to prioritize his mental health over hypothetical effects on parameters like stature.*

Following pubertal suppression, the next step in medical transition is typically gender-affirming hormone therapy, also known as cross-sex hormones or hormone replacement therapy. However, for individuals who begin their transition later and have already progressed through puberty, puberty blockers may not be an option. In these cases, they may go directly to cross-sex hormones as part of their medical transition. Prior to 2014, the recommendation was to start this therapy around the age of sixteen, but recent practices, supported by both medical and psychological professionals and with the backing of the child's family, have seen these hormones prescribed at younger ages (Hudson et al. 2018; Nos et al. 2022). These treatments involve administering estrogen or testosterone, which are also used in various medical interventions for cisgender individuals. These hormones can be administered through injections, pills, patches, or creams.

For most transgender individuals, taking these hormones will result in masculinizing or feminizing physical changes, affecting everything from the depth of the voice and hair growth patterns to bone density and even subtle changes in brain structures. It's important to note that, unlike pubertal suppression, the effects of hormone therapy are not fully reversible. This makes the decision to start hormone therapy a significant one, requiring careful consideration of the youth's emotional and psychological readiness, as well as their comfort with taking this step in their gender journey.

Despite the irreversible nature of some of their effects, gender-affirming hormone therapies are generally safe and have been used successfully by hundreds of thousands of transgender individuals to align their physical bodies with their gender identity. Like all medical treatments, there are risks involved, though these risks are comparable to those we all experience from our naturally produced hormones. Transgender youth taking testosterone may face an increased risk of heart disease, acne, and infertility, while those taking estrogen may be more susceptible to blood clots and strokes, particularly if they smoke. Parents and caregivers are often concerned that there are not enough randomized control trials to demonstrate the efficacy of the intervention, but Dr. Mandy Coles, physician and director of CATCH, Boston Medical Center's Child and Adolescent Transgender Center for Health, explains, "We lack randomized control trials because it's unethical to withhold what we know is a lifesaving treatment." In short, randomized trials would require doctors to withhold treatment from some individuals seeking care, which risks the health and well-being of individuals involved in the study.

It is crucial for families to discuss these risks openly, understanding them not as obstacles but as considerations to manage carefully on the path of transition. As with all major healthcare decisions, a thorough understanding of a patient's family medical history is an important component of providing appropriate care. These considerations carry even more weight when the individual is a minor, as the involvement of parents and healthcare professionals is essential.

Some care facilities require therapy before starting hormones, while others operate under the informed consent model. Informed consent doesn't mean hormones are handed out without caution; rather, it ensures that families and individuals understand the full scope of the risks, benefits, and long-term implications of gender-affirming treatment. Under this model, healthcare providers take time to explain the medical, emotional, and social impacts of transitioning, ensuring everyone involved is fully informed before moving forward. For top surgery, an evaluation and a letter of medical necessity from one mental health professional are required, whereas bottom surgery necessitates two letters from two separate clinicians to confirm the appropriateness of the procedure.

Gender-affirming hormone therapy can have a remarkably positive impact on the lives of trans people, but it's important to also recognize their limitations, especially for people who have begun or completed puberty that aligns with their sex assigned at birth. When a trans youth who was assigned male at birth takes estrogen, the hormone will not reverse changes to the voice that occurred during male puberty, such as the deepening of pitch and timbre. Testosterone causes the vocal cords to lengthen, a change that is irreversible without specialized voice training. Similarly, for youth assigned female at birth who take testosterone, the hormone will not reverse breast development that occurs during female puberty. While binders can be used during social transition to compress and minimize the appearance of breasts, permanent removal requires surgical intervention.

These nuances—the inability of hormones to reverse certain physical changes that occur during puberty, like voice deepening or breast development—highlight the specific effects and limitations of hormone therapy. They underscore the importance of timing and the careful choice of interventions in gender-affirming care. Understanding these details helps families and youth set realistic expectations for what hormone therapy can and cannot achieve, ensuring a well-informed approach to managing the transition process.

In the ongoing debate about gender-affirming care, detractors frequently cite high rates of regret associated with medical transition to argue against providing necessary healthcare to both transgender youths and adults. However, this myth has been robustly challenged by a systematic review from

*The American Journal of Surgery*, which presents compelling evidence to the contrary. The review, which was conducted by specialists at the University of Wisconsin School of Medicine and Public Health, analyzed over fifty-five studies concerning regret rates related to transgender surgeries and found that the incidence of regret following these surgeries is extremely low, under 1% (Bustos et al. 2021). This figure is significantly lower than regret rates observed in other medical procedures and major life decisions, such as tubal sterilization and facial rejuvenation, which often exceed 10%, and decisions like marriage and parenting, with regret rates of 31% and 13%, respectively (Thornton et al. 2024).

The use of regret in anti-transgender arguments is not only misleading but actively harmful, as demonstrated by narratives disseminated by sources like the Cass Review in England. The Cass Review, commissioned by the NHS, raised concerns about the safety and efficacy of gender-affirming care for minors. It cast doubt on the treatment protocols of gender clinics, fueling the misconception that regret is common among those who undergo gender-affirming care. This has led to severe restrictions on transgender care in England, skewing public perception and making it harder for transgender individuals and their care providers to make informed decisions about their health and has been cited in anti-trans legislation in the United States.

Critics, including a comprehensive review by Cornell University, have called out these manipulative tactics and the double standards applied to gender-affirming surgeries compared to other medical interventions. The *Cornell Review*, which analyzed numerous studies on transgender healthcare, found that regret is exceedingly rare in those who undergo gender-affirming care (What We Know Project 2018). Similarly, the 2022 US Transgender Survey confirms that competent gender-affirming care significantly enhances the well-being of transgender individuals (James et al. 2024). These findings emphasize the importance of access to informed, affirming healthcare, countering the harmful narratives that promote unnecessary fear and misunderstanding.

The persistence of the myth that transgender individuals frequently regret their transitions is also deeply disrespectful. Misleading claims about regret rates undermine the autonomy of transgender people and ignores the thorough, multidisciplinary process involved in gender-affirming surgeries. A preponderance of evidence from high-quality sources confirms that evidence clearly indicates that gender-affirming care is not only beneficial but essential for the health and happiness of transgender individuals. As such, it is imperative that public policy and public opinion evolve to reflect these realities, ensuring that transgender individuals receive the supportive and affirming healthcare they deserve.

Change, evolution, and growth are natural parts of life, and they are central to our understanding of gender identity and transition. Like any significant life event, transitioning comes with its own set of challenges and uncertainties. It's understandable to worry about whether your child might change their mind, experience regret, or face side effects. But uncertainty is a given in all areas of life—there is no path free of risks, consequences, or difficult choices. It's important to recognize that fluidity is inherent to being human. Many transgender and gender nonconforming individuals continue to adjust aspects of their transition throughout their lives, reflecting their personal growth and deepening self-understanding. Just as cisgender people may change their names, appearance, or other elements of themselves, transgender individuals may also evolve over time. These changes are part of the broader human experience, where identity is not fixed but continually unfolding.

Understanding that identity is fluid can help ease some of the anxieties associated with the transition process. Embracing the concept that everyone, whether transgender or cisgender, undergoes changes in social identity can foster a more supportive and flexible environment for your child. This perspective not only normalizes the experience of transition but also highlights it as a natural aspect of human life, encouraging an open and accepting approach to each person's unique journey.

Initially, discovering your child's identity might have brought feelings of fear and concern about the dangers of medical intervention. However, I encourage you to embrace a more empowering perspective:

"I am committed to helping my child make thoughtful and informed decisions that support their unique journey, wherever it may lead."

## KEY POINTS

**Transitioning Is Multifaceted:** Transitioning can involve social, medical, and sometimes legal steps. It's not just a binary process of transitioning from male to female or vice versa but includes a range of changes tailored to the individual's needs.

**Early Social Transition:** Social transitioning, such as changing pronouns, names, and presentation, can significantly improve mental and physical health and self-esteem in transgender youth.

**Pubertal Suppression:** Pubertal suppression provides time for young transgender individuals to explore their gender identity without the added stress of unwanted physical changes. This is reversible and provides a psychological buffer against gender dysphoria.

**Hormone Therapy Considerations:** Hormone therapy, while more permanent than puberty blockers, plays a crucial role in aligning one's physical appearance with their gender identity. Risks associated with hormone therapy need to be managed but are generally well understood and similar to other medical treatments.

**Importance of Informed Support:** Understanding and supporting your child's transition journey involves recognizing the individualized nature of transitioning and ensuring access to competent healthcare and supportive environments.

## REFLECTION QUESTIONS

1. What are your initial hopes, fears, or questions about the transitioning processes (social, medical, legal) described in this chapter?
2. How can you support your child in exploring their gender identity safely and positively?
3. Who can you talk with to get more information about the medical aspects of transitioning? Who might be a part of your child's support network if they pursue medical transition?
4. How do you feel about the reversibility of pubertal suppression and the permanence of hormone therapy? How does this information impact your perspective on your child's transition options?
5. Reflect on how societal perceptions of transitioning might influence your feelings. What can you do to ensure these perceptions do not hinder your support for your child?

## GENDER-AFFIRMING INTERVENTIONS

| TYPE | PROCEDURE | DESCRIPTION | APPROXIMATE AGE INTRODUCED |
|---|---|---|---|
| Social/ Legal | Name Change | Changing legal name to match gender identity | Any age |
| Social | Pronoun Change | Using pronouns that align with gender identity | Any age |
| Social | Dressing According to Gender Identity | Wearing clothes that align with gender identity | Any age |
| Social | Haircuts and Styling | Choosing haircuts and styles that align with gender identity | Any age |
| Social | Binding | Using binders to flatten the chest | Teens (13+) |
| Social | Tucking | Using garments or techniques to create a flatter appearance in the groin area | Teens (13+) |
| Social | Makeup and Grooming | Using makeup and grooming techniques to enhance gender presentation | Preteen & Teens (10+) |
| Medical | Puberty Blockers | Medications to delay puberty | Preteens (9–14) |

| TYPE | PROCEDURE | DESCRIPTION | APPROXIMATE AGE INTRODUCED |
|---|---|---|---|
| Medical | Hormone Replacement Therapy (HRT) | Estrogen or testosterone to develop secondary sex characteristics | Teens (14+) depending on development |
| Medical | Top Surgery | Surgery to remove or augment breast tissue | Teens (16+) to Adults |
| Medical | Facial Feminization Surgery (FFS) | Surgery to modify facial features to be more typically feminine | Adults |
| Medical | Bottom Surgery | Surgery to alter genitalia | Adults (with rare exception for 17+) |

13

# WILL THEY EVER BE SAFE?

**One of the most visceral fears** parents of transgender children express is their concern for the child's safety and well-being as they navigate the world. The pervasive narratives about violence, discrimination, and marginalization experienced by the transgender community can feel daunting. It's common for parents to wonder, "Will my child ever truly be safe living as their authentic self?"

This fear often stems from widespread misinformation that exaggerates the risks transgender people face. For example, claims that the life expectancy of trans women is only thirty-three or thirty-five years old are not based on credible evidence. Parents should pause when they encounter alarming statistics like these—if something seems scary and unbelievable, there's good reason to question its accuracy. Unfortunately, many reputable news sources have repeated this statistic without proper citation, making it difficult to trace the original source, which has led to its spread without verification (Herzog 2019). While trans people, particularly transgender women of color and those without access to quality care, do face heightened safety concerns, there are proven strategies to mitigate these risks and foster affirming environments where transgender individuals can thrive. Addressing safety concerns head-on means understanding the data, examining the reasons behind it, and recognizing that the risks transgender people face are not inherent to their identities but stem from a social and political climate that weaponizes their existence. It is true that transgender individuals experience significant safety risks, as indicated by various studies. Transgender individuals, especially transgender women of color, face disproportionately higher rates of violence, sexual assault, and hate crimes, (Human Rights Campaign 2020). In educational environments, trans people experience elevated risks of bullying, harassment, and discrimination, which create hostile atmospheres that hinder transgender students' ability to learn and develop (GLSEN 2020). The absence of legal protections and inclusive policies in many areas perpetuates discrimination in employment, housing, public accommodations, and access to services, further intensifying safety risks for transgender individuals (Movement Advancement Project 2024). Additionally, the mental health of transgender individuals is severely impacted, with alarming rates of suicidal thoughts and actions, highlighting the critical need for supportive measures (The Trevor Project 2024).

## LOST AND FOUND

### A Journey from Estrangement to Reconnection

*Ava grew up in a conservative town with no legal protections for LGBTQ+ people. When she came out as transgender at* fifteen, *Ava's family was unsupportive and unwilling to use her name and pronouns. "It was like they thought if they didn't affirm my identity, I wouldn't actually be trans," Ava recalls.*

*At school, the lack of trans-inclusive policies enabled relentless bullying and harassment from peers and staff. Ava was barred from using bathrooms aligning with her gender and was regularly misgendered by teachers. The hostile environment made her feel profoundly unsafe. "There were times I had to leave school out of fear for my physical safety," Ava says. "The stigma and discrimination felt inescapable."*

*After graduating, Ava moved to a city with robust nondiscrimination protections covering gender identity in employment, housing, and public accommodations. She was finally able to get her name and gender marker updated on legal documents. "It was like a weight lifted knowing I couldn't be legally fired, evicted, or denied services just for being myself," Ava says. "I finally felt safe to exist in public without fear of discrimination."*

*Ava also reconnected with her family after they attended PFLAG meetings and began to learn from other families' experiences. With open communication and affirmation from loved ones, Ava's mental health improved dramatically. "Having my family's support after years of rejection allowed me to heal from that trauma," she says. "Their acceptance, combined with living in an area with legal protections, made me feel safe in ways I never could before."*

Despite the safety concerns and risk of discrimination, significant protective factors can help mitigate these dangers. Family support and acceptance, in particular, have been shown to have a transformative impact on the well-being of transgender individuals. Research consistently shows that transgender youth with supportive families and strong parental relationships experience significantly better mental health outcomes and lower rates of substance abuse, homelessness, and other risk factors (The Trevor Project 2024). Family affirmation acts as a critical buffer against the hardships imposed by external marginalization.

Moreover, trans people who live in regions with robust nondiscrimination laws that protect gender identity in employment, housing, education, and public spaces typically exhibit markedly lower rates of poverty, homelessness, and other destabilizing factors that heighten safety risks. Affirming legal landscapes are crucial for reducing the dangers faced by transgender individuals.

Schools and communities that actively support transgender rights in their communities through clear anti-bullying policies, LGBTQ+ student groups, inclusive curriculum, and training for staff create safer, more supportive environments. Cities and towns that celebrate LGBTQ+ identity through events like Pride and provide community resources such as LGBTQ+ community centers, transgender-specific support groups, healthcare services offering gender-affirming care, legal aid for name and gender marker changes, and

LGBTQ+-friendly homeless shelters also foster resilience among transgender individuals.

### CREATING SAFE SPACES

#### Affirming Schools and Medical Care for Trans Youth

*As a transgender boy, Eric faced challenges at his local high school that lacked LGBTQ+-inclusive policies or resources. He was routinely bullied, lacked affirmative counseling, and had no social supports on campus.*

*"I felt completely alone and unsafe being my authentic self at school," Eric says. "My gender identity was treated like a disruption rather than validated."*

*Eric's mental health suffered until he transferred to a larger district with a Gender and Sexuality Alliance club, protections against discrimination, gender-neutral bathrooms, and LGBTQ+-inclusive curricula and training for staff.*

*"Just having a physical space where I could be myself without judgment was life-changing," Eric recalls. "I finally felt safe to take steps in my transition journey."*

*Eric's new school helped him connect with an affirming gender clinic with experienced providers who guided him through gender-affirming hormone therapy and other medical care. Having competent treatment made a pivotal difference. "My dysphoria eased so much once I began masculinizing," Eric says. "Knowing I had a care team supporting my transition allowed me to thrive rather than just survive." Eric also found an accepting community by getting involved with the local LGBTQ+ center's youth programming and support groups. Having multiple layers of affirmation created a powerful protective network.*

*"Between my affirming school, gender-affirming medical care, and the community I found, I went from feeling hopeless and unsafe to empowered as my true self," Eric states. "Those supports quite literally saved my life."*

The statistics on suicidal thoughts and actions among transgender individuals in the United States reveal deeply concerning trends. The 2022 US Transgender Survey by the National Center for Transgender Equality reveals alarmingly high rates of suicidal ideation and attempts that disproportionately impact the transgender community, especially youth. A staggering 56% of transgender and nonbinary youth ages thirteen to seventeen seriously considered suicide in the past year, nearly four times higher than their cisgender peers at 14%. One in five transgender youth (20%) attempted suicide over the same period, a rate almost three times that of cisgender youth (7%). Among transgender adults, 38% had serious thoughts of suicide and 7% made a suicide attempt in the past year. The data shows heightened vulnerability based on socioeconomic factors, with suicidal ideation highest among unemployed transgender adults (55%), those with household incomes under $25,000 (51%), and those who experienced homelessness (54%). Transgender people of color faced elevated suicide risk compared to their white transgender peers (James et al. 2024). Studies report that key drivers of suicidal ideation and attempts among transgender individuals include family and community rejection, violence, and lack of access to gender-affirming care. Kids aren't killing themselves because they are transgender—they are doing so because the world around them fails to accept and support them as transgender.

As a parent, this information can feel overwhelming and frightening, but it's important to understand it so you're empowered to help mitigate these risks. The factors contributing to suicide among transgender individuals are varied and complex. Rejection from family, friends, or society plays a significant role. When transgender people face discrimination in schools, workplaces, housing, healthcare, or from law enforcement, the likelihood of a suicide attempt doubles. Rejection from a spouse, partner, or even their own children further increase the risk, as does religious exclusion and the trauma of conversion therapy. Physical violence, particularly intimate partner violence, is also closely linked to higher rates of suicidal thoughts and attempts.

Trans deaths by suicide are preventable, and you, as a parent or caregiver, have the power to be the difference maker for your kid. Key protective factors include strong familial support, access to gender-affirming healthcare, and protections through nondiscrimination laws. Each of these elements, whether on their own or combined, plays a crucial role in reducing the likelihood of suicidal thoughts and attempts among transgender youth. Many trans people who do not have family support still thrive, but trans folks who do have support networks in their family and community have better outcomes and can lead successful, fulfilling lives. They achieve personal and professional milestones, form meaningful relationships, and engage in hobbies and passions that bring them joy. Being transgender can be a cause for celebration—a unique aspect of an individual's identity that enriches their perspective and experience.

The presence of supportive organizations and communities that highlight the positive aspects of transgender experiences is invaluable. They provide not only a counternarrative to the challenges but also a source of hope and affirmation. Your child's ability to advocate for themself and their self-awareness are testaments to their strength. Embracing and supporting your child for who they are is perhaps the most impactful action you can take, ensuring they thrive regardless of their gender identity. Research shows that having just one accepting adult—whether it's a parent, neighbor, coach, or mentor—can reduce the risk of a suicide attempt by 40% (The Trevor Project 2019). You have the power to be that person.

### A GAME-CHANGER

#### How Coach Peterson Created an Inclusive Team

*From an early age, Alex knew they were transgender but feared being rejected by their deeply religious family. As Alex entered high school, they struggled profoundly with their identity, experiencing crippling gender dysphoria and suicidal ideation.*

*"I felt so alone and disconnected from myself," Alex says. "The idea of living authentically seemed impossible. I didn't know if I could go on like that." Alex's lifeline came unexpectedly through their high school track coach, Samantha Peterson. Coach Peterson had undergone training on supporting LGBTQ+ athletes and creating an affirmative environment for her team. She noticed Alex's withdrawal and reached out with compassion.*

*"Coach pulled me aside and said she had my back no matter what," Alex recalls. "She was the first adult who seemed to truly see and accept me as my authentic self." Having that one trusted, affirming adult made an incredible difference for Alex. Research shows that LGBTQ+ youth who feel accepted by even one adult, no matter their role, have around 40%*

*lower odds of attempting suicide compared to those without acceptance (Trevor Project 2024).*

*Coach Peterson's allyship provided Alex sanctuary during a critical time. She advocated for Alex to be able to use the correct restroom, referred to them by their name and pronouns, and created a safe space to process their identity. "Coach gave me the courage to come out to my family," Alex says. "Having her in my corner helped me believe I deserved to live fully as myself."*

*While Alex's family initially struggled with acceptance, having Coach Peterson's steadfast support was an anchor through that turbulent period. Her affirmation quite literally saved Alex's life. "There were so many days the only thing stopping me from giving up was knowing I had Coach's acceptance," they admit. "She showed me a future was possible as my authentic self."*

*For many transgender youth facing rejection or lacking affirmation at home, having just one supportive voice like Coach Peterson can make all the difference in their resilience and safety. Her actions exemplify how cultivating pockets of acceptance, even outside the home, provides crucial protective factors against despair.*

Trans people do face greater risks, but these risks stem from external factors. As parents and caregivers, you have both the opportunity and responsibility to help mitigate these risks, not only within your home but also in your broader community. It is not avoiding our children's transgender identity out of fear but boldly leaning into cultivating the protective factors that will allow them to live authentically and thrive. Our children deserve no less than to feel safe, loved, and empowered as their full selves.

While initially discovering your child's identity may have sparked anxiety and concerns about their safety, I encourage you to adopt this empowering perspective moving forward:

> "I trust that by cultivating a strong support system and accessing affirmative resources, my child can thrive safely as their authentic self."

## KEY POINTS

**Misconceptions of Safety Risks:** While it's true that transgender individuals face significant risks, these are often exacerbated by misconceptions that portray these risks as universal and insurmountable.

**Impact of Discrimination and Marginalization:** Transgender people, particularly transgender women of color, experience high rates of violence, discrimination, and marginalization that significantly impact their safety.

**Importance of Supportive Environments:** Supportive family environments, inclusive policies, and affirming educational and healthcare settings can dramatically reduce risks and improve mental health outcomes for transgender individuals.

**Role of Legal and Community Support:** States, cities, and towns with robust nondiscrimination laws and community support structures offer better protection and quality of life for transgender individuals, highlighting the importance of legal and political advocacy.

**Legal Protections:** Understanding the legal protections available to trans youth and their families can provide a sense of security and empowerment. This includes antidiscrimination laws and rights related to name changes and gender marker updates.

**Empowering Rather Than Limiting:** Shifting the focus from vulnerability to empowerment by cultivating protective factors helps transgender individuals live authentically and safely.

## REFLECTION QUESTIONS

1. What stories have you told yourself about the safety of transgender individuals, and how do these compare with the realities presented?
2. Reflect on the support systems currently in place for transgender individuals in your community. (If you don't know any off the top of your head, take a moment to look some up.) What improvements can be made to enhance safety and acceptance?
3. How might discrimination in different areas of life (such as school, work, healthcare) compound the safety risks for transgender individuals? Can you think of ways to mitigate these risks locally?
4. What can you do to ensure the safety of your child to the best of your ability?
5. How can parents and loved ones move from a state of fear regarding their transgender child's safety to actively fostering an environment where they can thrive?

14

# WILL THEY EVER FIND LOVE?

**Parents of transgender youth** often harbor deep concerns about their child's future, particularly around social integration and personal relationships. There's a pervasive fear that transitioning might not only expose their child to potential hardship but could also limit their opportunities for a fulfilling social and romantic life. Many parents worry that being transgender might complicate their child's ability to find a romantic partner who fully appreciates and loves them for who they truly are.

The quality of life for transgender individuals is significantly impacted by societal stigma and widespread anti-transgender bigotry. This external prejudice can lead to the breakdown of long-standing social relationships, as friends or family members may struggle or refuse to accept the transgender individual's identity. Even relationships that do endure are often not immune to strain and tension, as the process of transition can be emotionally and logistically complex for both the person transitioning and their family and friends.

The challenges associated with transition are exacerbated by the difficulties many transgender youth face in accessing necessary medical care and social support. The increasing wave of anti-trans legislation across the United

States compounds these challenges, adding layers of external stress that can further complicate a young person's ability to maintain and manage relationships with peers and loved ones. While romantic relationships may not be as immediate a concern for younger children who are transitioning, friendships play an equally vital role in their social and emotional development. Many transgender youth find acceptance and support within their peer groups, where friends can serve as a powerful source of validation and connection. Friendships offer a sense of belonging and are essential in helping your child navigate the complexities of their identity. Social connections, especially with other trans or LGBTQ+ individuals, can also be transformative, providing a community where your child feels seen, understood, and supported. These relationships are a crucial foundation for developing healthy social skills and self-confidence, which later helps them navigate romantic relationships with a strong sense of self. For those living in non-affirming environments or struggling to find supportive friends, the internet can be a powerful tool. Online platforms, forums, and social media offer transgender individuals the opportunity to connect with others, share experiences, and build networks of support. These virtual communities often become lifelines, helping your child form meaningful connections even when local resources may be lacking. As they grow, these connections—whether online or in person—build resilience and self-acceptance, laying the groundwork for healthy, loving partnerships in the future.

It's natural to worry that if your child transitions, they may lose an existing romantic partner or find it more challenging to form new relationships in the future. The impact of transitioning on romantic relationships can be significant, as it often shifts dynamics and expectations within that intimate context. Both the transgender person and their partner often find themselves renegotiating their identities, roles, and compatibility as the transition unfolds.

While research remains limited, existing studies indicate some transgender people do end preexisting romantic relationships during their transition process (Marshall et al. 2020). It's important to recognize that, while there may be genuine love between your child and their current partner, some trans youth who have not yet come out or transitioned might choose their partners as a way to blend in and avoid stigmatization and bullying. As your child takes the significant step of transitioning, their preferences in romantic partners may naturally evolve, and that's perfectly okay. Most young people do not end up marrying their high school or even college partners. Yet, as a parent, it's understandable to view the ending of a youthful relationship as tragic, especially if you've watched your child build what seems like a loving partnership. You may feel protective, wanting to shield your child from the emotional pain of a breakup, and perhaps you even saw their partner as someone who could provide stability during their transition. The fear that your child might struggle to find love or acceptance in the future can intensify these feelings. However, ending a youthful relationship—whether initiated by your child or their partner—should not be seen as tragic. Instead, it can be recognized as a valuable growth experience for both individuals as they navigate their paths toward long-term partnerships or other life choices.

Although your child may experience changes or even the end of a romantic relationship during their transition, it doesn't mean they won't form meaningful, lasting partnerships in the future. Many transgender individuals in long-term relationships or marriages can maintain healthy, loving connections throughout their transition, especially when both partners engage with open communication, education, and a commitment to grow together (Van Acker et al. 2023). Transition does not limit the ability to find or sustain a fulfilling intimate partnership.

### DYLAN AND CARA

#### Navigating Identity, Love, and Family Together

*Dylan, seventeen, and Cara, eighteen, had been dating since sophomore year of high school when Dylan began to explore his gender identity. After much self-reflection and support from his school counselor, Dylan came out as a transgender man and started using he/him pronouns during their senior year. Cara, who had always identified as a lesbian, was initially supportive but struggled with her feelings as Dylan's appearance and identity evolved.*

*As Dylan began his transition, he experienced the complicated reality of being in a straight-presenting relationship while still in high school. Despite being open about his transgender identity, he found that classmates and teachers often assumed he was cisgender and straight when they saw him with Cara. This led to feelings of invisibility and erasure of his queer identity. Dylan grappled with the confusing mix of "straight-passing" privilege and the loss of his previous identity within their school's LGBTQ+ community. He often felt out of place at GSA meetings, unsure if he still belonged.*

*Cara, now a freshman in college, also struggled with how others perceived their relationship. As a lesbian, she felt her own queer identity was being erased when people assumed they were a heterosexual couple. This led to complicated feelings of guilt and resentment, especially as she navigated her new college environment and LGBTQ+ spaces there.*

*Despite their strong emotional connection, Cara realized that she was no longer physically attracted to Dylan as his transition progressed. After months of trying to make it work and renegotiating their roles within the relationship, they decided to end their romantic partnership. Both were heartbroken, but they recognized that forcing the relationship would be unfair to both of them as they entered new phases of their lives.*

*Dylan's parents were concerned about the breakup and its impact on Dylan's transition and final year of high school. However, they focused on supporting him through this challenging time. They emphasized that the end of this relationship didn't invalidate Dylan's identity or his worth as a person. They reassured him that it was better to be true to oneself than to compromise his identity for a relationship and reminded him that there would be many opportunities to meet people who would love and value him for who he truly is, especially as he looked forward to college.*

*Dylan's parents encouraged him to stay active in his school's GSA and to seek out LGBTQ+ youth groups in their area. They also helped him process his emotions about the breakup and the complex feelings of erasure he experienced, reminding him that it's okay to grieve the end of a relationship while still moving forward with his transition and future plans.*

*Over time, Dylan began to heal from the breakup and became more confident in his identity. He learned to navigate the complexities of being perceived as straight while still honoring his queer identity, which helped prepare him for college life. As he started his freshman year, he found a supportive LGBTQ+ community on campus and eventually met a partner who fully embraced his identity as a transgender man.*

## GROWING TOGETHER

### A Relationship Through Transition

*Jamie and Taylor had been a couple for six years when Jamie came out as a transgender woman at age twenty-eight. While Taylor initially struggled with the news, her love for Jamie helped her reevaluate her sexuality which allowed her to recommit to the relationship with newfound understanding. This motivated her to educate herself on what Jamie's transition would entail.*

*"Those first few months were really hard," Taylor admits. "I had to let go of the male partner I thought I knew, while also learning to see and love Jamie for who she truly is." With patience and open communication, the couple was able to navigate Jamie's social and medical transition together as a team. Taylor made efforts to use Jamie's new name and pronouns, attended LGBTQ+ counseling, and joined a partners' support group.*

*"Having a community of other partners of trans folks showed me I wasn't alone," Taylor says. "It helped me process the changes our relationship was going through." As Jamie began gender-affirming hormone therapy and presented more femininely, their intimacy required adjustment too. But their foundation of love and trust allowed for vulnerability.*

*"Our sex life definitely changed, but we worked together to figure out new ways to connect physically that felt authentic to who Jamie is," Taylor explains. Taylor learned that gender was not as important as she thought in her attraction to her partner and instead it was about their love and connection. Five years after her initial coming out, Jamie had gender confirmation surgery. Taylor was her greatest support system through the whole process. "Seeing Jamie become her true self and thrive has been one of the most beautiful things I've witnessed," Taylor says. "Our relationship today is stronger than ever because we faced this challenge together with empathy."*

*Now married, Jamie and Taylor's partnership demonstrates that a gender transition can strengthen a loving, intimate relationship when both partners navigate the journey with care and mutual support. "Transition reinvigorated our commitment to each other," Jamie shares. "By showing up for one another through this vulnerable process, we've built an incredible bond that we know will last a lifetime."*

*This case illustrates how clear communication, mutual commitment, community support systems, and an abundance of love can enable an intimate relationship to evolve and even deepen through a partner's gender transition when both people are willing to do the work together.*

For those entering new romantic relationships post-transition, the reality of societal bias means some transgender individuals face outright rejection or struggle with deciding when/how to disclose their identity and transition history. At the same time, increasing trans visibility has expanded opportunities to find affirmative partners. Ultimately, the evidence is inconclusive about how precisely these factors affect the ability of transgender individuals to form positive romantic relationships overall (Marshall et al. 2020). While transition can disrupt or complicate existing partnerships, it does not inherently prevent transgender people from experiencing loving connections, intimacy, and fulfilling romantic bonds when both partners navigate it with care and mutual understanding (Fuller and Riggs 2021). In some cases, the nature of the relationship may evolve, but the bond can remain just as strong or even grow deeper in new ways.

Despite the many social and political challenges they face, transgender people can and do form meaningful, positive, and supportive romantic relationships that significantly enhance their social and emotional well-being. Establishing these connections is made easier with stable support systems from affirming parents or caregivers. In contrast, hiding their trans identity can make it difficult to find a partner who genuinely understands and affirms their authentic self.

## FINDING LOVE, FINDING SELF

### Rowan's Path to Authenticity

*After years of hiding their true self, Rowan made the courageous decision at age twenty-one to begin embracing their nonbinary identity. While they felt a huge weight lifted living authentically, Rowan worried about what that would mean for their dating prospects. "I spent so long burying that part of myself out of fear and shame," Rowan says. "The idea of allowing myself to be truly seen and putting my nonbinary identity out there was terrifying at first."*

*In previous dating experiences, Rowan avoided any discussions of gender identity. But they knew if they wanted to find a partner who celebrated them for who they truly were, they would have to lead with vulnerability. After building up their confidence, Rowan made the decision to be upfront about their nonbinary identity on dating app profiles. Their bio simply stated they were a proud nonbinary person looking for a loving, respectful partner.*

*"I braced myself for ignorance and rejection, but I also remained hopeful that my authenticity would resonate with the right person," Rowan recalls. While they did face some offensive reactions, Rowan was amazed by the outpouring of positive responses from people inspired by their courage and authenticity. One person in particular, Casey, stood out with especially affirming and supportive messages.*

*From their first date, Casey made it clear they celebrated Rowan's identity fully and had intentionally read up about how to support a nonbinary partner. Their connection continued to deepen with time. "With Casey, I've never once had to sacrifice any part of myself." Rowan beams. "They embrace me for who I am, without labels or boxes. I finally have the authentic love I deserve."*

*Now two years into a committed relationship, Rowan and Casey's partnership demonstrates that by living one's truth with confidence, nonbinary individuals can absolutely find partners who will love them for their whole, authentic selves. "If I had never worked up the courage to be vulnerable about my identity, I may have missed out on this incredible love," Rowan says. "I'm so grateful I took that risk to be truly seen."*

Any relationship will have stressors and challenges. Transgender people are just as able to form a healthy relationship as cisgender individuals. More broadly, transitioning allows your child to connect with a community that celebrates their full identity and seek support from others with shared experiences (Aldridge et al. 2022). Your child can form relationships as their authentic self, ultimately leading to healthier bonds than self-denial or shame from delaying transition.

Although many parents of younger children or teens may not be immediately focused on surgical options, it's important to understand what the future might hold as your child grows and explores their identity. One common concern is whether bottom surgery will affect their child's ability to experience pleasure or attract a loving partner. To help address these worries, here's a case study that illustrates how some individuals navigate these aspects of transition and maintain fulfilling, intimate relationships.

### PLEASURE WITHOUT SHAME

#### Reclaiming Joy in Identity

*When their teenage son Jacob came out as transgender, the Wilsons had a multitude of worries—including fears about Jacob's future ability to develop healthy relationships and sexual intimacy after transitioning. "We wanted Jacob to be able to experience all the joys of romantic love and physical intimacy," his mother Susan said. "But we didn't understand how bottom surgery or using masculinizing hormones would impact things like sexual function and pleasure."*

*The Wilsons' concerns stemmed partly from misinformation and lack of knowledge about the diverse ways transgender people can experience sexuality and intimacy. Jacob's father Michael also worried about Jacob's future dating prospects.*

*To address their concerns, the Wilsons sought out resources from trusted medical professionals and connected with other parents of transgender children online. They learned that there are many paths to sexual fulfillment for transgender individuals that go beyond penile-vaginal penetration. The resources highlighted how queer people, like straight people, utilize a wide range of intimate practices like sensual massage, toy play, oral pleasuring, and more to experience pleasure with or without surgeries. They found examples of trans men in happy, fulfilling relationships and marriages facilitated by an open-minded approach to sexuality.*

*The Wilsons also learned about the capabilities of gender-affirming genital surgeries and prosthetics that can support erogenous sensation and intimacy in different ways. An educational seminar by a transgender man who had undergone phalloplasty provided particularly impactful firsthand insights. "Hearing his story showed us there are all kinds of ways Jacob could experience pleasure and connection with future partners," Susan said. "The decisions will ultimately be up to him based on his needs and comfort levels."*

*With this expanded understanding, the Wilsons overcame their worries about Jacob's future sexuality and relationships. They recognized those concerns stemmed more from their own lack of awareness than any true limitations Jacob would face. "We realized we had been making unfounded assumptions instead of listening to the full range of possibilities," Michael stated. "Once we opened our minds, we could separate misinformation from reality."*

*Now the Wilsons are supportive as Jacob explores his options for gender-affirming care. Their journey reminds parents to seek accurate information from credible sources and firsthand voices in order to overcome unfounded fears about their transgender child's capacity for intimacy and relationships. By staying open-minded, parents can support and celebrate the different ways their child may experience love and connection.*

Connecting with the larger transgender community and embracing their identity can lead to more fulfilling and affirming relationships—whether romantic, sexual, or platonic. The key isn't avoiding social challenges but developing the resilience and skills to navigate them. By supporting and affirming your child's identity, you'll be in the best position to help them build that resilience and thrive through this journey.

When your child first came out to you, this revelation may have sparked worries about them living a lonely life and having difficulty finding love, I encourage you to embrace this empowering perspective instead:

"By surrounding my child with unconditional love and support, they will develop the self-confidence to build and maintain healthy, fulfilling relationships and create their own loving family."

## KEY POINTS

**Social and Romantic Challenges:** Parents often worry that transitioning may expose their transgender child to hardship and limit their opportunities for fulfilling social and romantic relationships.

**Impact of Societal Stigma:** The quality of life for transgender individuals can be significantly affected by societal stigma and anti-transgender bigotry, potentially leading to the breakdown of social relationships.

**Navigating Romantic Relationships:** Transitioning can fundamentally shift dynamics within romantic relationships, requiring renegotiation of identities, roles, and expectations.

**Positive Outcomes with Support:** Many transgender individuals maintain healthy, loving relationships through their transition when both partners communicate openly and commit to evolving together.

**Community and Visibility:** Increased trans visibility and support can expand opportunities for transgender individuals to find affirmative partners and form positive relationships.

## REFLECTION QUESTIONS

1. What specific fears do you have about your child's ability to form and sustain romantic relationships?

2. In what ways can societal stigma influence your child's romantic life, and what steps can you take to mitigate its effects?

3. How can you as a parent support your child in developing healthy romantic relationships throughout their transition?

4. How can you help your child celebrate their identity in a way that enhances their self-confidence and attractiveness to potential partners?

5. What can you learn from the experiences of other families and transgender individuals that could help you better support your child in their relationships?

PART FOUR

# FAMILY, SOCIAL, AND CULTURAL IMPACTS

15

# WILL PEOPLE THINK I'M A BAD CAREGIVER?

**Nobody wants to be seen as a "bad" parent.** When their child comes out or begins exploring their gender in nontraditional ways, parents of trans youth often worry about how they'll be perceived by others, especially other parents. They may fear that affirming their child's identity will invite extra scrutiny and judgment on their parenting choices. In communities that aren't supportive of transgender identities, parents may feel as though others are quietly asking, "What did they do wrong?" There's also the worry that their own friends and peers might distance themselves—a topic we'll explore further in the next chapter, "What If We Lose Family, Friends, and Our Connection to Culture?"

Unfortunately, the fears that parents of trans youth experience are grounded in reality. Academic research based on interviews and surveys with parents across various countries reveals that they often face "secondary stigma." This stigma doesn't stem from anything inherent about the parents themselves but rather from their connection to a child or family member who is transgender (Johnson and Benson 2014). Parents may face negative judgments or discrimination simply because they are associated with someone who has a nonconforming gender identity. The discrimination directed at trans children—whether from institutions like schools and hospitals or from social interactions, including with extended family—can significantly impact the mental health and well-being of both the child and the parent (Hidalgo and Chen 2019). When supporting their child through this journey, parents often face added stress and strain in their own social relationships.

The challenges faced by parents of trans youth extend far beyond their immediate social circles. State governments across the United States have increasingly imposed restrictions since 2020 that severely limit parents' ability to support their trans children. Over the past few years, numerous states have introduced or passed laws that not only prohibit gender-affirming medical care for trans adolescents but also threaten to remove children from their homes or subject parents to jail time for affirming their child's identity (Movement Advancement Project 2024). This is not just extreme—it's a direct attack on parental rights and freedom. These laws deprive parents of their basic right to make decisions in the best interest of their own children. Moreover, this legislation stigmatizes trans identities and criminalizes those who simply want to support their kids. Alongside these measures, far-right political groups amplify inflammatory rhetoric to demonize those who stand by trans youth. Together, these actions are designed to intimidate parents into denying their child's identity, promoting this denial as the only "acceptable" form of parenting for trans children.

In some cases, families are forced to make the painful decision to relocate to states that protect their rights and allow access to lifesaving, medically necessary care. These families, often referred to as "gender refugees" within their own country, are cut off from their communities, friends, and support networks. The impact extends beyond the parents and the trans youth—it affects siblings too, who also face the disruption of leaving behind schools, friends, and the stability of their home life. Not every family has the financial means to relocate, adding yet another layer of distress for those who cannot leave hostile environments.

Despite these hardships, many parents courageously stand by their children's sides, even in the face of intense societal pressure. Trans identities have been under attack for generations, but when parents take the time to listen, understand, and trust their kids, they realize there's only one option:

to love their child for who they are and fight like hell for their right to be that person.

### THE RAINERS

#### Learning, Unlearning, and Embracing Change

*Evelyn and Samuel Rainer were pillars of their small, conservative Midwestern community. Active in their church and local politics, they prided themselves on raising their three children with traditional values. When their youngest child, fourteen-year-old Avery, came out as a transgender girl, the Rainers' reality was completely shaken.*

*Initially, Evelyn and Samuel struggled to understand and accept Avery's identity. They worried about what others in their tight-knit community would think. Would they be seen as bad parents who had somehow caused this? Would their church reject them? Despite their fears, the Rainers sought out resources, attending LGBTQ+ support groups, reading books about gender identity, and consulting with healthcare professionals. Through this process, they realized that supporting Avery's transition was the best way to ensure their child's well-being and happiness. They chose love over fear, understanding that embracing Avery's true identity was essential to protecting their mental and emotional health.*

*The backlash was swift. Several church members openly criticized their parenting, suggesting they were "enabling sin." Old friends stopped inviting them to social gatherings. Evelyn overheard whispers at the grocery store about how she must have "feminized" her child too much. Samuel faced scrutiny at work, with colleagues questioning his leadership abilities if he couldn't "control" his own child.*

*Despite the painful loss of some relationships, the Rainers stood firm in supporting Avery. They found a supportive therapist and connected with other parents of trans youth online. Evelyn became an outspoken advocate, testifying against anti-trans legislation at their state capitol. She also started a local support group for parents of transgender children, providing a safe space for others navigating similar challenges. Samuel, though initially more reserved, also began to speak out at community meetings and support Evelyn's advocacy efforts.*

*At home, the Rainers focused on creating a nurturing environment for Avery. They educated their other children about Avery's identity, ensuring they were supportive and understanding. Family dinners became a time for open conversations, where Avery could express her feelings and concerns without fear of judgment. Evelyn and Samuel made it clear that their home was a safe haven where Avery could be her authentic self.*

*Navigating the school system was another significant challenge. The Rainers met with school administrators to ensure that Avery's pronouns were respected and that she could use the bathroom that matched her gender identity. They also advocated for inclusive policies and anti-bullying measures to protect Avery and other transgender students. Though the school initially resisted, the Rainers' persistence paid off, and the administration eventually implemented more inclusive practices.*

*The emotional toll on Avery was significant, but the strong foundation of love and affirmation at home helped mitigate the damage. She struggled with anxiety and depression due to the lack of acceptance from some community members, but her parents' unwavering support provided a crucial emotional anchor. Avery's grades improved, and she became more involved in extracurricular activities, gaining confidence as she saw her family standing by her.*

*Over time, the Rainers' efforts began to bear fruit. Avery's mental health and overall well-being improved significantly. She felt empowered to continue exploring her gender identity and make informed decisions about her future, including potential gender-affirming medical care. Seeing their child thrive and hearing Avery say, "Thank you for believing in me," made weathering the community's judgment worthwhile.*

*Evelyn and Samuel's journey from initial confusion and fear to advocacy and support highlights the significant impact that parental acceptance can have on a transgender child's life. Despite the challenges and societal pressures, their commitment to Avery's well-being and happiness underscored the true essence of parental love and dedication. By prioritizing their child's needs and educating themselves, they not only strengthened their family bond but also contributed to a more inclusive and understanding community.*

Support for trans youth can take many forms, allowing parents to show up for their children in creative and meaningful ways. Parents can actively advocate for their children by engaging in social and political activism that promotes trans-supportive policies. They can be fierce advocates for their children, helping to protect them from the harm that anti-trans politicians and organizations have already caused and resist further attempts to pass legislation restricting their child's freedom to live as their authentic selves. The most important forms of support, however, are the ones that impact trans youth's lives and relationships with their parents most directly: helping them access needed services, affirming their identity (such as through the use of the correct name and pronouns), and helping to facilitate their transition socially by helping to communicate with the other people in their community about it (as long as they have their child's consent to do so). Through advocating for and supporting their children, parents can empower themselves and strengthen their relationships.

Supporting a child's transition may lead to judgment from others and could even cost parents some friendships or affect their relationship with certain communities. However, it will also open doors to new communities of supportive families who share the same commitment to loving and advocating for their children's right to live authentically. Most importantly, it will earn them the respect and trust of their children.

### THE GARCIA FAMILY

#### Navigating Tradition and Identity

*Elena and Carlos Garcia were progressive parents living in a diverse urban area. When their twelve-year-old child Maya (assigned male at birth) began exploring a more feminine gender expression, they approached it with open minds. However, they still grappled with fears about Maya's safety and future.*

*The Garcias allowed Maya to grow out her hair and wear feminine clothing at home but hesitated to let her present as female at school. They worried other parents would judge them for "pushing" a transgender identity on their child. What if Maya changed her mind later? Were they making the right choices?*

*Their fears intensified when several states began passing laws restricting transgender rights and medical care. The Garcias lived in a progressive state, but the harsh rhetoric from politicians made them anxious. They read stories of Child Protective Services investigating affirming parents in other states. Carlos's immigrant parents pressured them to force Maya to "act like a boy," causing family tension.*

*After connecting with a support group for families of transgender children, the Garcia's gained confidence in affirming Maya's identity. They worked with her school to support her social transition and found an affirming pediatrician to discuss future medical options. Elena started volunteering for a local chapter of an organization advocating for trans youth rights.*

*They still faced some criticism and, most painfully, lost touch with Carlos's parents, and the Garcias wrestled with the heartbreak of that loss. The decision to support Maya came with a heavy emotional toll, as cutting ties with close family members wasn't something they ever imagined. Losing that connection weighed on them deeply, but over time, they realized that supporting their daughter was more important than maintaining relationships with those who couldn't accept her. Despite the pain, they felt empowered by actively standing by Maya. Seeing their once-withdrawn child blossom into a confident, happy girl reassured them that they were making the right choice, even if it came at a personal cost.*

Parents' concerns about how they are perceived and treated within their community are understandable, but it's crucial to remember that at the heart of this journey is your child's well-being. The medical community strongly endorses this support, recognizing the profound positive impact parental support has on young people's lives. By focusing on your child's needs rather than external judgments, you're making decisions that truly serve their best interests—an approach that aligns with best practices in child development and mental health care.

To support your child effectively, it's important to build a support system for yourself as well. Consider identifying five people in your life—friends, family, or colleagues—whom you trust to be supportive and understanding. You might also reach out to a local or online community organization, such as an LGBTQ+ family group or counseling service, that can offer guidance and reassurance. Parents need strong support systems to be the best advocates for their children, and by surrounding yourself with caring individuals, you'll be better equipped to provide the unwavering support your child needs to thrive, regardless of outside opinions.

While initially learning about your child's identity may have raised concerns about how others view you and your parenting, I encourage you to adopt this empowering perspective instead:

> "I stand firm in supporting my child's true identity, seeking connection and support from those who share my commitment to their well-being, and focusing on the love and understanding that surround us."

## KEY POINTS

**Fear of Judgment and Stigma:** Parents often worry about facing severe judgment and stigma from their community when supporting their trans child's identity. This fear is grounded in reality, as many parents experience "secondary stigma" simply for being associated with a transgender family member. This discrimination can significantly impact the mental health and well-being of both the child and the parent.

**Legal and Societal Pressures:** State governments across the United States and countries throughout Europe are imposing restrictions that limit parents' ability to support their trans children. Laws are being passed that prohibit gender-affirming medical care for trans adolescents and may even criminalize affirming parenting practices.

**Importance of Parental Support:** Parental acceptance and support are crucial for the well-being of trans youth. Supporting your child's identity benefits their mental and emotional health and aligns with best practices in child development and mental health care.

**Forms of Support:** Support for trans youth can take many forms, including social and political advocacy, helping them access needed services, affirming their identity, and facilitating their social transition.

**Positive Impact of Support:** Parental support has a significant positive impact on trans youth, reducing suicidal thoughts and attempts and improving overall mental health and well-being. Despite societal pressures, the most important outcome is a happy, healthy child who feels seen, loved, and supported for who they truly are.

## REFLECTION QUESTIONS

1. What people or social circles are you worried will judge or reject you while supporting your child's authentic identity?
2. What support systems, both emotional and practical, can I build to help my family navigate the potential challenges of supporting my child?
3. How can you create a supportive and nurturing environment at home for your trans child?

4. What forms of social and political advocacy can you engage in to support your child's rights and the rights of other trans youth?

5. How can you communicate with your child's school and other institutions to ensure they respect and affirm your child's identity?

16

# WHAT IF WE LOSE FAMILY, FRIENDS, AND OUR CONNECTION TO CULTURE?

**Many parents worry** that supporting their child's transition might jeopardize their relationships with family and friends. These fears are real—as illustrated by Carlos's parents in the previous chapter—and often cause hesitation in affirming their trans child's true identity. Parents who choose to support their child's transition may face judgment from others who might claim, perhaps with good intentions, that the child's gender expression is "just a phase" or that supporting it is indulging problematic behavior. Additionally, some individuals may mock or ridicule trans youth and their parents or argue that accessing transition-related care is harmful. As anti-trans rhetoric has intensified in recent years, so too has the potential for judgmental responses when a trans youth comes out. This kind of judgment can make it harder for parents to rely on the social supports they usually depend on, potentially leading to social isolation and the breakdown of long-standing relationships.

While supporting your child's transition may lead to the loss of some relationships, which can be deeply painful, it can also strengthen others.

Friends and family members may view your support as a sign of thoughtful, courageous parenting, deepening those connections. Setting clear boundaries with those who cannot support your decisions is essential. This might involve limiting interactions, having honest conversations about the support you need, or even temporarily stepping back from certain relationships. Surround yourself with people who respect your role as a parent, even if they don't fully understand.

Cultural backgrounds deeply shape how families and communities respond to a trans youth's identity, intertwining social roles, gender expectations, and identity in complex ways. Historical contexts of systemic discrimination and struggles for equality often inform these reactions. Strong family and community ties, valued in many cultures, can provide vital support but also pose challenges when traditions conflict with acceptance of LGBTQ+ identities. Religious institutions, particularly those with fundamentalist views, often offer spiritual guidance but may promote teachings that conflict with affirming gender diversity, adding layers of discrimination such as racism, transphobia, and classism to a trans youth's journey.

Traditional gender roles in many cultures can create barriers to acceptance, especially when they clash with a child's gender identity. However, these same cultures often place great value on family unity and resilience, which can motivate families to rally around their child, even if acceptance takes time. The involvement of extended family—grandparents, aunts, uncles, and cousins—can amplify both challenges and opportunities for support as a child's transition affects the broader family system. Despite societal stereotypes, many parents choose to prioritize their child's well-being, reframing acceptance as both an act of love and resistance against cultural expectations.

In many cultures, the emphasis on family honor and reputation can heavily influence how families respond to a child's gender identity. Initially, some family members may reject their child out of fear of how the community will perceive them. Yet this same focus on family reputation can also motivate families to support their child to preserve family unity. At the same time, the cultural expectation of respecting elders and adhering to traditional family roles can create additional challenges as a child's transition may be seen as disrupting these norms. Despite societal pressures, there are always parents who rise above these challenges to unconditionally support their children.

Some cultures offer a unique perspective by historically recognizing and respecting diverse gender identities. For example, many Indigenous cultures in North America honored (and still honor) Two-Spirit individuals who embody both masculine and feminine qualities, while hijra communities in South Asia have long been recognized as a distinct gender identity. These traditional understandings can provide a framework for acceptance in communities today. However, the impact of colonization, external influences, and forced assimilation has often eroded these perspectives. Families may find strength in reclaiming these traditional views grounded in intergenerational values such as freedom, self-determination, and authenticity. Even as they contend with the pressures of binary gender norms imposed over generations, many parents are finding ways to prioritize their child's well-being and embrace a loving approach—values deeply rooted across cultures and histories.

## GENDERED CULTURAL TRADITIONS REIMAGINED

Cultural traditions often hold deeply ingrained gender roles, which can create unique challenges for trans and nonbinary youth and their families. However, many families have found creative ways to adapt and reinterpret these traditions to align with their values, honoring their cultural heritage while affirming their child's identity. The following examples illustrate how various cultures can navigate this delicate balance:

### Quinceañera in Latine Culture

In many Latine cultures, the quinceañera marks a girl's transition from childhood to womanhood, making it a deeply gendered tradition. When fourteen-year-old Maria came out as a trans girl, her family hesitated, unsure if hosting a quinceañera would feel authentic or be accepted by their community. Seeking guidance, they connected with an LGBTQ+ family support group and community leaders, who helped them see that Maria deserved the same celebration as any other girl. With renewed confidence, her family organized a traditional quinceañera, including the dress, ceremony, and festivities, but added personal touches such as decorations in trans flag colors and a speech from Maria about her journey to self-discovery. The event became a powerful affirmation of Maria's womanhood, blending cultural tradition with her family's unconditional love and support, and showing how gendered rituals can be reimagined to honor both identity and heritage.

### Bar/Bat Mitzvah in Jewish Culture

Jewish coming-of-age ceremonies, such as the bar and bat mitzvah, are steeped in tradition and often reinforce gender roles. When Alexi, who identifies as nonbinary, approached their bar mitzvah, their family collaborated with a progressive rabbi to create a "B'nai Mitzvah" ceremony that honored both Alexi's Jewish faith and their gender identity. The family incorporated gender-neutral language in blessings and used the term "mi-beit" (from the house of) instead of traditional gendered phrases like "ben" (son of) or "bat" (daughter of). Alexi wore a tallit incorporating masculine and feminine colors, and their d'var Torah explored themes of gender diversity in Jewish texts. By symbolically stepping through a doorway to mark their transition into adulthood, Alexi's ceremony affirmed their identity and sparked meaningful conversations within their synagogue about inclusivity, paving the way for other families to adapt these traditions.

### Prom and Coming-of-Age Dances in American Culture

Prom holds special significance as a rite of passage for many American teens, but for Ryder, a trans boy, it initially raised questions about how best to celebrate. His parents, unsure how to navigate this milestone, sought guidance from their pastor and worked with Ryder's school to ensure he could attend confidently. They supported him in choosing attire that made him feel affirmed and advocated for gender-inclusive practices, including respectful use of names and pronouns and access to gender-neutral restrooms. Ryder's prom ultimately became not only a celebration of his senior year but also a reflection of his family's commitment to supporting his identity. By embracing this milestone on Ryder's terms, his parents showed how traditions like prom can evolve into affirming and inclusive celebrations.

### Debutante Balls in the Southern United States

Debutante balls are a long-standing tradition in the Southern United States, steeped in formality and gender norms that can pose challenges for trans youth. When Thomas, a sixteen-year-old trans girl, expressed her desire to participate, her parents hesitated, concerned about community reactions. With the support of event organizers—who had personal connections to transgender issues—the family found a way to adapt the tradition. Thomas donned the traditional white gown and was formally presented to society, while the event's focus shifted to celebrating her individuality rather than rigid gender roles. This adaptation not only affirmed Thomas's identity but also sparked conversations among attendees, illustrating how even the most traditional customs can evolve to embrace inclusivity and authenticity.

### Genpuku in Japanese Culture

In traditional Japanese culture, the genpuku ceremony marks a boy's transition into adulthood, with rituals centered on readiness for societal roles such as work or marriage. For Hiro, a transgender girl, this deeply gendered tradition presented unique challenges. Her family worked closely with cultural advisers to adapt the ceremony, blending elements of male and female rites to reflect Hiro's journey into adulthood rather than manhood. By focusing on the core values of maturity and growth, they honored both their cultural heritage and Hiro's authentic self, showing that even time-honored traditions can be reshaped to affirm individuality while preserving cultural meaning.

### Sweet Sixteen in American Culture

The Sweet Sixteen celebration, often associated with young girls, has become more inclusive in recent years. When Eli, a trans boy, approached his sixteenth birthday, his family decided to adapt the tradition, reframing it as a "Coming of Age" party. The celebration highlighted Eli's journey into young adulthood, with heartfelt speeches and a memory book created by loved ones. These personal touches affirmed Eli's identity while preserving the celebratory nature of the milestone. By shifting the focus away from gendered expectations, Eli's family created a meaningful and affirming tradition that honored his individuality while maintaining the spirit of the occasion.

### Navajo Kinaaldá Ceremony

The Kinaaldá ceremony, central to Navajo culture, marks a girl's transition to womanhood and her connection to the goddess Changing Woman. When Sky, a trans boy, approached this milestone, his family faced the challenge of balancing traditional expectations with his gender identity. Guided by tribal elders, who drew on Navajo culture's recognition of gender diversity, including the Nádleehi, the family adapted the Kinaaldá to focus on Sky's transition to adulthood rather than womanhood. This thoughtful modification honored both Sky's identity and the sacredness of the ceremony, creating a meaningful experience that upheld cultural values while fostering inclusivity.

### Chinese Hair Combing Ceremony

The Chinese Hair Combing Ceremony is a traditional pre-wedding ritual marking a bride's transition to womanhood. For Mei, a trans woman preparing for her wedding, her family embraced the opportunity to honor her identity through this meaningful tradition. By focusing on the ritual's themes of blessings and marital happiness, rather than gendered expectations, the ceremony became a powerful affirmation of Mei's womanhood. This act of inclusion not only celebrated Mei as a bride but also provided a framework for more traditional family members to embrace and understand her identity within the context of cultural heritage.

When family members initially reject your child's identity, it's essential to understand that your first responsibility is to protect your child. This might involve setting firm boundaries to prevent exposure to any negativity or judgment that could cause emotional harm. In some cases, this may mean limiting contact with those family members or having difficult conversations about the need for respect. You can explain that while you understand their perspective, disrespect or harmful behavior toward your child will not be tolerated.

As you set these boundaries, it's important to be clear about your expectations for future interactions. If you decide that you're open to maintaining or eventually rebuilding a relationship, let them know that respecting your child's identity is nonnegotiable. In the meantime, you may need to restrict family gatherings or control communication until a level of understanding and respect is reached. Protecting your child from rejection and hurtful attitudes must be your top priority. Leaning on supportive friends, family members, or even therapy and community resources can help you navigate this challenging time.

Should you choose to rebuild relationships with these family members, understand that it will likely be a gradual process. Begin by setting clear boundaries around respecting your child's identity in all interactions. You can share educational resources to help them understand trans identities but take care not to overwhelm them with too much information at once. Family therapy can also be a valuable tool, providing a safe space for discussion while leaving the emotional labor to a professional.

As progress is made, celebrate small steps forward, such as occasional use of your child's correct name or pronouns. Share positive updates about your child's life to show that they are thriving, helping to reshape their understanding of your child's identity. Be patient; acceptance often comes in stages and can take years. Even as you work on these relationships, always prioritize your child's emotional well-being, ensuring that they are not exposed to harmful behavior throughout the process.

### WHEN FAITH AND LOVE COLLIDE

#### A Family's Choice to Support Their Daughter

*The Jacksons were a close-knit Christian family living in Atlanta, where their faith played a significant role in their daily lives. They regularly attended church services and participated in community activities, which fostered strong relationships with fellow congregants. Their home was filled with discussions about faith, values, and the importance of supporting one another through life's challenges. Family gatherings often included prayer and reflection, reinforcing their commitment to their beliefs. As they navigated various life events, including milestones like graduations and weddings, the Jacksons relied on their church community for guidance and support, making faith an integral part of their family's identity and interactions. So, when their youngest child, sixteen-year-old Jasmine, revealed she was transgender, it threatened to upend their entire support system and way of life.*

*Jasmine's father, Deacon Robert Jackson, was a highly respected leader in their Baptist church. He had always taken immense pride in raising his child to be a "strong Black man"—a protector, a leader, an unwavering pillar of the community. Jasmine's transition represented an affront to everything he understood about manhood, masculinity, and his own identity as a father.*

*For Jasmine's mother Sarah, the turmoil was equally devastating. As a devout woman of faith, she had been taught that transgender identities were an abomination—a "sinful" choice that could jeopardize her child's soul. Yet she loved Jasmine fiercely and couldn't fathom losing her relationship and worried about her daughter's safety given what she had heard about the high rates of homelessness, violence, and suicide that impacted so many trans youth rejected by their families.*

*Perhaps most terrifying for the Jacksons was the prospect of being outcast by their entire church community and extended family if they accepted Jasmine's identity. Their church's doctrine explicitly condemned transgender people, framing it as a "confused phase" and any acceptance as validating "unnatural" behavior.*

*The Jacksons watched as former friends at church immediately turned their backs on Jasmine, refusing to use her name and pronouns. Jasmine's grandparents, aunts, and uncles also reacted with outright rejection, leaving her feeling isolated and depressed. The family feared they could lose everything—their spiritual community, their long-standing relationships, even potentially their jobs and housing if they were ostracized from their community.*

*For years, the Jacksons remained torn between their love for Jasmine and the church's strict fundamentalist teachings. Through agonizing family therapy and extensive research, they came to understand that Jasmine's identity was not a choice but an intrinsic part of who she is. As they reflected more deeply on their faith, they began to see that their religious teachings—particularly the values of love, compassion, and treating others with dignity—supported their acceptance of Jasmine. They realized that embracing Jasmine was not in conflict with their faith but aligned with its highest principles. While the broader doctrine of their church may not have shifted, they found that by focusing on the core tenets of love and acceptance, they could support Jasmine fully, living out their faith in a way that honored both their child and their spiritual beliefs.*

*In a heart-wrenching decision, the Jacksons ultimately chose their daughter, prioritizing her life and self-worth over the rigid expectations of their church community. They risked losing everything they had built—friends, social ties, and spiritual support—to embrace Jasmine fully. By committing to unconditional love, they learned to use her chosen name and pronouns, even when doing so publicly meant facing inevitable rejection. The process wasn't easy, marked by setbacks and the struggle to unlearn generations of ingrained beliefs.*

*To the Jacksons' surprise, while they lost some friends and faced harsh judgment from their former church, they also experienced an outpouring of support from unexpected places. Family members, coworkers, and others in the broader community rallied around them with open hearts and minds. In time, the Jacksons realized that those who couldn't accept their family's truth were never truly their people. Though the cost was high, their journey led them to a more authentic community—one that embraced and celebrated Jasmine's identity without hesitation or caveats. Empowered by their experience, the Jacksons became advocates, using their voices to support other families caught between the love for their LGBTQ+ children and the constraints of fundamentalist faiths.*

Faith communities often play a crucial role in either exacerbating or alleviating the social isolation that trans individuals and their loved ones might face. Many trans people find themselves disconnected from their previous faith communities after coming out, losing a vital source of support during the challenging transition process. Additionally, family conflicts involving religion can further strain a trans person's relationships with both their family and their spiritual beliefs. However, disconnection and rejection aren't always the outcome. For some, their religious community can provide crucial support and act as a protective factor, helping to shield them from greater harm and distress.

There are faith communities such as Unitarian Universalism, Reform Judaism, and certain progressive Christian denominations that openly affirm trans identities and welcome trans parishioners and their families. If faith is an important part of your life and you're struggling with your current faith community's stance on transgender issues, it's worth knowing that affirming options exist. However, changing one's faith tradition is a deeply personal decision that involves many factors beyond just LGBTQ+ acceptance. Some families may choose to stay within their current faith tradition and work toward greater understanding and acceptance from within. Others might seek out LGBTQ+-affirming congregations within their existing denomination. For those open to exploring other faith communities, finding an affirming religious group can provide additional spiritual support and acceptance for both you and your child. Whatever path you choose, it's important to prioritize your family's well-being and spiritual needs.

While cultural contexts significantly influence family reactions to transgender youth, individual responses within any culture can vary widely. Approaching each situation with cultural sensitivity, empathy, and openness to learning is crucial. Seeking guidance from culturally specific LGBTQ+ organizations can provide invaluable, tailored support. Rather than viewing culture as an obstacle, explore how cultural values can be reframed to affirm and support trans youth. Connecting with families who share similar cultural or spiritual backgrounds and have successfully navigated this journey can provide valuable insights and build a strong, supportive network.

At first, learning about your child's identity might have brought concerns about losing friends or family. However, I encourage you to shift toward an empowering perspective:

> "We will find our people—those who wholeheartedly support and celebrate our child's authenticity, allowing us to honor their true self and uphold our values."

## KEY POINTS

**Cultural Considerations:** Different cultural backgrounds can significantly influence family and community reactions to a trans youth's identity. Recognizing and navigating these cultural nuances can help in finding acceptance and support. Ceremonies and traditions can be adapted to honor both the young person's cultural and gender identities.

**Rebuilding Relationships:** Rebuilding relationships with family members who initially reject your child's identity is a gradual process that requires open communication, patience, and setting clear boundaries that protect your child.

**Faith Communities:** Faith communities can play a significant role in either exacerbating or alleviating social isolation. Finding inclusive faith communities can provide crucial support for both you and your child.

## REFLECTION QUESTIONS

1. How do you feel about the potential changes in your family dynamics since your child has come out?
2. What steps can you take to communicate effectively with family members who are struggling to accept your child's identity?
3. How can you find and join supportive communities, both online and offline, to help you and your child?
4. How does your child's gender identity interact with your religious or spiritual beliefs (if relevant)?
5. In what ways can you set boundaries with family and friends who are not supportive of your child's identity?

# 17

# DO WE NEED TO REWRITE HISTORY?

**Every family creates and maintains its own narrative,** a collection of memories, stories, and even physical objects that frame the members' understanding of their lives and their interactions with one another. This narrative helps define roles within the family system and shapes the collective history that influences current ways of living and relating to each other. Within a family, these stories and memories serve as a foundation for understanding individual and group identities. Family members may interpret their roles and the broader family narrative differently based on their personal experiences. These perspectives can vary greatly, leading to agreements or conflict about the nature of their shared history and each person's place within it.

Each family's narrative is deeply imbued with emotion, capturing moments of joy, celebration, and love, as well as times of hardship and trauma. The way a family chooses to remember and tell these stories adds layers of meaning to their collective identity and has a profound impact on each member's sense of self. It's through these stories that family members learn about their heritage, understand their personal and familial identities, and form bonds that can either strengthen or strain their connections to one another. By reflecting on and occasionally reshaping these narratives, families can resolve past misunderstandings and begin to heal old wounds. In this dynamic process, the narrative isn't just a record of the past but a living, evolving understanding that continues to shape the family's present and future interactions.

Families with trans, nonbinary, or gender nonconforming youth experience unique challenges as they navigate changes in the family narrative. When a child comes out, it often feels to parents like they are being asked to "rewrite" their understanding of their child's development and history. This rewriting is not just about adjusting to a new idea; it involves rethinking the roles and relationships within the family that may shift significantly as parents and other family members learn to understand and accept the child's identity.

During the initial stages of a child's transition, families often encounter a period of confusion and adjustment regarding roles and boundaries. This phase can be particularly overwhelming as both caregivers and children work through the complex emotions and logistic changes involved. The ambiguity and uncertainty about family dynamics during this time can be a source of stress and can be difficult for everyone, especially for the trans youth at the center of these changes.

As the family navigates the child's gender transition, the challenge often lies in how readily parents and siblings can adapt to and embrace the child's authentic self. Successfully adjusting to the child's gender identity and expression can lead to a deeper, more empathetic understanding within the family, reinforcing bonds and building a foundation of acceptance and support. However, this journey requires patience, open communication, and, often, external support from counselors or support groups that can provide guidance and reassurance during this transformative time. Ultimately, embracing a child's true identity may reshape the family narrative, but it also enriches it, adding layers of resilience and unity. While it doesn't change the past, it allows the family to understand it more fully, creating space for healing and growth. This adaptation not only supports the trans youth but also strengthens the entire family, fostering a more open and supportive environment for everyone.

Parents of trans, nonbinary, or gender nonconforming children and adolescents often experience a significant shift in how they understand their child's history, which can lead to a sense of needing to "rewrite" their family narrative. This challenge is distinct from the concept of ambiguous loss, which was addressed in chapter nine. Here, the focus is more on the disorienting experience of rethinking the past and the family story you've held onto for years. The process of rewriting your understanding of your child's history can be emotionally complex because it feels like altering core memories, values, and the narrative that has shaped your relationship with your child.

The process of embracing a child's authentic gender identity can often feel like a reframing of family history, stirring up complex emotions for parents. One of the most profound challenges is mourning the vision of the past. Parents might experience a deep sense of loss over who they thought their child was or who they envisioned their child becoming. Earlier memories, family narratives, and milestones—reflected in photographs, documents, and rituals—are often rooted in the gender assigned at birth, making it difficult to reconcile these cherished moments with the child's true identity. For many parents, this shift can be especially hard, catching them by surprise, as photos and memories that once symbolized pride and love now feel hurtful or out of place.

However, drastic changes are not always required. Even if you feel the need to take down some photos, you don't have to throw them away. Not all children mind seeing older photographs, and some are proud of the journey it took to become who they truly are. One client shared with me that seeing her old photos made her feel grateful that the younger version of herself stuck around long enough for her to grow into her true identity. For some families, these moments can still represent love, resilience, and the path to becoming one's authentic self. It's important to have open conversations with your child about how they feel, as these decisions can be deeply personal and unique to each individual.

This emotional journey can also include releasing attachment to the name they lovingly chose. Parents often pick a name with deep care and intention, perhaps to honor a relative or continue a family tradition. To have that name now referred to as a "deadname" can feel jarring and even painful, as it may seem to erase the significance it once held. The term "deadname" itself can be hard for parents to hear because it carries connotations of finality and loss. However, it's important to note that not all trans people use or prefer this term. Some prefer the language of "birth name" and "chosen name," as they see the act of choosing a new name not as a rejection of the past but as a reflection of survival and a celebration of their true identity. For parents, shifting their relationship with the name they once chose with love can be a difficult process, but understanding this perspective can help reframe the narrative in a more positive, affirming light.

Affirming a child's authentic gender identity can also bring a struggle between affirmation and denial. Some parents may feel that affirming their child's true self means denying or erasing the image they had of their child in the past. This conflict is often tied to a deep emotional investment in the original narrative, where parents raised their child with certain gender assumptions in mind. Letting go of this narrative isn't just about accepting new information; it's about reshaping the entire framework of their relationship with their child. For some parents, this leads to the perception that their child is now a "different person." Even though their child remains fundamentally the same, the shift in gender identity can create a disconnect between the child they once knew and the person they now see.

Adapting family traditions often requires thoughtful change. Many customs—whether during holidays, birthdays, or other significant events—are shaped by gender roles. Parents and siblings may need to rethink or rework these traditions to be more inclusive of the child's authentic identity. While this process can feel like letting go of long-held rituals, it also opens the door to discovering new ways to honor and celebrate the evolving identities within the family.

This "rewriting" process isn't about erasing the past but finding ways to integrate both the old and new understandings of your child's identity into a cohesive, evolving family story. Embracing this transformation can ultimately strengthen your connection with your child and deepen your shared history, but it requires patience, self-compassion, and a willingness to let go of rigid expectations.

The need to reconcile past memories with the present reality can be particularly challenging when it comes to cherished family narratives preserved through photographs, keepsakes, and official documents. These artifacts, once viewed as affirming a particular understanding of your child's identity, may now feel at odds with who they are today as they assert their true gender identity. For parents who have built strong emotional connections to these narratives, accepting and affirming their child's evolving identity can feel like an emotional tightrope walk. This integration can take many forms: updating family photo displays to include both past and present images, adapting how you recount family stories by using your child's current name and pronouns even for past events, or creating new family traditions that allow for more flexible gender expressions. This shift isn't about erasing the past but about integrating it into a fuller, more accurate story—one that honors both the history you've shared and the authenticity of who your child is becoming.

This process of reweaving the family narrative allows for continuity and connection as your understanding of your child deepens. Recognizing that the past still holds value and meaning, even as you update it to reflect new truths, becomes an essential part of this journey. Learning to navigate this emotional terrain is crucial not just for your child's well-being but for the health of your entire family as you move forward together. By embracing both your shared history and your child's authentic self, you create a more inclusive and affirming family story that can strengthen bonds and foster resilience in the face of change.

## MORE THAN A DOCUMENT

### The Meaning Behind Amending a Birth Certificate

*At a parent support group meeting, Brittany shared her struggle with amending her transgender son Ryan's birth certificate. Brittany is the mother of sixteen-year-old Ryan, who was assigned female at birth but came out as a transgender boy at age fourteen. Brittany has been very supportive of Ryan's transition so far—she enthusiastically embraced his new name and pronouns, took him to get a legal name change, and helped him pursue gender-affirming hormone therapy. Brittany has also committed to attending this weekly parent support group to learn how to best support her transgender son.*

*Recently, Ryan asked Brittany to take the next step and amend his birth certificate to reflect his accurate gender marker and male name. While Brittany expected this request at some point, being faced with officially "rewriting history" by changing that founding document stopped her in her tracks.*

*Brittany shared, "I know Ryan is my son, and I want to validate his identity fully. But that birth certificate is the permanent record of me giving birth to my baby girl. Changing it now feels like it's erasing that real experience and cherished memory for me as his mother."*

*Many parents in the group nodded, relating to Brittany's sense of ambiguous loss. One mother named Jenna said, "I remember so vividly cradling my newborn daughter in my arms that first day. Now my child wants me to go back and put an 'M' on that certificate, and it makes me feel like I'm being asked to deny that moment ever happened for me."*

*Another parent, Carlos, expressed, "It's almost like my child is saying 'No, you're wrong, you didn't actually give birth to a daughter that day.' Of course I support my child, but it's still hard not to feel invalidated about my own memory and experience." The facilitator acknowledged the painful ambiguous loss the parents described. They reminded the group that amending a birth certificate does not erase or invalidate birth memories and experiences of mothers and birthing parents. It simply updates the documentation to reflect their children's true identities.*

*As a practical matter, the facilitator explained, parents are rarely required to present birth certificates for their adult children. However, individuals often need to present their own birth certificates, such as when planning to marry. Allowing this change would make their children's futures easier and less painful by providing proper documentation of their identities. The facilitator suggested reframing the situation this way: "The birth certificate amendment doesn't change the fact that you gave birth to and loved a beautiful baby on that day. It just corrects the inaccurate gender marker based on what was known at the time before your child could self-identify."*

*For Brittany, this reframing helped. While still emotionally complex, she decided to embrace amending the certificate as honoring Ryan's authentic self and their family's evolution, rather than deleting the birth experience itself from her memory and identity as a mother. Amending a birth certificate is a significant milestone that can stir up complex emotions. But I encouraged them to see it as an affirmation of their child's identity, not an erasure of their own memories and experiences as parents. With support and reframing, these parents can find a way to honor both their child's truth and their own cherished birth stories.*

Navigating a child's gender transition can bring about shifts in family dynamics, especially if your family strongly identifies with certain gender roles or traditions. For example, if you've always been a "#BoyMom" or "#GirlDad" and suddenly that changes, or if your family had traditions where the boys went fishing with dad while the girls got their nails done with mom—what happens when one of your children transitions? This shift can be particularly impactful, not only for you as a parent but also for the siblings, who may experience a range of emotions, from confusion to resentment to celebration.

Siblings might feel a sense of loss or even jealousy if they perceive that their trans sibling is receiving more attention, or they may struggle with the change in how the family identifies itself. It's crucial to be mindful of these dynamics and to regularly check in on your other children. Consciously set aside time to talk with them about their own experiences and challenges—not only relating to their sibling's transition but also, crucially, about their lives in general. While a child who is transitioning may require more attention, time, and care during this period, it's imperative that this does not detract from their siblings' feelings of being seen, heard, and supported. Acknowledge their feelings and reassure them that they are equally valued and loved within the family.

At the same time, siblings can also become their trans sibling's strongest allies. The bond between siblings, forged through mutual support and understanding, can become a powerful force for good. Witnessing this can be one of the greatest gifts of parenting—a testament to the values you've instilled in your children. So, while some of these changes may be challenging, they also offer opportunities for growth and deepening connections within your family. It's important to give yourself a pat on the back for guiding your children through this journey, helping them become supportive and compassionate individuals.

## THE HARRISON CREW

### Expanding Identity and Family Bonds

*The Harrison family was well known in their community, largely due to Coach Harrison's dedication to the local youth hockey league, where he coached his four sons. Hockey was more than just a sport for the Harrisons; it was a way of life. The "Harrison Boys," as they were fondly called, were a tight-knit squad, united on and off the ice. Mrs. Harrison proudly embraced having so many boys, often cheering from the stands, wearing her custom "Hockey Mom" gear and relishing her role in supporting her sons.*

*However, their family dynamic shifted when Skylar, one of the Harrison Boys, came out as transgender. This revelation challenged not just the family's identity, but also Coach Harrison's deeply ingrained ideas of masculinity and team camaraderie. He grappled with a mix of confusion and protectiveness, questioning how to reconcile being the coach and father of the "Harrison Boys" while embracing Skylar's new identity. It was a journey of unlearning and relearning, as he realized that his role was not just about fostering traditional masculinity but about teaching resilience, teamwork, and integrity—qualities that transcended gender.*

*For Mrs. Harrison, the news was equally challenging. She had always taken pride in being a #BoyMom, and the family's identity had been built around being a squad of boys—a shared bond over sports, competition, and all things traditionally "masculine." Now, with Skylar's transition, she felt an unsettling mix of love, uncertainty, and grief as she grappled with redefining her identity as a mother. Yet, through this emotional turmoil, she discovered a new pride in being a mother who could support all her children authentically.*

*The initial period was tough for everyone. Skylar's brothers found it hard to adjust, worrying that the family's traditions and dynamic would be thrown off course. There was also tension around how the extended community, especially in their hockey circles, would respond to this shift. Coach Harrison struggled internally, torn between his protective instincts as a father and his attachment to the camaraderie he had built among his children as their coach.*

*But as time passed, the Harrisons began to see that Skylar's transition didn't have to mean losing what made their family special—it could mean finding new ways to honor their bond. Skylar's siblings gradually moved from confusion to becoming Skylar's fiercest advocates. The family had to navigate new territory—like deciding whether Skylar would continue in the hockey league or if some of their long-held family traditions needed to change. They found ways to adjust without losing their closeness. Whether it was tweaking family rituals to be more inclusive or rethinking the dynamics of their weekend sports gatherings, the Harrisons leaned into communication and support.*

*In the end, the Harrisons didn't lose their identity—they redefined it. Their journey highlights that while family roles and traditions may shift, their love, support, and unity remain constant. By stepping up as allies and advocates, Coach Harrison and Mrs. Harrison not only supported Skylar but also strengthened the entire family, creating a new, more inclusive legacy for the "Harrison Crew."*

Parenting requires constantly adjusting to shifting relationships and roles within the family, even if your child identifies with the gender they were assigned at birth. Changes will occur in your family as a result of your child's transition, but some transformation is inevitable as your child grows. Embracing these changes can lead to profound positive outcomes for both you and your child. As discussed in previous chapters, affirming a trans young person's gender identity is not only essential for their well-being but can also forge a stronger, more courageous family unit. This journey often results in deeper connections and increased trust among family members. Your child may have known their gender didn't match others' expectations for a long time, but they were afraid to say it or lacked the language to do so. Now that they have, the most important way for you to help them is to encourage and support them in living as their authentic self. This process can foster resilience, empathy, and open communication, ultimately strengthening the bonds within your family and creating a more nurturing environment for everyone involved.

Supporting your child's transition does not require "rewriting" the past; rather, honoring a trans young person's past self can be a meaningful part of the transition process. There are many ways to do this—such as sharing cherished memories or including past photos in family discussions—and you can collaborate with your child to find what works best for your family. Whatever you choose, the underlying truth remains: you can celebrate the person your child is becoming while also honoring who they've been. This approach not only validates their journey but also reinforces the continuity of your family's narrative, allowing everyone to feel connected and valued throughout this transformative experience.

The family in this next case study found a thoughtful way to adapt their holiday traditions to affirm their child's identity while still preserving cherished memories.

### REWRITING TRADITIONS

#### How One Family Adapted with Love

*During the annual Christmas tree decorating, Eloise, a mom of two, realized how the family's customary ornaments, many personalized with her children's names, might affect her youngest child, who was assigned female at birth, and now goes by their gender-neutral family nickname "Scout" over their birth name. As Eloise pulled out the "Baby's First Christmas" ornament with Scout's birthname engraved on it, she paused, considering how this might make Scout feel. This moment of realization sparked an opportunity for Eloise to reassess and adapt these cherished traditions.*

*She gently approached Scout, asking how they'd like to handle the personalized ornaments. Together, they decided to create new ornaments using Scout's preferred nickname while also keeping the old ones as a part of their family history.*

*Determined to support her child's identity, Eloise lovingly updated all the family's ornaments. Every year, she would place angel ornaments representing each child on their chairs to show Santa where to leave gifts. The ornaments had been made years ago, including one for Scout, an angel dressed in pink with blond hair. But now, the angel no longer reflected Scout's true identity. Rather than discarding the original ornament, Eloise kept it for herself, as it still held fond memories of Scout's earlier years. For Scout, she created a new ornament, repainting the angel's dress blue, changing the hair to black with purple highlights, and adding rhinestones for a personal touch. She inscribed "Scout" across the front, ensuring the ornament truly represented Scout's identity.*

*This process was not just about Scout. Eloise decided to update the ornaments for all her children to reflect their current identities, appearances, and interests. For her older daughter, Mia, she added a paintbrush to her ornament, symbolizing her love of art. For her son, Theo, she included a small soccer ball, representing his passion for the game. By including all the siblings in the tradition, Eloise ensured that no one felt left out, and the entire family celebrated each member's evolving identity.*

*The reaction was overwhelmingly positive. "You painted it blue! And did my hair!" Scout exclaimed with joy upon seeing the transformed angel ornament. The recognition in their smile underscored the impact of this loving gesture. Additionally, a new tradition was introduced—a pride nutcracker holding a rainbow flag now welcomes guests at the entrance, symbolizing the family's embrace of diversity and acceptance. These small but meaningful updates transformed the family's traditions into a celebration of growth, identity, and unity.*

Modifying family traditions, while initially challenging, can greatly enhance inclusivity and support for trans or gender nonconforming family members. By taking thoughtful actions to respect and affirm her child's identity, Eloise not only preserved the spirit of their traditions but also reinforced a message of unconditional love and acceptance. Adapting these rituals fosters a sense of belonging and joy, ensuring many colorful, happy holidays to come. These changes can make all the difference in a child's experience of family and acceptance.

Whatever approach you take, the underlying truth remains: you can celebrate the person your child is becoming while also honoring the person they've been. By embracing both the past and the future, families can create meaningful new traditions that bring them closer than ever before.

At the beginning of this chapter, you may have felt weighed down by the idea that the past needed to be erased. However, the insights and case studies presented here offer a different perspective: one where the family narrative isn't rewritten but rewoven. It's about integrating past experiences with a deeper understanding of your child's identity, creating a richer, more inclusive story. Rather than focusing on erasure, you can embrace the possibility of honoring the past while adapting to the present, allowing both to coexist in meaningful ways. Ultimately, I encourage you to embrace this empowering belief:

"I have the capacity to cherish our shared past while fully acknowledging and affirming their present identity."

## KEY POINTS

**Family Narratives:** Every family creates and maintains its own narrative, comprising memories, stories, and physical objects that define roles and shape the collective history. This narrative helps members understand individual and group identities, influencing current ways of living and relating.

**Emotion in Family Narratives:** Family narratives are deeply emotional, capturing moments of joy, love, hardship, and trauma. These stories add layers of meaning to the family's collective identity and impact each member's sense of self, shaping their understanding of heritage and personal identity.

**Challenges for Families with Trans Youth:** Families with trans, nonbinary, or gender nonconforming youth face unique challenges. When a child comes out, it can feel like a significant shift in the family narrative, requiring adjustments in roles and relationships.

**Updating Documentation:** Updating legal documents to reflect a child's true gender identity is an important step in their transition. Amending a birth certificate can pave the way for updating other crucial documents such as a social security card, passport, and driver's license as the child gets older. This process of updating a child's documents helps ensure that all official records align with the child's gender identity, reducing the potential for discrimination and enhancing their ability to navigate the world confidently.

**Adapting Family Narratives:** Successfully navigating the transition process involves open communication, external support, and patience. Embracing a child's true identity enriches the family narrative, adding resilience and unity while supporting the well-being of the trans youth and the entire family.

## REFLECTION QUESTIONS

1. What has changed in the family narrative since your child has come out?
2. In what ways can you support your child while maintaining and respecting the family history?
3. What steps can you take to ensure all family members feel included and respected during this transition?
4. How can external support (e.g., counseling, support groups) aid your family during this time?
5. What are some meaningful ways you could preserve old memories while also embracing your child's authentic self?

## 18

# WILL I HAVE GRANDKIDS?

**For many parents of transgender children,** one of the most challenging concerns is the fear that their child's transition could affect their ability to have biological children in the future. You've likely envisioned what it would be like to have grandchildren—playing with them, watching them grow, passing on family traditions. The idea that your child's path could make that dream more difficult or perhaps impossible is challenging to grapple with.

These concerns about grandchildren may stem from broader worries about your transgender child's ability to experience significant life milestones, such as finding a loving partnership, getting married, or starting a family of their own. You want your child to have the opportunity for those joys, should they desire them. Worries about fertility preservation and future reproductive options can weigh heavily. The desire for grandchildren is not selfish; rather, it often reflects a deep love for your child and a hope that they, too, can experience the joy of parenthood. You may yearn for grandchildren because of how much fulfillment being a parent has brought you, and you want your child to have that same opportunity for happiness.

Gender-affirming care may involve treatments that can impact fertility, so it's important for families to consider this when navigating medical options like puberty suppression, estrogen, or testosterone therapies, which can affect future fertility potential. For transgender adolescents who may wish to have biological children in the future, discussing fertility preservation options before starting pubertal suppression or gender-affirming hormones is crucial. One of the most common options is gamete preservation, which involves freezing sperm, eggs, or ovarian/testicular tissue, allowing individuals to retain the potential for biological reproduction.

However, there are barriers that can make fertility preservation challenging. Cost is often a major obstacle, as these procedures are generally not covered by insurance. There may also be geographic limitations if reproductive clinics offering these services are not locally available. Some transgender youth may prefer to forgo fertility preservation due to personal circumstances or their preferences and perceptions of future fertility needs.

Although fertility preservation is often significant to parents and caregivers who are concerned about their child's future reproductive options, studies show that the rates of transgender adolescents utilizing these options remain relatively low. In one study of over two hundred trans youth, only around 5% chose to pursue fertility preservation prior to starting gender-affirming treatment. The most common reasons cited were no desire for future children, wanting to avoid delays in transition, and concerns about costs (Cheng et al. 2019).

Additionally, the process of fertility preservation can feel in direct opposition to the goals of transitioning. For example, harvesting eggs often requires taking estrogen and other medications to stimulate egg production, which can be distressing for someone seeking to transition away from a female-assigned body. For sperm preservation, adolescents must be old enough to produce viable sperm and may need to temporarily go off puberty blockers. These factors contribute to why many transgender adolescents choose to forgo fertility preservation.

Medical providers must have open, age-appropriate discussions about fertility from the first visit with transgender youth. Exploring your child's thoughts about future fertility desires and the full scope of family-building options allows young people and their care teams to make informed decisions aligned with their values and goals. With comprehensive counseling, transgender adolescents can carefully weigh the pros and cons of fertility preservation versus prioritizing gender-affirming interventions based on their specific needs.

While research is still limited, emerging evidence suggests many transgender individuals do want the opportunity to pursue having children, whether through assisted reproductive technology, adoption, or other pathways to parenthood. By prioritizing fertility counseling, providers can ensure transgender youth understand their options and have the chance to make choices they won't regret later in life. Considering future fertility possibilities allows for important flexibility, as life circumstances or the desire to start a family shift and evolve.

As a parent, it's natural to want the best for your children, and you may have imagined the joy of future grandchildren and the experience of becoming a grandparent. These hopes often come from a place of love and a desire for your child to experience the fulfillment that parenthood can bring. However, it's also important to reflect on where these expectations originate. Could they be shaped by societal stigma, discrimination, or misinformation? It's worth considering whether you might be unintentionally creating false distinctions between the lives that cisgender and transgender people can lead.

It's crucial to remember that fertility is not guaranteed for anyone, regardless of gender identity. Many heteronormative couples also face infertility and miscarriage or important choices regarding adoption, IVF, or other alternatives to biological children. By evaluating these factors, you can approach the topic with a broader understanding of the possibilities available to both cisgender and transgender individuals when it comes to starting families in the future.

It's completely natural for parents to struggle with letting go of the specific futures they had envisioned for their children. To help recognize and process these preconceived notions, try this exercise: Reflect on some key milestones or experiences you've imagined for your child's future, such as graduation, career, and relationships. Consider which aspects of these visions are tied to gender expectations and then reimagine these scenarios without those gender-specific elements. Ask yourself what core hopes and dreams remain unchanged and what new possibilities you can envision. This exercise aims to help you focus on your fundamental wishes for your child's happiness and success, independent of gender, encouraging flexibility in your expectations while reinforcing your enduring love and support for your child.

It's also important to ask yourself deeper, potentially uncomfortable questions: how important is your desire to have grandchildren, and why? Having children does not guarantee happiness or fulfillment, and not having biological grandchildren is just as possible for cisgender individuals as it is for transgender individuals. The desire for grandchildren is a common source of tension between parents and their adult children, regardless of gender identity, and should be explored separately from your child's transition. Many adult children, cis or trans, may not wish to pursue parenthood, and navigating this dynamic requires empathy and open communication.

## MORE THAN ACCEPTANCE

### A Family's Commitment to Affirmation

*For parents Diane and Mark, their youngest child Alicia's coming out as transgender at age fourteen was a moment that challenged many of their deeply held hopes and dreams for her future. Diane had long imagined the joy of someday becoming a grandparent through Alicia. She pictured herself holding Alicia's children, passing down family traditions, and sharing in the special moments of parenthood. "When Alicia told us she identified as a girl, I remember feeling this wave of sadness. I had always pictured her with a wife and children. In my mind, that dream was fading away," Diane said.*

*Mark, too, had specific images of the future in mind. He had always looked forward to standing beside Alicia on her wedding day, buttoning her cufflinks just as his own father had done for him. "I had always imagined walking my son down the aisle," Mark shared. "But suddenly, I realized that vision was changing, and I felt a little lost."*

*At first, Diane and Mark fixated on mourning the future they had imagined—grandchildren, weddings, and family milestones that felt like they were slipping away. But as they learned more and talked with a parent coach, they realized that their focus on these distant, hypothetical moments was preventing them from seeing what Alicia truly needed in the present.*

*"We had to stop and ask ourselves: what's more important, clinging to an imagined future or supporting our daughter who needed us right now?" Mark said. As they embraced this new perspective, they saw Alicia begin to flourish. With their affirmation and support in accessing gender-affirming care like puberty blockers and hormone therapy, Alicia's confidence blossomed. "I finally felt seen and loved for who I truly was," Alicia said. "That acceptance allowed me to thrive in ways I couldn't before when I was depressed and disconnected from myself."*

*Now in her twenties, Alicia shares a close and loving bond with her parents. "We still don't know what the future will look like in terms of relationships or kids, and that's okay," Diane reflected. "We've learned that the most important thing is showing up for Alicia in the present. By doing that, we get to share this incredible relationship with our amazing daughter, and that's what truly matters." Mark added with a smile, "I may not be buttoning cufflinks, but I'm looking forward to walking my daughter down the aisle someday."*

*Their journey shows that while hopes of grandchildren or traditional family milestones are understandable, fixating on those dreams can overshadow what truly matters—being there for your child now.*

These fertility-related issues are undoubtedly difficult to grapple with as a parent, but you don't have to navigate them alone. Countless other parents have worked through similar fears, emotions, and preconceived notions to become fully supportive of their transgender children, and there are support systems available and people who can relate to your experience. Remember the fundamental responsibility of being a parent: your greatest priority is to do everything you can to support your child's happiness and well-being.

Supporting your child through their transition not only enhances their happiness and well-being in the present but can also positively impact their future. By creating a supportive and affirming environment, you help set the foundation for healthier relationships, personal fulfillment, and even the possibility of future grandchildren. In fact, data shows that many transgender people report significant increases in confidence, life satisfaction, and overall well-being after transitioning. In the US Transgender Survey, 78% of respondents felt more confident at work post-transition (James et al. 2024). Another study found that 93% of transgender individuals experienced improvements in relationships, mental health, happiness, perceived financial status, and more after transitioning (What We Know Project 2018). Even in romantic relationships specifically, research indicates transgender individuals can reach the same baseline levels of satisfaction as cisgender couples (Marshall et al. 2020).

Ultimately, you have the opportunity to meet your transgender child with affirmation and an open mind, understanding that your concepts of family and love may have been shaped by cisgender, heteronormative ideals. While this isn't wrong, it's helpful to remember that many LGBTQ+ people have children in various ways.

When considering the possibility of grandchildren, it's important to recognize that your transgender child, like many others, has multiple pathways to parenthood. Options such as fertility preservation, adoption, fostering, and surrogacy are all possibilities. While they may face additional barriers, with your support and advocacy, these dreams can still be realized.

### REDEFINING FATHERHOOD

#### Marcus's Story of Pregnancy and Love

*Marcus had been on testosterone for over ten years since starting his medical transition at age eighteen. While he knew many trans men were able to get pregnant after stopping testosterone, Marcus worried that the decade of hormone therapy may have impacted his fertility.*

*"The doctors really didn't have a definitive answer for me," Marcus said. "There was a lot of 'we don't know for sure' about whether the long-term testosterone use could affect my ability to get pregnant or impact the pregnancy itself."*

*Despite the uncertainties, Marcus and his wife Rachel decided to try for a baby after Marcus went off testosterone. To their relief, Marcus's menstrual cycle returned within four months after stopping the hormone therapy.*

*"We naively thought it would happen really quickly once I was having regular periods again," Marcus said. "But it ended up taking us over a year of trying before I got pregnant." Marcus conceived through intrauterine insemination (IUI) using Rachel's eggs that had been frozen earlier due to her own fertility issues. The pregnancy went smoothly with no complications. "My ob-gyn said everything looked healthy and normal, despite my history on testosterone," Marcus said. "It helped ease my mind after all the uncertainty."*

*At thirty-nine weeks, Marcus gave birth to a healthy baby boy they named Micah. Father and baby went home just a couple days later. "Holding Micah in my arms, I couldn't believe I had been so worried about whether this was possible for me as a trans man," Marcus said. "This experience has shown me to have more faith in my body's resilience."*

*Marcus's story demonstrates that transgender men can successfully get pregnant and have healthy births even after an extended period of testosterone use, with the right medical support. His case provides a positive example to counter misconceptions about trans fertility potential.*

The challenges transgender individuals face stem largely from societal stigma and discrimination, rather than from their identity itself. While being transgender involves unique healthcare needs and experiences related to sexuality, these should not inherently be more difficult than those encountered by cisgender people. The real difficulties stem from a world that often stigmatizes and marginalizes trans identities. By providing your child a safe, affirmative environment to grow and discover themselves and connecting them to understanding communities, you can help them cultivate incredibly healthy relationships—likely healthier than a lifetime spent denying their authentic self. Showing them love in this way may in turn help them follow your example and become parents to children they love, accept, and support.

At first, learning about your child's identity might have raised concerns about your family's future and their ability to have children. However, I invite you to consider this more empowering perspective:

"By accepting and supporting my child, I am helping create a future where milestones like parenthood are possible for them, if that's what they choose."

## KEY POINTS

**Parental Concerns Over Grandchildren:** Parents of transgender children often worry that their child's transition might limit their ability to have biological children and, by extension, limit the parents' opportunities to have grandchildren.

**Impact of Medical Transition on Fertility:** Gender-affirming treatments like puberty blockers and hormones can impact fertility, making it crucial for families to consider and discuss fertility preservation options early in the transition process.

**Barriers to Fertility Preservation:** Although fertility preservation techniques such as gamete freezing are available, they often come with high costs and geographical limitations, making access challenging.

**Desire for Parenthood Among Transgender Individuals:** Despite the challenges, many transgender people still express a strong desire for children, exploring and pursuing various family-building options such as assisted reproductive technologies, adoption, and surrogacy.

**Importance of Open Discussions on Fertility:** Medical providers should engage in open and age-appropriate discussions with transgender youth about fertility, allowing them to make informed decisions that respect their future family planning desires.

## REFLECTION QUESTIONS

1. How does your understanding of fertility and transgender healthcare impact your feelings about your child's future family possibilities?
2. What steps can you take to support your child in preserving their fertility options, if they choose?
3. How can you reconcile your hopes for grandchildren with the reality of your child's needs and choices?
4. What resources and support networks are available to help you and your child navigate questions about reproduction and family building?
5. How can you foster an environment that respects and celebrates your child's potential pathways to parenthood, regardless of their gender identity?

PART FIVE

# FROM UNDERSTANDING TO ACTION

19

# HOW CAN I MAKE A BROADER IMPACT?

**Over the past eighteen chapters,** you've explored the history and limitations of the gender binary, asked yourself challenging questions, and broadened your understanding of what it means to support your transgender child. You've confronted your fears, reevaluated preconceived notions, and developed greater empathy for your child's journey. Now you're ready to take the next steps, equipped with deeper insight and a more open perspective. Now you're prepared to expand your focus beyond your immediate family. Now I invite you to consider the broader picture, recognizing the impact you can have on all transgender youth and society as a whole. It's time to channel your experiences and insights into advocating for systemic change and supporting the rights and well-being of all transgender individuals.

When you support your transgender child, you are not only impacting their life but also contributing to a broader societal shift toward a more just, free, and equitable world. Your acceptance and advocacy help create a more inclusive environment that benefits all transgender youth. As a vocal and visible ally, you can influence schools, workplaces, and communities to adopt more supportive policies and practices. Your actions can inspire other parents to embrace their children's identities, fostering a network of support that extends far beyond your family.

We are living in a time of significant political and social change. Laws are being proposed and passed that aim to limit the freedoms of transgender individuals, yet at the same time, the trans community is more visible, connected, and organized than ever before. Support systems are expanding, and there are more resources available for transgender people and their families. By the time this book is in your hands, the political landscape may look very different from today. Laws and policies affecting transgender rights can change rapidly, both for better or worse, and your actions will inevitably contribute to one direction or the other. You have the power to choose how you'll support your child and the broader community as these changes unfold.

To help you be part of the change, this book will be accompanied by a dedicated web page providing up-to-date information and resources to equip you with the tools needed to be an effective advocate. This page, located in Additional Resources at the end of the book, is designed to be a living document, reflecting the latest developments in transgender rights, and offering actionable steps to support not only your child but the broader transgender community. Whether it's contacting legislators, participating in community events, or educating others, you'll have easy access to the resources you need to make a meaningful impact.

Supporting transgender youth goes beyond individual families; it's about building a more just and equitable society. Advocacy can also be a powerful way to strengthen your relationships with your child, partner, family, and friends. By showing up together—whether contacting legislators, participating in community events, or simply having conversations—you not only advocate for transgender rights but also create deeper bonds with the people you care about, demonstrating your commitment to a more inclusive world.

## BUILDING BRIDGES

### The Chen Family's Role in Community Leadership

*Li and Wei Chen, first-generation immigrants from China, lived in a diverse suburban neighborhood with their two children. Their youngest,*

*Alex, came out as nonbinary at sixteen. The Chens, deeply rooted in their cultural traditions, initially struggled to understand Alex's identity. Determined to support their child, Li and Wei embarked on a journey of learning and growth. They sought resources in both English and Chinese, trying to bridge the gap between their cultural background and their child's identity. However, the available Chinese-language resources were sparse, making the process even more challenging.*

*Recognizing this gap, the Chens decided to take action and become a resource for other Chinese American families. They began by hosting informal gatherings at their home, where other parents of LGBTQ+ youth could share experiences and provide mutual support. What started as small, intimate conversations over tea quickly grew into a formal support group for Asian American families with transgender children.*

*Wei, a software engineer, took the lead in developing a bilingual website that provided both English and Chinese materials on gender identity, family resources, and personal stories. He spent months translating key materials, including articles and guides, and even reached out to experts to ensure the translations were culturally sensitive and accurate. His site featured a section of personal testimonies from parents like him, hoping to normalize these discussions within Chinese communities.*

*Meanwhile, Li, a teacher, faced her own challenges in advocating for LGBTQ+ inclusivity in her classroom. She began by adding LGBTQ+-inclusive books to her curriculum, introducing stories like* Julian Is a Mermaid *and* Red: A Crayon's Story*. She incorporated discussions about diverse families and identities into lessons on empathy and social justice. Additionally, Li faced some resistance when she displayed a small Pride flag in her classroom, sparking conversations among her colleagues and students alike. Despite pushback, she received support from her school administration, who encouraged her to continue her work in fostering an inclusive environment.*

*The Chens didn't stop there. They became active participants in local Pride events, marching with signs that read "Proud Asian Parents" in both English and Chinese. Their presence provided a visible example of Asian American parents embracing and advocating for their LGBTQ+ child, and their story became a source of inspiration for others.*

*One of their biggest challenges came when they decided to share Alex's journey with their extended family in China. Wei and Li carefully crafted a letter, explaining Alex's identity and the importance of supporting them. While some family members reacted with confusion or disapproval, others expressed gratitude for the education and support. Wei recalled an emotional phone call with his mother, who said, "I don't fully understand, but I love Alex, and I want to learn."*

*The family's advocacy reached new heights when they were invited to speak at a national conference for educators about supporting LGBTQ+ students from diverse cultural backgrounds. At the event, they shared a personal story of how Alex's nonbinary identity initially clashed with traditional Chinese gender roles during family gatherings and how, through trial and error, they found ways to honor their heritage while respecting Alex's identity, such as creating a gender-neutral Lunar New Year celebration. Their story resonated with the audience, many of whom were struggling with similar cultural intersections in their classrooms.*

*At home, the Chens continued to support Alex's journey, learning to use gender-neutral pronouns in both English and Chinese—a linguistic challenge they embraced with patience. Together, they explored ways to incorporate both Chinese traditions and Alex's identity, adapting rituals like ancestor worship and family celebrations to be more inclusive.*

*Over time, the Chen's saw the impact of their efforts. Chinese American families from across the country reached out for guidance, and their translated resources were shared widely in community groups. They even received emails from families in China, thanking them for providing access to information that was difficult to find in their country. Wei and Li had become pioneers in bridging cultural and gender-diverse identities, proving that acceptance and tradition can coexist. The Chen family's journey from confusion to acceptance to active advocacy demonstrated the power of cultural bridge-building and the importance of specific, diverse voices in the LGBTQ+ rights movement.*

Consider the broader implications of your advocacy. When schools implement inclusive policies, it creates a safer environment for all students. When workplaces adopt nondiscriminatory practices, it opens opportunities for everyone to thrive. When healthcare systems provide comprehensive care, it ensures that all individuals receive the support they need. Your efforts can help dismantle systemic barriers and secure equal rights and opportunities and promote a culture of acceptance and equality.

## TAKING ACTION: 5 PRACTICAL STEPS FOR ADVOCACY

1. **Stay Informed:** Regularly check the dedicated web page for updates on laws, policies, and advocacy opportunities. Knowledge is power, and staying informed is the first step in effective activism.

2. **Get Involved Locally:** Find and join or support local organizations that advocate for transgender rights. Attend school board meetings, participate in community forums, and volunteer your time to causes that support LGBTQ+ youth. Local elections are particularly important, as they're often the first line of defense against efforts to pack school boards with anti-LGBTQ+ agendas. These elections can come down to just a few votes, meaning your participation can have a truly transformative impact. Make sure your voice is heard and vote in every local election.

3. **Educate Others:** Use your experience and knowledge to educate friends, family, and community members. Share resources, organize workshops, or simply engage in conversations that challenge misconceptions and promote understanding.

4. **Support Legislation:** Advocate for laws and policies that protect and empower transgender individuals. Contact your representatives, sign petitions, and participate in advocacy campaigns. Make sure to vote in both local and national elections, as these have a direct impact on the

rights and protections for LGBTQ+ communities. Your voice and vote can help shape a more inclusive society.

5. **Create Inclusive Spaces:** Work to make your child's school, extracurricular activities, and community spaces more inclusive. This can involve everything from ensuring proper use of pronouns and promoting visibility of trans narratives, to advocating for gender-neutral bathrooms.

## A VISION FOR THE FUTURE

Supporting transgender youth goes far beyond the bounds of the immediate family. It's about cultivating a society where every individual, regardless of gender identity, is treated with dignity, respect, and equal opportunity. By staying informed, actively engaging in advocacy, and championing inclusive policies, you can help build a world that is safer, more compassionate, and supportive for all. Your efforts hold the power to create meaningful change—cultivating a community that not only values diversity but also actively uplifts and protects its most vulnerable members.

While you may have originally picked up this book because you were specifically concerned about your own child, you are now ready to embrace and embody this more empowering belief:

---

"My support for my child ripples outward, creating positive change not just for our family, but for all trans individuals. By advocating for inclusivity and understanding, I am helping to build a more accepting world for everyone."

---

## KEY POINTS

**Expanded Focus:** Having navigated personal challenges, you're now prepared to consider your broader impact on all transgender youth and society. This change in perspective allows you to use your experiences to create positive change beyond your immediate family.

**Societal Shift:** Your support contributes to creating a more inclusive environment for all transgender individuals. By openly supporting your child, you're helping to normalize acceptance and understanding in your community, which can have far-reaching effects.

**Advocacy Role:** Becoming vocal allies can influence schools, workplaces, and communities to adopt more supportive policies. Your personal experiences and insights can be powerful tools in educating others and pushing for systemic changes that benefit all transgender individuals.

**Political Awareness:** Staying informed about rapidly changing laws and policies affecting transgender rights is crucial. The political landscape surrounding transgender issues is complex and ever evolving, making it essential for advocates to stay up-to-date and ready to act. And most importantly—vote! Your vote has the power to shape the future and protect the rights of transgender individuals. Every election, whether local or national, plays a pivotal role in building a more inclusive society.

**Resource Availability:** A dedicated web page, which can be found in the back of the book, will provide up-to-date information and resources for effective advocacy. This tool can help you navigate the complexities of advocacy work and connect with other supporters and organizations. Be sure to share it with friends, family, and anyone interested in supporting transgender rights—together, we can make a larger impact.

**Systemic Change:** Supporting transgender youth extends to creating a more just and equitable society overall. Your efforts can contribute to dismantling systemic barriers and promoting a culture of acceptance and equality for all individuals, regardless of gender identity.

## REFLECTION QUESTIONS

1. How has your journey of supporting your transgender child prepared you to be an advocate for broader societal change?
2. What specific areas (e.g., schools, healthcare, legislation) do you feel most passionate about improving for transgender individuals?
3. How can you use your personal experiences to educate and influence others in your community?
4. What challenges do you anticipate in becoming a more vocal advocate, and how might you overcome them?
5. How can you involve your transgender child in advocacy efforts while respecting their privacy and comfort levels?

20

# WHAT'S NEXT FOR US?

**As you navigate** the complex and often challenging journey of raising a transgender or gender-diverse child, it's crucial to hold on to the empowering beliefs that have guided you this far. These beliefs will serve as your anchor, providing stability and strength when things get rocky at home or within our ever-changing political landscape. This final chapter is a reminder to embrace these empowering truths and use them as a foundation for your continued support and advocacy.

## CELEBRATE EXPLORATION AND GROWTH

Every step your child takes in exploring their identity is a step toward growth. Celebrate their journey, fostering their confidence and supporting them as they navigate their unique path. Your unwavering support will empower them to explore their identity fully and without fear.

"I support my child's journey by celebrating exploration and fostering their confidence, supporting their growth in whatever direction it takes."

## CHERISHING PAST AND PRESENT

Balancing the memories of the past with a full embrace of your child's present identity can be challenging but essential. By cherishing both, you affirm that all parts of their journey matter and create a safe space for them to flourish.

"I have the capacity to cherish our shared past while fully acknowledging and affirming their present identity."

## AFFIRMATION AND BOUNDARIES

Supporting your child sometimes means letting go of relationships that don't align with your values. Affirm your commitment to your child's authenticity and protect them from those who may not offer the acceptance they deserve.

"I accept losing connections with those who do not support my child's authenticity, as it's essential to honor their true self and uphold our values."

## ACCESSING COMPETENT CARE

Trust in the availability of resources and care. By seeking out knowledgeable providers, you equip your child with the tools they need to thrive, both in their transition and in life.

"Resources and care are available, and I can find competent providers who can equip my child with the education and services they need to thrive."

## INCLUSIVE FEMINISM

By expanding your understanding of feminism to be inclusive of all gender identities, you honor your child's individuality and uphold the core values of equality and autonomy that allow them to thrive.

"By affirming my child's gender identity and embracing a more inclusive view of feminism, I uphold the true values of equality and autonomy, ensuring my child can thrive as their authentic self."

## EMBRACING GENDER'S FLUIDITY

Recognizing and celebrating the fluidity of gender is crucial. Support your child in expressing their identity authentically and without limitations, knowing that gender is an evolving journey for everyone.

"I embrace the belief that gender is expansive and fluid, and I celebrate and support the diverse expressions of identity."

## LOVE AND RELATIONSHIPS

Encourage your child to live their truth with confidence. The right people will love and accept them for exactly who they are, and living authentically will lead to fulfilling relationships.

"By living one's truth with confidence, trans and gender-expansive individuals can find partners who will love them for their whole authentic selves."

## HONORING SELF-AWARENESS

Recognize and honor your neurodivergent child's deep sense of self-awareness. Support their right to explore their identity fully, trusting in their unique capacity to know themselves deeply.

"As a parent of a neurodivergent transgender child, I recognize their profound capacity for self-awareness and honor their right to explore their identity fully."

## STANDING FIRM

It's not about what others think—it's about standing firm in support of your child. Value the opinions of those who respect your child's journey and let go of those who do not.

"I stand firm in supporting my child's true identity, valuing the respect of those who truly understand while ignoring the opinions of those who don't."

## OPENNESS TO LEARNING

No matter your initial reaction, you have the capacity to grow and shift your understanding. Being open to learning will strengthen your relationship with your child and help you support them more effectively.

"Whether or not this was a surprise, I can learn, shift my perspective, and support my child's identity."

## RESPECTING MEDICAL DECISIONS

Medical decisions are deeply personal. Trust in your child's ability to make informed choices and offer your respect and compassion as they navigate their path to affirming their gender.

"As a parent, I acknowledge my child's capacity to make informed medical decisions and will support their journey with respect and compassion."

## FACING FEARS

Facing your fears head-on is a testament to the unconditional love you have for your child. Strengthening your bond with them comes from confronting those fears and supporting them wholeheartedly.

"I support my child unconditionally, facing my fears and strengthening our bond."

## FOSTERING FUTURE CHOICES

By seeing your child for who they are today, you help create a foundation for the future. Your acceptance now will pave the way for them to make empowered choices throughout their life.

> "By genuinely acknowledging and accepting the child before me, I am better equipped to foster their future choices."

## EMBRACING MILESTONES

Many of the milestones you've envisioned for your child are just as attainable for transgender individuals. Support them in reaching those milestones, whether it's parenthood, career success, or loving relationships.

> "I recognize that the milestones that hold significance for me are increasingly attainable for trans individuals."

## MOVING FORWARD

As you reach the final pages of this book, take a moment to reflect on the profound journey you and your family have undertaken. The empowering beliefs and insights you've embraced are more than just guideposts; they are lifelines, helping you navigate the complexities, challenges, and uncertainties of raising a transgender or gender-diverse child. Remember to appreciate the journey itself, not just the destination—life is an ongoing experience of becoming, and every phase of this process is meaningful and beautiful. Hold these beliefs close, especially during the toughest moments, as they are reminders of the deep strength and resilience both you and your child possess.

While the political landscape may shift, and societal attitudes may ebb and flow, one thing remains constant: your unshakable commitment to your child's well-being and authenticity. By holding fast to these beliefs, you are not only affirming your child's right to live as their true self but also actively contributing to a more inclusive, compassionate world. Keep these affirmations close to your heart, especially in moments of doubt or fear. They stand as powerful testaments to your love, your fierce dedication, and your unwavering support for your child.

Now, as you reflect on how far you've come, I invite you to retake the self-assessment you completed at the beginning of this book. Let it serve as a marker of your growth, a celebration of the insights you've gained, and a reaffirmation of your purpose. This simple exercise can provide clarity and a renewed sense of strength as you continue walking this journey, hand in hand with your child.

Together, you can face any challenge and continue to build a future where your child, and all children, can live authentically and without fear.

Remember, you don't have to worry or wonder alone.

# EVER-EVOLVING GLOSSARY OF GENDER AND SEXUALITY TERMS

**advocate**

1 *noun:* a person who actively works to end intolerance, educate others, and support social equity for a marginalized group. 2 *verb:* to actively support or be in favor of a particular cause, the action of working to end intolerance or educate others.

**agender**

*adj.:* a person with no (or very little) connection to the traditional system of gender, no personal alignment with the concepts of either man or woman, and/or someone who sees themselves as existing without gender. Sometimes called gender neutrois, gender-neutral, or genderless.

**ally**

*noun:* a (typically straight and/or cisgender) person who supports and respects members of the LGBTQ+ community. We consider people to be active allies who take meaningful actions to show this support and respect.

**androgyny/androgynous**

1 *noun:* a gender expression that has elements of both masculinity and femininity. 2 *adj.:* occasionally used in place of "intersex" to describe a person with both female and male anatomy, generally in the form "androgyne."

**androsexual/androphilic**

*adj.:* being primarily sexually, romantically, and/or emotionally attracted to men, males, and/or masculinity.

### aromantic

*adj.:* experiencing little or no romantic attraction to others and/or having a lack of interest in romantic relationships/behavior. Aromanticism exists on a continuum from people who experience no romantic attraction or have any desire for romantic activities, to those who experience low levels or romantic attraction only under specific conditions. Many of these different places on the continuum have their own identity labels *(see demiromantic)*. Sometimes abbreviated to "aro" (pronounced "arrow").

### asexual

*adj.:* experiencing little or no sexual attraction to others and or a lack of interest in sexual relationships/behavior. Asexuality exists on a continuum from people who experience no sexual attraction or have any desire for sex, to those who experience low levels or sexual attraction only under specific conditions. Many of these different places on the continuum have their own identity labels *(see demisexual)*. Sometimes abbreviated to "ace."

### autigender

*adj.:* a term that some autistic people use to describe their unique relationship with gender. Lyric Holmans (they/them, xe/xem) defines autigender as "the relationship between being autistic and how that can influence and impact someone's relationship with their gender identity and their experience of gender."

### bicurious

*adj.:* a curiosity toward experiencing attraction to people of the same gender/ sex *(similar to questioning)*.

### bigender

*adj.:* a person who fluctuates between traditionally "woman" and "man" gender-based behavior and identities, identifying with two genders (or sometimes identifying with either man or woman, as well as a third, different gender).

### binder/binding

1 *noun:* an undergarment used to alter or reduce the appearance of one's breasts (worn similarly to how one wears a sports bra). 2 *verb:* the (sometimes daily) process of wearing a binder. Binding is often used to change the way others' read/perceive one's anatomical sex characteristics, and/or as a form of gender expression.

### biological sex

*noun:* a medical term used to refer to the chromosomal, hormonal, and anatomical characteristics that are used to classify an individual as female or male or intersex. Often referred to as simply "sex," "physical sex," "anatomical sex," or specifically as "sex assigned at birth."

### biphobia/biphobic

1 *noun:* a range of negative attitudes (e.g., fear, anger, intolerance, resentment, erasure, or discomfort) that one may have or express toward bisexual individuals. Biphobia can come from and be seen within the LGBTQ+ community as well as straight society. 2 *adj.:* a word used to describe actions, behaviors, or individuals who demonstrate elements of this range of negative attitudes toward bisexual people.

### bisexual

1 *noun/adj.:* a person who experiences attraction to some men and women. 2 *noun/adj.:* a person who experiences attraction to some people of their gender and another gender. Bisexual attraction does not have to be equally split or indicate a level of interest that is the same across the genders an individual may be attracted to. Can be shortened to "bi" (pronounced "bye"). Often used interchangeably with "pansexual."

### bottom surgery

*noun:* a gender-affirming surgical procedure that modifies the genitalia to align with a person's gender identity. For trans women and transfeminine individuals, this may include vaginoplasty or orchiectomy; for trans men and transmasculine individuals, it may include phalloplasty, metoidioplasty, or hysterectomy.

**butch**

*noun/adj.:* a person who identifies themselves as masculine, whether it be physically, mentally, or emotionally. "Butch" is sometimes used as a derogatory term for lesbians, but is also claimed as an affirmative identity label.

**cisgender**

*adj.:* a gender description for when someone's sex assigned at birth and gender identity correspond (e.g., someone who was assigned female at birth and identifies as a woman). A simple way to think about it is if a person is not transgender, they are cisgender. The word cisgender can also be shortened to "cis" (pronounced "siss").

**cishet**

*adj.:* a description for someone who is cisgender *(see definition)* and heterosexual.

**cisnormativity**

*noun:* the assumption, in individuals and in institutions, that everyone is cisgender and that cisgender identities are superior to trans* identities and people. Leads to invisibility of non-cisgender identities.

**cissaviorism**

*noun:* a cisgender mindset that transgender people need to be "helped" and "saved" instead of listened to. The actions may be taken as a result of a cis person's misplaced guilt toward the way society treats trans people.

**cissexism**

*noun:* behavior that grants preferential treatment to cisgender people, reinforces the idea that being cisgender is somehow better or more "right" than being transgender, and/or makes other genders invisible.

**closeted**

*adj.:* an individual who is not open to themselves or others about their (queer) sexuality or gender identity. This may be by choice and/or for other reasons such as fear for one's safety, peer or family rejection or disapproval, and/or loss of housing, job, etc. Also known as being "in the closet." When someone chooses to break this silence they "come out" of the closet *(see coming out)*.

### coming out

1 *noun:* the process by which one accepts and/or comes to identify one's own sexuality or gender identity (to "come out" to oneself). 2 *verb:* the process by which one shares one's sexuality or gender identity with others.

### cross-dresser

*noun:* someone who wears clothes typically attributed to another gender.

### demiromantic

*adj.:* little or no capacity to experience romantic attraction until a strong emotional or sexual connection is formed with someone, often within a sexual relationship.

### demisexual

*adj.:* little or no capacity to experience sexual attraction until a strong emotional or romantic connection is formed with someone, often within a romantic relationship.

### down low

*adj.:* typically referring to men who identify as straight but who secretly have sex with men. Down low (or DL) originated in, and is most commonly used by, communities of color.

### drag king

*noun:* someone who performs masculinity theatrically.

### drag queen

*noun:* someone who performs femininity theatrically.

**dyke**

*noun:* referring to a masculine-presenting lesbian. While often used derogatorily, it is also reclaimed affirmatively by some lesbians and gay women as a positive self-identity term.

**emotional attraction**

*noun:* a capacity that evokes the want to engage in emotionally intimate behavior (e.g., sharing, confiding, trusting, interdepending), experienced in varying degrees (from little-to-none to intense). Often conflated with sexual attraction, romantic attraction, and/or spiritual attraction.

**fag(got)**

*noun:* a derogatory term referring to a gay person or someone perceived as queer. While often used derogatorily, it is also reclaimed by some gay people (often gay men) as a positive in-group term.

**feminine-of-center; masculine-of-center**

*adj.:* a phrase that indicates a range in terms of gender identity and expression for people who present, understand themselves, and/or relate to others in a generally more feminine/masculine way but don't necessarily identify as women or men. Feminine-of-center individuals may also identify as "femme," or "transfeminine"; masculine-of-center individuals may also identify as "butch," "stud," "boi," "transmasculine," etc.

**feminine-presenting; masculine-presenting**

*adj.:* a way to describe someone who expresses gender in a more feminine/masculine way. Often confused with feminine-of-center/masculine-of-center, which generally include a focus on identity as well as expression.

**femme**

*noun/adj.:* someone who identifies themselves as feminine, whether it be physically, mentally, or emotionally. Often used to refer to a feminine-presenting queer woman or person.

### fluid(ity)

*adj.:* generally with another term attached, like gender-fluid or fluid sexuality, fluid(ity) describes an identity that may change or shift over time between or within the mix of the options available.

### FtM/F2M; MtF/M2F

*abbr.:* female-to-male transgender person; male-to-female transgender person.

### gay

1 *adj.:* experiencing attraction solely (or primarily) to some members of the same gender. Can be used to refer to men who are attracted to other men and women who are attracted to women. 2 *adj.:* an umbrella term used to refer to the queer community as a whole or as an individual identity label for anyone who is not straight *(see LGBTQ and queer).*

### gender binary

*noun:* the socially constructed idea that there are only two genders and that every person is one of those two.

### gender-expansive

*adj.:* an umbrella term sometimes used to describe people who expand notions of gender expression and identity beyond perceived or expected societal gender norms.

### gender expression

*noun:* the external display of one's gender through a combination of clothing, grooming, demeanor, social behavior, and other factors, generally made sense of on scales of masculinity and femininity. Also referred to as "gender presentation."

### gender-fluid

*adj.:* refers to someone who experiences fluctuations in their gender expression or gender identity or both.

### gender identity

*noun:* the internal perception of one's gender and how they label themselves, based on how much they align or don't align with what they understand their options for gender to be. Often conflated with biological sex, or sex assigned at birth.

### gender neutrois

*adj.: see agender*

### gender nonconforming

1 *adj.:* a gender expression descriptor that indicates a nontraditional gender presentation (masculine woman or feminine man). 2 *adj.:* a gender identity label that indicates a person who identifies outside of the gender binary. Often abbreviated as "GNC."

### gender normative

*adj.:* someone whose gender presentation, whether by nature or by choice, aligns with society's gender-based expectations.

### genderqueer

1 *adj.:* a gender identity label often used by people who do not identify with the binary of man/woman. 2 *adj.:* an umbrella term for many gender nonconforming or nonbinary identities (e.g., agender, bigender, gender-fluid).

### gender variant

*adj.:* someone who either by nature or by choice does not conform to gender-based expectations of society (e.g., transgender, transsexual, intersex, genderqueer, cross-dresser, etc.).

### gynesexual/gynephilic

*adj.:* being primarily sexually, romantically, and/or emotionally attracted to women, females, and/or femininity.

### hermaphrodite

*noun:* an outdated medical term previously used to refer to someone who was born with some combination of typically male and typically female sex characteristics. It's considered stigmatizing and inaccurate (*see intersex*).

### heteronormativity

*noun:* the assumption, in individuals and/or in institutions, that everyone is heterosexual and that heterosexuality is superior to all other sexualities. Leads to invisibility and stigmatizing of other sexualities: when learning a woman is married, asking her what her husband's name is. Heteronormativity also leads us to assume that only masculine men and feminine women are straight.

### heterosexism

*noun:* behavior that grants preferential treatment to heterosexual people, reinforces the idea that heterosexuality is somehow better or more "right" than queerness, and/or makes other sexualities invisible.

### heterosexual/straight

*adj.:* experiencing attraction solely (or primarily) to some members of a different gender.

### homophobia/homophobic

1 *noun:* an umbrella term for a range of negative attitudes (e.g., fear, anger, intolerance, resentment, erasure, or discomfort) that one may have toward LGBTQ+ people. The term can also connote a fear, disgust, or dislike of being perceived as LGBTQ+. 2 *adj.:* a word used to describe actions, behaviors, or individuals who demonstrate elements of this range of negative attitudes toward LGBTQ+ people.

### homosexual

*noun/adj.:* a person primarily emotionally, physically, and/or sexually attracted to members of the same sex/gender. This [medical] term is considered stigmatizing (particularly as a noun) due to its history as a category of mental illness and is discouraged for common use (use gay or lesbian instead).

### intersex

*adj.:* term for a combination of chromosomes, gonads, hormones, internal sex organs, and genitals that differs from the two expected patterns of male or female. Formerly known as hermaphrodite (or hermaphroditic); these terms are now outdated and derogatory.

### lesbian

*noun/adj.:* non-men who are primarily attracted romantically, erotically, and/or emotionally to other non-men.

### LGBTQ+; GSM; DSG; TGNC

*abbr.:* shorthand or umbrella terms for all folks who have a non-normative (or queer) gender or sexuality, there are many different initialisms people prefer. LGBTQ is Lesbian Gay Bisexual Transgender and Queer and/or Questioning (sometimes people add a + at the end in an effort to be more inclusive); GSM is Gender and Sexual Minorities; DSG is Diverse Sexualities and Genders; TGNC is Transgender and Gender Nonconforming (sometimes you'll see "NB" added for nonbinary). Other options include the initialisms GLBT, LGBT, or TLBG, or the acronym QUILTBAG (Queer [or Questioning] Undecided Intersex Lesbian Trans* Bisexual Asexual [or Allied] and Gay [or Genderqueer]). When a "P" is included, it usually means pansexual; an "I" generally represents intersex. There is no "correct" or "official" initialism to represent everyone who is queer or LGBTQ+. If you're unsure of which one to use, defer to your local community.

### lipstick lesbian

*noun:* usually refers to a lesbian with a feminine gender expression. Can be used in a positive or a derogatory way. Is sometimes also used to refer to a lesbian who is assumed to be (or passes for) straight.

### metrosexual

*adj.:* a man with a strong aesthetic sense who spends more time, energy, or money on his appearance and grooming than is considered gender normative.

### MSM/WSW

*abbr.:* men who have sex with men or women who have sex with women, to distinguish sexual behaviors from sexual identities: because a man is straight, it doesn't mean he's not having sex with men. Often used in the field of HIV/AIDS education, prevention, and treatment.

### Mx.

*noun:* an honorific (e.g., Mr., Ms., Mrs., etc.) that is gender-neutral. It is often the option of choice for folks who do not identify within the gender binary: Mx. Smith is a great teacher.

### neopronoun

*noun:* a type of gender-neutral pronoun, coined after 1800 and used especially by nonbinary and genderqueer people, as in English *ze/hir/hirs, e/em/eirs,* or *xe/xem/xyrs.*

### nonbinary

*adj.:* a gender identity label used by some people who do not identify with the binary of man/woman. Alternatively spelled "non-binary." Often abbreviated as "enby" or "enbie" (based on the pronunciation of N-B) *(see genderqueer).*

### neuroqueer

1. *noun*: a term used to describe individuals whose identity, selfhood, gender performance, and/or neurocognitive style has been shaped by their engagement in practices of neuroqueering, highlighting the unique ways individuals may experience and express neurodivergence, gender, and sexuality. The term reflects the intersection of neurodivergence and queerness, and is not limited to any particular identity or diagnosis. 2. *verb*: to neuroqueer is to engage in practices—conscious or unconscious—that challenge dominant norms around neurotypicality and cisheteronormativity, reshaping one's ways of being, knowing, and relating to self and others. Neuroqueering is not restricted by gender identity, sexual orientation, or neurotype.

### outing

*verb:* involuntary or unwanted disclosure of another person's sexual orientation, gender identity, or intersex status.

### pansexual

*adj.:* a person who experiences sexual, romantic, physical, and/or spiritual attraction for members of all gender identities/expressions. Often shortened to "pan."

### passing

1 *adj./verb:* trans people being accepted as, or able to "pass for," a member of their self-identified gender identity (regardless of sex assigned at birth) without being identified as trans. 2 *adj.:* an LGB/queer individual who is believed to be or perceived as straight.

### polyamory/polyamorous

*noun:* refers to the practice of, desire for, or orientation toward having ethical, honest, and consensual nonmonogamous relationships, which may include multiple partners. Often shortened to "poly," this relationship style is not specific to transgender individuals but is included here for educational purposes, as it is becoming increasingly common across diverse communities. Understanding polyamory can help broaden perspectives on relationship dynamics and inclusivity.

### queer

1 *adj.:* an umbrella term to describe individuals who don't identify as straight and/or cisgender. 2 *noun:* a slur used to refer to someone who isn't straight and/or cisgender. Due to its historical use as a derogatory term, and how it is still used as a slur in many communities, it is not embraced or used by all LGBTQ+ people. The term "queer" can often be used interchangeably with LGBTQ+ (e.g., "queer people" instead of "LGBTQ+ people").

### questioning

*verb/adj.:* an individual who or time when someone is unsure about or exploring their own sexual orientation or gender identity.

### QPOC/QTPOC

*abbr.:* initialisms that stand for queer people of color and queer and/or trans people of color.

### romantic attraction

*noun:* a capacity that evokes the want to engage in romantic intimate behavior (e.g., dating, relationships, marriage), experienced in varying degrees (from little-to-none to intense). Often conflated with sexual attraction, emotional attraction, and/or spiritual attraction.

### same-gender loving (SGL)

*adj.:* sometimes used by some members of the Black community to express a non-straight sexual orientation without relying on terms and symbols of European descent.

### sex assigned at birth (SAAB)

*abbr.:* a phrase used to intentionally recognize a person's assigned sex (not gender identity). Sometimes called "designated sex at birth" (DSAB) or "sex coercively assigned at birth" (SCAB) or specifically used as "assigned male at birth" (AMAB) or "assigned female at birth" (AFAB): Jenny was assigned male at birth but identifies as a woman.

### sexual attraction

*noun:* a capacity that evokes the want to engage in physically intimate behavior (e.g., kissing, touching, intercourse), experienced in varying degrees (from little-to-none to intense). Often conflated with romantic attraction, emotional attraction, and/or spiritual attraction.

### sexual orientation

*noun:* the type of sexual, romantic, emotional/spiritual attraction one has the capacity to feel for some others, generally labeled based on the gender relationship between the person and the people they are attracted to. Often confused with sexual preference.

### sexual preference

*noun:* the types of sexual intercourse, stimulation, and gratification one likes to receive and participate in. Generally when this term is used, it is being mistakenly interchanged with "sexual orientation," creating an illusion that one has a choice (or "preference") in who they are attracted to.

### sex reassignment surgery (SRS)

*noun:* used by some medical professionals to refer to a group of surgical options that alter a person's biological sex. "Gender affirmation surgery" is considered by many to be a more affirming term. In many cases, one or multiple surgeries are required to achieve legal recognition of gender. Some refer to different surgical procedures as "top" surgery and "bottom" surgery to discuss what type of surgery they are having without having to be more explicit.

### skoliosexual

*adj.:* being primarily sexually, romantically, and/or emotionally attracted to some genderqueer, transgender, transsexual, and/or nonbinary people.

### social transition

*adj.:* the social portion of a transition in which a person may tell people about their gender identity, change their name or pronouns, and/or change elements of their gender expression or presentation.

### spiritual attraction

*noun:* a capacity that evokes the want to engage in intimate behavior based on one's experience with, interpretation of, or belief in the supernatural (e.g., religious teachings, messages from a deity), experienced in varying degrees (from little-to-none to intense). Often conflated with sexual attraction, romantic attraction, and/or emotional attraction.

### stealth

*adj.:* a trans person who is not "out" as trans and is perceived/known by others as cisgender.

### straight

*adj.:* a person primarily emotionally, physically, and/or sexually attracted to some people who are not their same sex/gender. A more colloquial term for the word heterosexual.

### stud

*noun:* most commonly used to indicate a Black and Latine masculine, lesbian/queer woman. Also known as "butch."

### third gender

*noun:* for a person who does not identify with either man or woman but identifies with another gender. This gender category is used by societies that recognize three or more genders, both contemporary and historic, and is also a conceptual term meaning different things to different people who use it as a way to move beyond the gender binary.

### top surgery

*noun:* a gender-affirming surgical procedure that modifies the chest to align with a person's gender identity. It typically refers to the removal of breast tissue to create a more masculine chest for transgender men and some nonbinary individuals, but it can also include breast augmentation for transfeminine individuals.

### trans

*adj.:* an umbrella term covering a range of identities that transgress socially defined gender norms. Trans* with an asterisk is often used in written forms (not spoken) to indicate that you are referring to the larger group nature of the term, and specifically including nonbinary identities, as well as transgender men (trans men) and transgender women (trans women).

### transgender

*adj.:* an umbrella term for anyone whose sex assigned at birth and gender identity do not correspond (e.g., someone who was assigned male at birth but does not identify as a man).

### transition/transitioning

*noun/verb:* referring to the process of a transgender person changing aspects of themself (e.g., their appearance, name, pronouns) or making physical changes to their body to be more congruent with the gender they know themself to be (as opposed to the gender they lived as pre-transitioning). Some transition socially, medically, legally, or some combination thereof. Transition looks different for everyone!

### trans man; trans woman; trans person

*noun:* a person who was not assigned that gender via sex at birth and transitioned (socially, medically, and/or legally) from that assignment to their gender identity, signified by the second part of the term. Also referred to as men and women (though some/many trans people prefer to keep the modifier "trans" in their identity label).

### transmisia/transmisic

1 *noun*: a systemized discrimination or antagonism directed against trans/nonbinary/genderqueer/agender persons. 2 *adj.:* a word used to describe an individual who discriminates and antagonizes trans people (also called transantagonism).

### transphobia/transphobic

1 *noun:* the fear of, discrimination against, or hatred of trans* people, the trans* community, or gender ambiguity. Transphobia can be seen within the queer community, as well as in general society. 2 *adj.:* a word used to describe an individual who harbors some elements of this range of negative attitudes, thoughts, and/or intents toward trans* people.

### transsexual

*noun/adj.* a person who identifies as a gender/sex other than the one to which they were assigned at birth. Transsexual is not a term that is often used anymore but would be used to distinguish trans folks who had medically transitioned.

### tucking

*verb:* a practice used by some transgender women and nonbinary individuals to create a flatter appearance in the groin area. This involves moving the testicles up into the groin area and tucking the penis back between the legs. Various methods can be used to achieve this, including specialized underwear, tape, or tucking garments. Tucking can help alleviate gender dysphoria for some individuals by aligning their physical appearance with their gender identity.

### Two-Spirit

*noun:* refers to a person who identifies as having both a masculine and a feminine spirit, and is used by some Indigenous people to describe their sexual, gender, and/or spiritual identity. As an umbrella term, it may encompass same-sex attraction and a wide variety of gender variance, including people who might be described in Western culture as gay, lesbian, bisexual, transsexual, transgender, genderqueer, cross-dressers, or who have multiple gender identities. Two-Spirit can also include relationships that could be considered poly.

### ze/zir

neopronouns that are gender-neutral and preferred by some trans* people. They replace "he" and "she," and "his" and "hers," respectively. Alternatively some people who are not comfortable/do not embrace he/she use the plural pronoun "they/their" as a gender-neutral singular pronoun.

# BIBLIOGRAPHY


Abreu, Roberto L., Jules P. Sostre, Kirsten A. Gonzalez, Gabriel M. Lockett, Em Matsuno, and Della V. Mosley. "Impact of Gender-Affirming Care Bans on Transgender and Gender Diverse Youth: Parental Figures' Perspective." *Journal of Family Psychology* 36 (5), 643–52, 2022. https://doi.org/10.1037/fam0000987.

Aldridge, Z., N. Thorne, E. Marshall, et al. "Understanding Factors That Affect Wellbeing in Trans People 'Later' in Transition: A Qualitative Study." *Quality of Life Research* 31 (9), 2695–703, 2022. https://doi.org/10.1007/s11136-022-03134-x.

Anderson, Sloan Okrey, and Jenifer K. McGuire. "'I Feel Like God Doesn't Like Me': Faith and Ambiguous Loss Among Transgender Youth." *Family Relations* 70 (2), 390–401, 2021. https://doi.org/10.1111/fare.12536.

Andrzejewski, Jack, Sanjana Pampati, Riley J. Steiner, Lorin Boyce, and Michelle M. Johns. "Perspectives of Transgender Youth on Parental Support: Qualitative Findings from the Resilience and Transgender Youth Study." *Health Education & Behavior* 48 (1), 74–81, 2020. https://doi.org/10.1177/1090198120965504.

Ashley, Florence. "Thinking an Ethics of Gender Exploration: Against Delaying Transition for Transgender and Gender Creative Youth." *Clinical Child Psychology and Psychiatry* 24 (2), 223–36, 2019. https://doi.org/10.1177/1359104519836462.

Backhaus, Wibke. "Judith Butler: Gender Trouble. Feminism and the Subversion of Identity, Routledge: New York 1990, 172 S. (dt. Das Unbehagen der Geschlechter, Frankfurt: Suhrkamp 1991, 236 S.)." In *Klassiker der Sozialwissenschaften*. Springer VS, Wiesbaden, 2016. https://doi.org/10.1007/978-3-658-13213-2_87.

Baker, Kellan E., Lisa M. Wilson, Ritu Sharma, Vadim Dukhanin, Kristen McArthur, and Karen A. Robinson. "Hormone Therapy, Mental Health, and Quality of Life Among Transgender People: A Systematic Review." *Journal of the Endocrine Society* 5 (4), 2021. https://doi.org/10.1210/jendso/bvab011.

Bockting, Walter, Eli Coleman, Madeline B. Deutsch, et al. "Adult Development and Quality of Life of Transgender and Gender Nonconforming People." *Current Opinion in Endocrinology & Diabetes and Obesity* 23 (2), 188–97, 2016. https://doi.org/10.1097/med.0000000000000232.

Bosse, Jordan D., Kimberly A. Dion, Sally Campbell Galman, and Lisa M. Chiodo. "Transgender and Nonbinary Young Adults' Perception of Sibling and Parental

Support for Gender Identity." *Research in Nursing & Health* 45 (5), 569–79, 2022. https://doi.org/10.1002/nur.22251.

Bull, Brooke, and Justine D'Arrigo-Patrick. "Parent Experiences of a Child's Social Transition: Moving Beyond the Loss Narrative." *Journal of Feminist Family Therapy* 30 (3), 170–90, 2018. https://doi.org/10.1080/08952833.2018.1448965.

Bustos, Valeria P., Samyd S. Bustos, Andres Mascaro, et al. "Regret After Gender-Affirmation Surgery: A Systematic Review and Meta-Analysis of Prevalence." *Plastic and Reconstructive Surgery—Global Open* 9 (3), e3477, 2021. https://doi.org/10.1097/gox.0000000000003477.

Butler, Judith. *Gender Trouble*. Routledge Classics. London, England: Routledge, 2006.

Campbell, Olivia. "Why Gender Stereotypes in Kids' Shows Are A REALLY Big Deal." *Refinery29*, December 5, 2017. https://www.refinery29.com/en-us/kids-shows-gender-roles-stereotypes.

Catalpa, Jory M., and Jenifer K. McGuire. "Family Boundary Ambiguity Among Transgender Youth." *Family Relations* 67 (1), 88–103, 2018. https://doi.org/10.1111/fare.12304.

Capous-Desyllas, Moshoula, and Cecillia Barron. "Identifying and Navigating Social and Institutional Challenges of Transgender Children and Families." *Child and Adolescent Social Work Journal* 34, 527–42, 2017. https://doi.org/10.1007/s10560-017-0491-7.

Cheng, Philip J., Alexander W. Pastuszak, Jeremy B. Myers, Isak A. Goodwin, and James M. Hotaling. "Fertility Concerns of the Transgender Patient." *Translational Andrology and Urology* 8 (3), 209–18, 2019. https://doi.org/10.21037/tau.2019.05.09.

Choi, Young-Joon, and Ho Jong Ra. "Patient Satisfaction After Total Knee Arthroplasty." *Knee Surgery & Related Research* 28 (1), 1–15, 2016. https://doi.org/10.5792/ksrr.2016.28.1.1.

Cleveland Clinic. n.d. "Transgender Health & Gender Affirming Medical Services." https://my.clevelandclinic.org/about/community/lgbt-health/transgender-medical-services.

Cohen-Kettenis, Peggy T., and Friedemann Pfäfflin. "Transgenderism and Intersexuality in Childhood and Adolescence: Making Choices." SAGE Publications, 2003. https://doi.org/10.4135/9781452233628.

Coleman, E., A. E. Radix, W. P. Bouman, et al. "Standards of Care for the Health of Transgender and Gender Diverse People, Version 8." *International Journal of Transgender Health* 23 (sup1), S1–259, 2022. https://doi.org/10.1080/26895269.2022.2100644.

De Abreu, Paula Daniella, Rubia Laine de Paula Andrade, Israel Lucas da Silva Maza, Mariana Gaspar Botelho Funari de Faria, Jordana de Almeida Nogueira, and Aline Aparecida Monroe. "Dynamics of Primary Social Networks to Support Mothers, Fathers, or Guardians of Transgender Children and Adolescents: A Systematic

Review." *International Journal of Environmental Research and Public Health* 19 (13), 7941, 2022. https://doi.org/10.3390/ijerph19137941.

Durwood, Lily, Katie A. McLaughlin, and Kristina R. Olson. "Mental Health and Self-Worth in Socially Transitioned Transgender Youth." *Journal of the American Academy of Child & Adolescent Psychiatry* 56 (2), 116-123.E2, 2016. https://doi.org/10.1016/j.jaac.2016.10.016.

Elischberger, Holger B., Jessica J. Glazier, Eric D. Hill, and Lynn Verduzco-Baker. "'Boys Don't Cry'—or Do They? Adult Attitudes Toward and Beliefs About Transgender Youth." *Sex Roles* 75, 197–214, 2016. https://doi.org/10.1007/s11199-016-0609-y.

Etengoff, C., and C. Daiute. "Family Members' Uses of Religion in Post–Coming-Out Conflicts with Their Gay Relative." *Psychology of Religion and Spirituality* 6 (1), 33–43, 2014. https://psycnet.apa.org/doi/10.1037/a0035198.

Fast, Anne A., and Kristina R. Olson. "Gender Development in Transgender Preschool Children." *Child Development* 89 (2), 620–37, 2017. https://doi.org/10.1111/cdev.12758.

Fuller, Kimberly A., and Damien W. Riggs. "Intimate Relationship Strengths and Challenges Amongst a Sample of Transgender People Living in the United States." *Sexual and Relationship Therapy* 36 (4), 399–412, 2021. https://doi.org/10.1080/14681994.2019.1679765.

Garcia-Navarro, Lulu. "Woman Who Popularized Gender-Reveal Parties Says Her Views on Gender Have Changed." *NPR*, July 28, 2019. https://www.npr.org/2019/07/28/745990073/woman-who-popularized-gender-reveal-parties-says-her-views-on-gender-have-change.

GLAAD. "Medical Association Statements in Support of Health Care for Transgender People and Youth." 2023. https://glaad.org/medical-association-statements-supporting-trans-youth-healthcare-and-against-discriminatory/.

GLSEN. "The 2019 National School Climate Survey." Last modified November 20, 2020. https://www.glsen.org/research/2019-national-school-climate-survey.

Gottlieb, Jeremy. "Enacting Transgender: An Ethnography of Transgender Ontology in a Pediatric Gender Clinic." Honors thesis, Duke University, 2018. https://dukespace.lib.duke.edu/dspace/handle/10161/16613.

Graham, Philip. "Transgender Children and Young People: How the Evidence Can Point the Way Forward." *BJPsych Bulletin* 47 (2), 98–104, 2022. https://doi.org/10.1192/bjb.2022.3.

Gray, Sarah A. O., Kristen K. Sweeney, Renee Randazzo, and Heidi M. Levitt. "'Am I Doing the Right Thing?': Pathways to Parenting a Gender Variant Child." *Family Process* 55 (1), 123–38, 2015. https://doi.org/10.1111/famp.12128.

Gülgöz, Selin, Jessica J. Glazier, Elizabeth A. Enright, et al. "Similarity in Transgender and Cisgender Children's Gender Development." *Proceedings of the National*

*Academy of Sciences* 116 (49), 24480–85, 2019. https://doi.org/10.1073/pnas.1909367116.

Guss, Carly, and Catherine M. Gordon. "Pubertal Blockade and Subsequent Gender-Affirming Therapy." *JAMA Network Open* 5 (11), e2239763, 2022. https://doi.org/10.1001/jamanetworkopen.2022.39763.

Hasenbush, Amira, Andrew R. Flores, and Jody L. Herman. "Gender Identity Nondiscrimination Laws in Public Accommodations: A Review of Evidence Regarding Safety and Privacy in Public Restrooms, Locker Rooms, and Changing Rooms." *Sexuality Research and Social Policy* 16 (1), 70–83, 2018. https://doi.org/10.1007/s13178-018-0335-z.

Hassouri, Paria. "Op-Ed: What I Didn't Know About My Transgender Child." *Los Angeles Times*, July 19, 2019. https://www.latimes.com/opinion/story/2019-07-18/doctor-transgender-child-lgbtq-healthcare?.

Hatchel, Tyler, Gabriel J. Merrin, and Dorothy Espelage. "Peer Victimization and Suicidality Among LGBTQ Youth: The Roles of School Belonging, Self-Compassion, and Parental Support." *Journal of LGBT Youth* 16 (2), 134–56, 2016. https://doi.org/10.1080/19361653.2018.1543036.

Herzog, Katie. "Is the Life Expectancy of Trans Women in the U.S. Just 35? No." *The Stranger*, September 23, 2019. https://www.thestranger.com/slog/2019/09/23/41471629/is-the-life-expectancy-of-trans-women-in-the-us-just-35-no.

Heyam, Kit. *Before We Were Trans: A New History of Gender*. Seal Press, 2022.

Hidalgo, Marco A., and Diane Chen. "Experiences of Gender Minority Stress in Cisgender Parents of Transgender/Gender-Expansive Prepubertal Children: A Qualitative Study." *Journal of Family Issues* 40 (7), 865–86, 2019. https://doi.org/10.1177/0192513x19829502.

Hinchy, Jessica. *Governing Gender and Sexuality in Colonial India: The Hijra, c.1850–1900*. Cambridge University Press, 2019.

Hisle-Gorman, Elizabeth, Corinne A. Landis, Apryl Susi, et al. "Gender Dysphoria in Children with Autism Spectrum Disorder." *LGBT Health* 6 (3), 95–100, 2019. https://doi.org/10.1089/lgbt.2018.0252.

Holiday, Steven, Bradley J. Bond, and Eric E. Rasmussen. "Coming Attractions: Parental Mediation Responses to Transgender and Cisgender Film Trailer Content Targeting Adolescents." *Sexuality & Culture* 22 (4), 1154–70, 2018. https://doi.org/10.1007/s12119-018-9517-3.

Holmans, Lyric. "What Is AutiGender?—The Relationship Between Autism & Gender—An Autistic Perspective." *Neurodivergent Rebel*, January 6, 2021. https://neurodivergentrebel.com/2021/01/06/what-is-autigender-the-relationship-between-Autism-gender-an-Autistic-perspective/.

Holt, Martin, Timothy Broady, Denton Callander, et al. "Sexual Experience, Relationships, and Factors Associated with Sexual and Romantic Satisfaction in the First Australian Trans & Gender Diverse Sexual Health Survey." *International Journal of Transgender Health* 24 (1), 34–38, 2022. https://doi.org/10.1080/26895269.2021.2016540.

Horton, Cal. "'I Never Wanted Her to Feel Shame': Parent Reflections on Supporting a Transgender Child." *Journal of LGBT Youth* 20 (2), 231–47, 2021. https://doi.org/10.1080/19361653.2022.2034079.

Hudson, Janella, Leena Nahata, Elizabeth Dietz, and Gwendolyn P Quinn. "Fertility Counseling for Transgender AYAs." *Clinical Practice in Pediatric Psychology* 6 (1), 84–92, 2018. https://doi.org/10.1037/cpp0000180.

Human Rights Campaign. "Dismantling a Culture of Violence: Understanding Anti-Transgender Violence and Ending the Crisis." 2020. https://hrc-prod-requests.s3-us-west-2.amazonaws.com/files/assets/resources/Dismantling-a-Culture-of-Violence-010721.pdf.

James, S.E., J.L Herman, L.E. Durso, and R. Heng-Lehtinen. "Early Insights: A Report of the 2022 U.S. Transgender Survey." National Center for Transgender Equality, Washington, DC, 2024. https://www.queercme.com/blog/early-insights-from-the-u-s-trans-survey-2022.

Jedrzejewski, Breanna Y., Mary C. Marsiglio, Jess Guerriero, Amy Penkin, Kara J. Connelly, and Jens U. Berli. "Regret After Gender-Affirming Surgery: A Multidisciplinary Approach to a Multifaceted Patient Experience." *Plastic and Reconstructive Surgery* 152 (1), 206–14, 2023. https://doi.org/10.1097/prs.0000000000010243.

Johnson, Susan L., and Kristen E. Benson. "'It's Always the Mother's Fault': Secondary Stigma of Mothering a Transgender Child." *Journal of GLBT Family Studies* 10 (1–2), 124–44, 2014. https://doi.org/10.1080/1550428x.2014.857236.

Kay, April, Brenda Davison, Elizabeth Badley, and Susan Wagstaff. "Hip Arthroplasty: Patient Satisfaction." *Rheumatology* 22 (4), 243–49, 1983. https://doi.org/10.1093/rheumatology/22.4.243.

Vanderbilt University Medical Center. "Key Transgender Health Concerns." Program for LGBTQ Health, 2012. https://www.vumc.org/lgbtq/key-transgender-health-concerns.

Kolbuck, Victoria D., Abigail L. Muldoon, Karen Rychlik, Marco A. Hidalgo, and Diane Chen. "Psychological Functioning, Parenting Stress, and Parental Support Among Clinic-Referred Prepubertal Gender-Expansive Children." *Clinical Practice in Pediatric Psychology* 7 (3), 254–66, 2019. https://doi.org/10.1037/cpp0000293.

Littman, Lisa. "Correction: Parent Reports of Adolescents and Young Adults Perceived to Show Signs of a Rapid Onset of Gender Dysphoria." *PLOS ONE* 14 (3), e0214157, 2019. https://doi.org/10.1371/journal.pone.0214157.

Littman, Lisa. "Parent Reports of Adolescents and Young Adults Perceived to Show Signs of a Rapid Onset of Gender Dysphoria." *PLOS ONE*, 2018. https://doi.org/10.1371/journal.pone.0202330.

Lemish, Dafna, and Colleen Russo Johnson. "The Landscape of Children's Television in the US & Canada." Center for Scholars & Storytellers, 2019.

Lorber, Judith. "The Social Construction of Gender." *The Inequality Reader*, April, 318–25, 2018. https://doi.org/10.4324/9780429494468-36.

Malpas, Jean, Michael J. Pellicane, and Elizabeth Glaeser. "Family-Based Interventions with Transgender and Gender Expansive Youth: Systematic Review and Best Practice Recommendations." *Transgender Health* 7 (1), 7–29, 2022. https://doi.org/10.1089/trgh.2020.0165.

Marshall, Ellen, Cris Glazebrook, Sally Robbins-Cherry, Serge Nicholson, Nat Thorne, and Jon Arcelus. "The Quality and Satisfaction of Romantic Relationships in Transgender People: A Systematic Review of the Literature." *International Journal of Transgender Health* 21 (4), 373–90, 2020. https://doi.org/10.1080/26895269.2020.1765446.

Marshall, Kravitz. "The Gender Binary Is a Tool of White Supremacy." *Medium*, June 18, 2020. https://aninjusticemag.com/the-gender-binary-is-a-tool-of-white-supremacy-db89d0bc9044.

Martinez, Dawn Belkin, and Ann Fleck-Henderson. *Social Justice in Clinical Practice: A Liberation Health Framework for Social Work*. Routledge, 2014.

Martinez, M. Anais, Alisha Osornio, May Ling D. Halim, and Kristina M. Zosuls. "Gender: Awareness, Identity, and Stereotyping." In *Encyclopedia of Infant and Early Childhood Development (Second Edition)*, edited by Janette B. Benson. Elsevier eBooks, 2020. https://doi.org/10.1016/b978-0-12-809324-5.21818-x.

Mayo Clinic. "Puberty Blockers for Transgender and Gender-Diverse Youth." Effective June 14, 2023. https://www.mayoclinic.org/diseases-conditions/gender-dysphoria/in-depth/pubertal-blockers/art-20459075.

Mayo Clinic. "Health Concerns for Transgender People." Effective March 7, 2024. https://www.mayoclinic.org/healthy-lifestyle/adult-health/in-depth/transgender-health/art-20154721.

McGregor, Kerry, John L. McKenna, Coleen R. Williams, Ellis P. Barrera, and Elizabeth R. Boskey. "Association of Pubertal Blockade at Tanner 2/3 with Psychosocial Benefits in Transgender and Gender Diverse Youth at Hormone Readiness Assessment." *The Journal of Adolescent Health: Official Publication of the Society for Adolescent Medicine*, S1054-139X(23)005608, 2024. https://doi.org/10.1016/j.jadohealth.2023.10.028.

Mills-Koonce, W. Roger, Peter D. Rehder, and Amy L. McCurdy. "The Significance of Parenting and Parent-Child Relationships for Sexual and Gender Minority

Adolescents." *Journal of Research on Adolescence* 28 (3), 637–49, 2018. https://doi.org/10.1111/jora.12404.

Miseo, Mel Constantine. "Grieving the Transgender (Assumed-Cisgender) Child: What Gendered Mourning Among Midwestern Parents Tells Us About Familial Cisnormativity and Creating Livable Trans Futures." *Bulletin of Applied Transgender Studies* 1 (3–4), 211–33, 2022. https://doi.org/10.57814/e4gh-9q03.

Movement Advancement Project. "Bans on Best Practice Medical Care for Transgender Youth." Last modified December 10, 2024. https://www.lgbtmap.org/equality-maps/healthcare/youth_medical_care_bans.

Movement Advancement Project. "Snapshot: LGBTQ Equality by State." Last modified December 10, 2024. https://www.lgbtmap.org/equality-maps.

NAEYC. n.d. "What the Research Says: Gender-Typed Toys." Accessed December 13, 2024. https://www.naeyc.org/resources/topics/play/gender-typed-toys.

Nagoski, Emily, and Amelia Nagoski. *Burnout: The Secret to Unlocking the Stress Cycle*. Ballantine Books, 2019.

National Center for Transgender Equality; Gay & Lesbian Advocates & Defenders. n.d. "Marriage Equality and Transgender People." Accessed December 20, 2024. https://transequality.org/sites/default/files/docs/resources/NCTEMarriageFAQ_Z-Fold_0.pdf.

Newcomb, Michael E., Brian A. Feinstein, Margaret Matson, Kathryn Macapagal, and Brian Mustanski. "'I Have No Idea What's Going On Out There:' Parents' Perspectives on Promoting Sexual Health in Lesbian, Gay, Bisexual, and Transgender Adolescents." *Sexuality Research and Social Policy* 15 (2), 111–22, 2018. https://doi.org/10.1007/s13178-018-0326-0.

Nobili, Anna, Cris Glazebrook, and Jon Arcelus. "Quality of Life of Treatment-Seeking Transgender Adults: A Systematic Review and Meta-Analysis." *Reviews in Endocrine and Metabolic Disorders* 19 (3), 199–220, 2018. https://doi.org/10.1007/s11154-018-9459-y.

Norwood, Kristen. "Grieving Gender: Trans-Identities, Transition, and Ambiguous Loss." *Communication Monographs* 80 (1), 24–45, 2012. https://doi.org/10.1080/03637751.2012.739705.

Nos, Andrea L., David A. Klein, Terry A. Adirim, et al. "Association of Gonadotropin-Releasing Hormone Analogue Use with Subsequent Use of Gender-Affirming Hormones Among Transgender Adolescents." *JAMA Network Open* 5 (11), e2239758, 2022. https://doi.org/10.1001/jamanetworkopen.2022.39758.

Olson, Kristina R., and Selin Gülgöz. "Early Findings from the TransYouth Project: Gender Development in Transgender Children." *Child Development Perspectives* 12 (2), 93–97, 2017. https://doi.org/10.1111/cdep.12268.

Olson, Kristina R., Lily Durwood, Rachel Horton, Natalie M. Gallagher, and Aaron Devor. "Gender Identity 5 Years After Social Transition." *PEDIATRICS* 150 (2), e2021056082, 2022. https://doi.org/10.1542/peds.2021-056082.

Olson, Kristina R., Lily Durwood, Madeleine DeMeules, and Katie A. McLaughlin. "Mental Health of Transgender Children Who Are Supported in Their Identities." *PEDIATRICS* 137 (3), e20153223, 2016. https://doi.org/10.1542/peds.2015-3223.

Parker-Pope, Tara. "Regrets After Prostate Surgery." *Well*, August 27, 2008. https://archive.nytimes.com/well.blogs.nytimes.com/2008/08/27/regrets-after-prostate-surgery/.

Payne, Jenny Gunnarsson, and Theo Erbenius. "Conceptions of Transgender Parenthood in Fertility Care and Family Planning in Sweden: From Reproductive Rights to Concrete Practices." *Anthropology & Medicine* 25 (3), 329–43, 2018. https://doi.org/10.1080/13648470.2018.1507485.

Price, Myeshia N., and Amy E. Green. "Association of Gender Identity Acceptance with Fewer Suicide Attempts Among Transgender and Nonbinary Youth." *Transgender Health* 8 (1), 56–63, 2023. https://doi.org/10.1089/trgh.2021.0079.

Priest, Maura. "Transgender Children and the Right to Transition: Medical Ethics When Parents Mean Well but Cause Harm." *The American Journal of Bioethics* 19 (2), 45–59, 2019. https://doi.org/10.1080/15265161.2018.1557276.

Rae, James R., Selin Gülgöz, Lily Durwood, et al. "Predicting Early-Childhood Gender Transitions." *Psychological Science* 30 (5), 669–81, 2019. https://doi.org/10.1177/0956797619830649.

Reczek, Rin, and Emma Bosley⊠Smith. "How LGBTQ Adults Maintain Ties with Rejecting Parents: Theorizing 'Conflict Work' as Family Work." *Journal of Marriage and Family* 83 (4), 1134–53, 2021. https://doi.org/10.1111/jomf.12765.

Riley, Elizabeth Anne, Lindy Clemson, Gomathi Sitharthan, and Milton Diamond. "Surviving a Gender-Variant Childhood: The Views of Transgender Adults on the Needs of Gender-Variant Children and Their Parents." *Journal of Sex & Marital Therapy* 39 (3), 241–63, 2013. https://doi.org/10.1080/0092623x.2011.628439.

Rodsky, Eve. *Fair Play: A Game-Changing Solution for When You Have Too Much to Do (and More Life to Live)*. Penguin Random House, 2021.

Russell, Stephen T., Amanda M. Pollitt, Gu Li, and Arnold H. Grossman. "Chosen Name Use Is Linked to Reduced Depressive Symptoms, Suicidal Ideation, and Suicidal Behavior Among Transgender Youth." *Journal of Adolescent Health* 63 (4), 503–5, 2018. https://doi.org/10.1016/j.jadohealth.2018.02.003.

Sansfaçon, Annie Pullen, Denise Medico, Morgane Gelly, Valeria Kirichenko, and Frank Suerich-Gulick. "Blossoming Child, Mourning Parent: A Qualitative Study of Trans Children and Their Parents Navigating Transition." *Journal of Child and Family Studies* 31 (7), 1771–84, 2022. https://doi.org/10.1007/s10826-021-02178-w.

Schlehofer, Michèle M., Lori Cortez-Regan, and Domonique Bush. "Experiences of Parent-Advocates of Trans and Gender Non-Conforming Youth." *Journal of GLBT Family Studies* 17 (5), 450–469, 2021. https://doi.org/10.1080/1550428X.2021.1902447.

Schlehofer, Michèle M., Lori Cortez-Regan, and Jessica Harbaugh. "'If Extended Family Can't Deal . . .' Disclosing Trans and Gender Non-Conforming Children's Identity." *Child and Adolescent Social Work Journal* 39 (1), 29–43, 2020. https://doi.org/10.1007/s10560-020-00709-w.

Seo, Hannah. "First-of-a-Kind Study Shows Encouraging Data for Trans Kids Who Socially Transition." *Popular Science*, May 5, 2022. https://www.popsci.com/science/transgender-children-gender-identity/.

Simons, Lisa, Sheree M. Schrager, Leslie F. Clark, Marvin Belzer, and Johanna Olson. "Parental Support and Mental Health Among Transgender Adolescents." *Journal of Adolescent Health* 53 (6), 791–93, 2013. https://doi.org/10.1016/j.jadohealth.2013.07.019.

Smothers, Hannah. "Hm, No One Had a Problem With Puberty Blockers When Only Cis Kids Took Them." *VICE*, July 27, 2024. https://www.vice.com/en/article/no-one-had-a-problem-with-puberty-blockers-when-only-cis-kids-took-them/.

Snorton, C. Riley. *Black on Both Sides: A Racial History of Trans Identity*. University of Minnesota Press, 2017.

Steyer, Isabella. "Gender Representations in Children's Media and Their Influence." *Campus-Wide Information Systems* 31 (2/3), 171–80, 2014. https://doi.org/10.1108/cwis-11-2013-0065.

St. James, Emily. "What's So Scary About a Transgender Child?" *Vox*, September 29, 2022. https://www.vox.com/policy-and-politics/23281683/trans-kids-transition-medicine-surgery.

Talusan, Meredith. "Celebrate Your Kid's Transition. Don't Grieve It." *New York Times*, October 18, 2019. https://www.nytimes.com/2019/10/18/opinion/sunday/gender-transition-death-grief.html.

Tasker, Fiona, and Jorge Gato. "Gender Identity and Future Thinking About Parenthood: A Qualitative Analysis of Focus Group Data with Transgender and Non-Binary People in the United Kingdom." *Frontiers in Psychology* 11, 2020. https://doi.org/10.3389/fpsyg.2020.00865.

Testoni, Ines, and Manuela Anna Pinducciu. "Grieving Those Who Still Live: Loss Experienced by Parents of Transgender Children." *Gender Studies* 18 (1), 142–62, 2020. https://doi.org/10.2478/genst-2020-0011.

The Trevor Project. "Accepting Adults Reduce Suicide Attempts Among LGBTQ Youth." The Trevor Project, June 27, 2019. https://www.thetrevorproject.org/research-briefs/accepting-adults-reduce-suicide-attempts-among-lgbtq-youth/.

The Trevor Project. "2024 U.S. National Survey on the Mental Health of LGBTQ+ Young People." 2024. https://www.thetrevorproject.org/survey-2024/.

Thornton, Sarah, Armin Edalatpour, and Katherine Gast. "A Systematic Review of Patient Regret After Surgery—A Common Phenomenon in Many Specialties but Rare Within Gender-Affirmation Surgery." *The American Journal of Surgery* 234, 68–73, 2024. https://doi.org/10.1016/j.amjsurg.2024.04.021.

Tobin, Valerie, and Kathleen R. Delaney. "Child Abuse Victimization Among Transgender and Gender Nonconforming People: A Systematic Review." *Perspectives in Psychiatric Care* 55 (4), 576–83, 2019. https://doi.org/10.1111/ppc.12398.

Trans PULSE. "Impacts of Strong Parental Support for Trans Youth: A Report Prepared for Children's Aid Society of Toronto and Delisle Youth Services." October 2, 2012. https://transpulseproject.ca/wp-content/uploads/2012/10/Impacts-of-Strong-Parental-Support-for-Trans-Youth-vFINAL.pdf.

Troia, Bailey. "'I'm *Technically* Not Disowned': Familial Strain, Trans Resilience, and Bargaining for Belonging." In *Advances in Trans Studies: Moving Toward Gender Expansion and Trans Hope*, edited by Austin Johnson, Baker Rogers, and Tiffany Taylor. Emerald Publishing Limited, 2021. https://doi.org/10.1108/s1529-212620210000032011.

Tsfati, Maya. "Stigma, Resistance and Hope: The Experiences of Parents of Young Transgender Adults." *Journal of Family Studies* 29 (1), 1–16, 2021. https://doi.org/10.1080/13229400.2021.1911830.

Turban, Jack L., Dana King, Jeremi M. Carswell, and Alex S. Keuroghlian. "Pubertal Suppression for Transgender Youth and Risk of Suicidal Ideation." *PEDIATRICS* 145 (2), e20191725, 2020. https://doi.org/10.1542/peds.2019-1725.

Turban, Jack L., Stephanie S. Loo, Anthony N. Almazan, and Alex S. Keuroghlian. "Factors Leading to 'Detransition' Among Transgender and Gender Diverse People in the United States: A Mixed-Methods Analysis." *LGBT Health* 8 (4), 273–80, 2021. https://doi.org/10.1089/lgbt.2020.0437.

Valente, Pablo K., Eric W. Schrimshaw, Curtis Dolezal, Allen J. LeBlanc, Anneliese A. Singh, and Walter O. Bockting. "Stigmatization, Resilience, and Mental Health Among a Diverse Community Sample of Transgender and Gender Nonbinary Individuals in the U.S." *Archives of Sexual Behavior* 49 (7), 2649–60, 2020. https://doi.org/10.1007/s10508-020-01761-4.

Van Acker, Isabeau, Alexis Dewaele, Els Elaut, and Kariann Baetens. "Exploring Care Needs of Partners of Transgender and Gender Diverse Individuals in Co-Transition: A Qualitative Interview Study." *Healthcare* 11 (11), 1535, 2023. https://doi.org/10.3390/healthcare11111535.

Vandello, Joseph A., Jennifer K. Bosson, Dov Cohen, Rochelle M. Burnaford, and Jonathan R. Weaver. "Precarious Manhood." *Journal of Personality and Social Psychology* 95 (6), 1325–39, 2008. https://doi.org/10.1037/a0012453.

Von Doussa, Henry, Jennifer Power, and Damien Riggs. "Imagining Parenthood: The Possibilities and Experiences of Parenthood Among Transgender People."

*Culture, Health & Sexuality* 17 (9), 1119–31, 2015. https://doi.org/10.1080/13691058.2015.1042919.

Wahlig, Jeni L. "Losing the Child They Thought They Had: Therapeutic Suggestions for an Ambiguous Loss Perspective with Parents of a Transgender Child." *Journal of GLBT Family Studies* 11 (4), 305–26, 2014. https://doi.org/10.1080/1550428x.2014.945676.

Walker, Nick. "Neuroqueer Heresies: Notes on the Neurodiversity Paradigm, Autistic Empowerment, and Postnormal Possibilities." Autonomous Press, 2021.

Ward, L. Monique, and Jennifer Stevens Aubrey. "Watching Gender: How Stereotypes in Movies and on TV Impact Kids' Development." *Common Sense*, 2017. https://www.commonsensemedia.org/sites/default/files/research/report/2017_commonsense_watchinggender_fullreport_0620.pdf.

Warrier, Varun, David M. Greenberg, Elizabeth Weir, et al. "Elevated Rates of Autism, Other Neurodevelopmental and Psychiatric Diagnoses, and Autistic Traits in Transgender and Gender-Diverse Individuals." *Nature Communications* 11, 3959, 2020. https://doi.org/10.1038/s41467-020-17794-1.

Wernick, Laura J., Alex Kulick, and Matthew Chin. "Gender Identity Disparities in Bathroom Safety and Wellbeing Among High School Students." *Journal of Youth and Adolescence* 46, 917–30, 2017. https://doi.org/10.1007/s10964-017-0652-1.

What We Know Project. "What Does the Scholarly Research Say about the Effect of Gender Transition on Transgender Well-Being?" Cornell University, 2018. https://whatweknow.inequality.cornell.edu/topics/lgbt-equality/what-does-the-scholarly-research-say-about-the-well-being-of-transgender-people/.

Williams Institute at UCLA School of Law. "How Many Adults and Youth Identify as Transgender in the United States?" 2022. https://williamsinstitute.law.ucla.edu/publications/trans-adults-united-states/.

Williams Institute at UCLA School of Law. "Suicide Thoughts and Attempts Among Transgender Adults." 2020. https://williamsinstitute.law.ucla.edu/publications/suicidality-transgender-adults/.

Wilson, Erin C., Ellen Iverson, Robert Garofalo, and Marvin Belzer. "Parental Support and Condom Use Among Transgender Female Youth." *Journal of the Association of Nurses in AIDS Care* 23 (4), 306–17, 2012. https://doi.org/10.1016/j.jana.2011.09.001.

Wilson, Erin C., Yea-Hung Chen, Sean Arayasirikul, H. Fisher Raymond, and Willi McFarland. "The Impact of Discrimination on the Mental Health of Trans*Female Youth and the Protective Effect of Parental Support." *AIDS and Behavior* 20, 2203–11, 2016. https://doi.org/10.1007/s10461-016-1409-7.

Wood, Julia. *Gendered Lives: Communication, Gender, and Culture (Eighth Edition)*. Wadsworth Publishing, 1994.

## ADDITIONAL RESOURCES

PROTECT TRANS YOUTH ADVOCACY PAGE

EVER-EVOLVING GLOSSARY OF TERMS

# INDEX

# ACKNOWLEDGMENTS

To the clients and families who trusted me on their gender journeys—this book exists because of your courage and belief in our work together. Thank you for trusting me.

To the first publisher who rejected this book: Thank you for challenging me to grow, for pushing me to hone my vision, and for sparing me from writing a book I wasn't yet ready to create. Your "no" became the catalyst for my "yes."

To the undergraduate students, Molly Roitman and Jack Rowland, who supported me in creating my first proposal and annotated bibliography in 2020—your early contributions laid the foundation for this work.

To my graduate research assistants, Alanah Hodges and Isaiah Newman, your unwavering dedication and passion for this field have been a constant source of inspiration and support. The field of social work is fortunate to have you.

To my colleagues, who challenge, inspire, and motivate me to think deeper and push further. This book would not exist without your invaluable insights and encouragement.

To my family, for raising me to be curious, to never be a bystander, and to always be in service.

To my spouse, who tolerated the late nights, the rewrites, and the moments of fear that this book would be banned before it even got in the hands of those who needed it most. Your patience and partnership made this book possible.

And to the trans elders who paved the way—your courage and resilience have made this work possible for generations to come.

# ABOUT THE AUTHOR

REBECCA MINOR, LICSW, is a queer clinician, consultant, and educator specializing in trauma, gender, and sexuality. As a gender specialist, she works with trans and gender nonconforming youth and their families, equipping parents with the tools to affirm and support their children. With more than ten thousand hours of experience, Rebecca has helped countless families build stronger relationships and create affirming environments where everyone can thrive.

She is the founder of Prism Therapy Collective, a group practice offering trauma-informed, neurodiversity-affirming care. Rebecca's internationally recognized consulting and parent-coaching work supports schools, businesses, and organizations in becoming more culturally responsive and inclusive.

Rebecca also serves as an adjunct faculty member and lecturer at Boston University School of Social Work, where she helps train the next generation of affirming clinicians.

She is frequently quoted as an expert on gender-affirming care, and has authored articles on LGBTQ+ youth and contributed to textbooks on the subject. A sought-after speaker, she presents at conferences for clinicians, trans and gender-expansive people, and their allies.

Rebecca's mission is to help families show up for their children with love, confidence, and unwavering commitment—because every child deserves to be seen, affirmed, and celebrated for who they truly are.